£3-50

Elizabeth of York

Elizabeth
of YORK

The Mother of HENRY VIII

BY NANCY LENZ HARVEY

Macmillan Publishing Co, Inc.

NEW YORK

Macmillan Publishing Co., Inc.
866 Third Avenue, New York, N.Y. 10022
Collier-Macmillan Canada Ltd., Toronto, Ontario

Library of Congress Catalog Card Number: 72–11952

First Printing 1973

Printed in the United States of America

To my mother and father

CONTENTS

Contents

ILLUSTRATIONS

HOUSE OF YORK

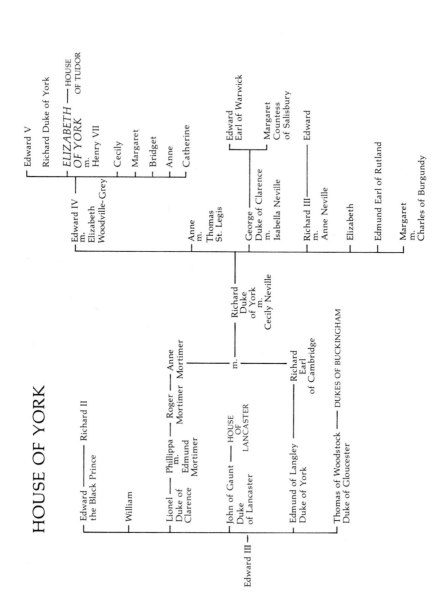

HOUSE OF LANCASTER

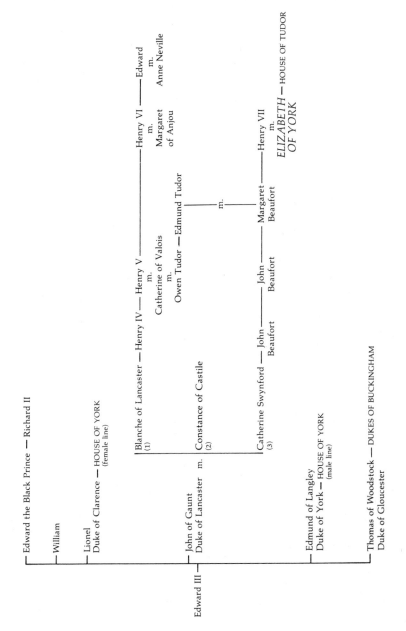

HOUSE OF TUDOR

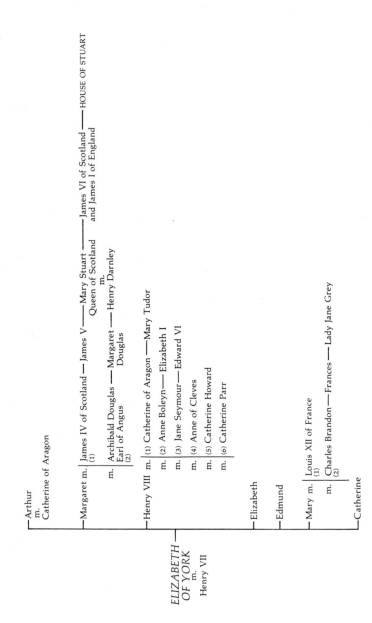

PREFACE

THE story of Elizabeth of York reveals a life of reaction rather than action. Hurled by destiny into the gore of the War of the Roses, surrounded by a multitude of colorful and ambitious men and women, locked into a time of great emotional stress, she walked the thin line of survival. Although she was the daughter of a king and heiress to his throne, she was, ironically, without power and a captive of her blood. She became a pawn within the power structure, sought by all factions as the most important marriageable quantity.

In a way her life becomes the War of the Roses retold; but in most accounts Elizabeth of York is covered over by more dramatic events and persons. She is, however, a study in contrast, the eye in the midst of the hurricane. And the events which swirled about her molded and directed her life; where the stronger forces moved, so must she follow. But all these things she witnessed and endured. It seems fitting therefore to tell her story as she lived it and as she reacted to it. The result is a reflection, a life relived. In order to shape the narrative, I have adapted some techniques of the novel—a method somewhat unusual in biography, but seemingly fitting here; and the narrative moves from her mind in and out of others' in an attempt to understand, as she must have attempted to understand, the holocaust of her world. Such a method runs the risk of hypothesis, but every attempt has been made to keep the narrative from fiction and surmise. The major liberty is with the brief mention of Elizabeth's sister Bridget, whose life is telescoped. Here Bridget contemplates entering the convent, which she did; however, at the point noted in the narrative, she would have been only a small child. Quotations have been used sparingly, but when they occur the spelling has been modernized while the original syntax has been kept.

One, of course, does not write a book alone but builds upon the work of ancient historians and modern scholars and draws heavily on the critical and moral support of friends and family. It is impossible to thank them all. I do, however, wish to thank Jane Allen and Jeannie Musterman of the University of Cincinnati Library; the staffs of the Library of Congress and the British Museum; Carole Bowman, who brought good sense to the arrangement of the genealogy charts; Julie Dietrich and Georgia Jackson, who helped with the research; Elizabeth Armstrong, Pauline Riley, and Wayne Miller for their comments and support; Mary-Berenice McCall for her careful scrutiny of the text; Alvena Stanfield for typing the manuscript; and Ray Roberts of the Macmillan Company for his interest, understanding, and guidance.

N. L. H.

Cincinnati, 1972

FEBRUARY 8, 1503

THE *morning of February 8, 1503, was a glooming day. The winds off the Thames and the freezing rains beat against the Tower walls. The tapestries shivered about the stones. The chill would not be put down. Inside the royal apartments, high at the top of the White Tower, the candles flickered with each gust, and the light chased about the mirrors wrapped in gold, about the frames of ancestors long dead, along the polished tables, and pushed into the darkness of the quiet halls. Servants, huddled in woolen wraps against the cold, moved quickly between the kitchens and the private chambers of the queen. One by one they knocked upon the door; it opened and hands reached out and took away the linens, the bowls of broth, the vessels of water, the gifts of friends. Here there were few sounds, only the whispered exchanges and the softened footsteps.*

The quiet within contrasted sharply to the noise without. As though to challenge the rain and ice, the cannons of the Tower crashed through the dawn. Volley after volley shook the walls and echoed throughout London, and the bells of the city took up the sounds of celebration. During the night a princess had been born.

For the queen herself, the movements of the servants and the sounds of the guns and the shaking of the Tower walls had little meaning. She had had a life of ceremony. And what was ceremony compared to the life now beside her, to the children she had borne and those she had lost? Elizabeth of York rested among her pillows and dreamed. For every beginning provokes a search for beginnings, just as every end foreshadows the final end.

1 · THE DAUGHTER OF THE KING

HER own birth had caused great and unusual anticipation, for Elizabeth was the firstborn of the handsome King Edward IV and his queen Elizabeth Woodville-Grey. The father, it is true, had hoped for, was promised, a boy —an heir to his throne. The astrologers and wise men had been consulted. One astrologer, Master Dominic, had been so certain of his prediction that he wished to be the first to tell King Edward the gladsome news. Through the days of confinement and the hours of labor, Dominic hovered, his ear to the door of the queen's chamber. At last the child's cries sounded, and Dominic beat at the door and demanded what the queen had. The midwife shouted back: "Whatsoever the queen's grace hath here within, sure it is a fool standeth there without." Seeing neither the child nor the king, Dominic, with charts and maps under his arm, slunk from the palace.[1]

Elizabeth was born February 11, 1465, at Westminster Palace. On the following Wednesday, robed in crimson and gold, carried beneath a canopy fringed and jeweled, she was brought in pomp and procession to her christening in Westminster Abbey. With her grandmothers Cecily Duchess of York and Jacqueline Duchess of Bedford and her father's chief ally Richard

Neville Earl of Warwick as godparents, the child was baptized and named Elizabeth for her mother. Then, as the lights of a thousand candles played against the tapestries on the walls, as the images and statues seemed to move in the shadows, as the choir chanted its litanies of celebration, the child was confirmed. With the help of her godfather, the child held in her hand a lighted candle and placed it upon the altar. This first public performance became a symbol of her life. For it was an act of reverence and humility, a posture she maintained throughout the years and manifested in the words of her motto, Humble and Reverent.

In spite of his initial disappointment, the king came to dote on this, his firstborn child. In infancy he carried her into court to display her to his subjects; in childhood he commanded her presence with increasing frequency. At his table she moved quickly from the bench to his lap and ate from his trencher. In moments of leisure, he guided her fingers over the strings of the lute. Often the family traveled from one home to the next, from the Tower to Westminster, Greenwich, Windsor, Fotheringay, or to the princess' own manor of Great Lynford in Buckinghamshire.[2] As the family settled into one home or the other, the days of childhood were filled with the stories of intrigue that became part of the War of the Roses.

Only five years before, Elizabeth's grandfather, Richard Plantagenet Duke of York, had challenged the weak-minded King Henry VI of the House of Lancaster for the throne. The fortunes of victory were tossed between the two factions until suddenly the Duke of York was disadvantaged and his head posted on the gates of the city of York. His fallen standard of the sunburst and white rose was raised immediately by his eldest son, the handsome Edward Earl of March, nineteen years old, towering six feet four, with a retentive steel-trap mind, an eagerness for leadership, and a genius for war and politics.[3]

Edward's victories came swiftly if bloodily. It was said, for instance, that at the conclusive battle of Pomfret thirty-eight thousand men feil in the field besides those drowned in the neighboring river. Since it was winter, the blood of the wounded and dead covered the land, and "afterwards ran down in the furrows and ditches along with the melted snow . . . for a distance of two or three miles."[4] In the end, Henry was captured and brought to the keep of the Tower of London where he stayed for eight uninterrupted years.[5] His queen Margaret and their son Edward were forced to the safety of Scotland and the support of France. Other Lancastrian followers were either dead or placed outside the law. Peace settled and Edward had himself crowned with pomp and ceremony amidst the song of the citizenry: "Let us walk in a new wineyard, and let us make a gay garden in the month of March with this fair white rose and herb, the Earl of March."[6]

Once in command of crown and country, Edward sought to enjoy all that kingship meant. He savored the wealth and worship, the pleasures of pomp at court, the freedom to hunt in the royal forests, the thrill of power. Let Warwick, for the time, handle the problems of government, for Edward with his flair for magnificent display indulged his senses with the pleasures of living. Dressed in robes of velvet garnished with gold and set with jewels, he awed the most stalwart and mummified the less sophisticated. But with easy familiarity—a hand on the shoulder, a smile into the eyes, a genuine sympathy and humanity—he intentionally dispelled fear of the royal presence. For this warmth and understanding, he became by his people widely loved.[7] Thus he sought to fulfill the words of the song, to make his court into a happy glittering setting for its virile white rose. The rose, however, was a lusty one which almost uprooted itself and its entire garden.

It was well enough to behead one's enemies, to hunt the stag and boar, to coin money in one's image, to fill the courts with sunshine and laughter and song, to sail the Thames in

golden barges, to dally with the ladies.[8] But he married one of
the ladies. The marriage resulted from a morning's hunt. The
king, hot and thirsty from the chase, sought refreshment at the
manor of Grafton near Stony Stratford, home of the Duchess
of Bedford, wife to Sir Richard Woodville. With her was a
daughter, Elizabeth, widow of Sir John Grey who had died for
the Lancastrians and Henry VI. No matter, the lady was comely.
Although she was five years older than Edward and the mother
of two young sons, Elizabeth seemed helpless as she petitioned
for lands lost in the political scuffle. Her tongue was winning,
her face was pleasing, and the king soon favored both her
suit and her person.

Elizabeth Woodville, however, resisted the king's pursuit.
No, she would not be his paramour, but she would be his queen.
Edward knew he must have the lady at any price. Thus he ignored policy and politics, and the fact that Warwick—who
considered himself solely responsible for Edward's elevation to
the crown—was at the moment lobbying in France for the
hand of a princess, Bona of Savoy, sister-in-law to the French
Louis XI.[9] The Duchess of York, hearing of Edward's intention,
much preferred a princess as a daughter-in-law. She heatedly
argued that Elizabeth Woodville was not a fitting consort to a
king, since her father was only a knight. Desperate to halt the
match, the Duchess further maintained that a pre-contract of
marriage already existed between Edward and the Lady Elizabeth Boulton. Edward would not be moved.[10]

On a May morning in 1464 Edward rode once more to the
Grafton manor and married in secret Lady Elizabeth Woodville-
Grey. The only witnesses were the bride's mother, two ladies
of quality, and the priest. The service over, the king bedded the
bride, returned to the court, and slept. He told no one of the
morning's adventure. Three and a half months later, while
meeting with his council at Reading, Edward announced his
marriage. The council was stunned into "great displeasure."

Warwick, upon hearing the news, began to seethe and to think of rebellion.[11]

Fall turned into winter, and the lady formally became queen. First in the coronation procession as it left the Tower of London were the representatives of the Church, carrying the holy relics of a footprint of Christ from the Mount of Olives and the girdle of the Virgin. Next came the singing scholars with their lighted torches. Then in stately profusion rode the noble ladies of the realm, the trumpeters, pipers, and players with stringed instruments, forty-two of the king's minstrels, twenty-four heralds, sixty knights, and under a canopy the queen herself, sitting in a richly decorated litter. Behind her walked her mother, the Duchess of Bedford, and sixty ladies more. The king, as etiquette demanded, attended neither the coronation nor the banquet; but he understood the princely quality of magnificence and provided the sumptuous setting for these events. After the service, the queen alone enjoyed her banquet. For three hours she dipped into the scores of dishes while her ladies, including her mother and the king's sister, knelt, and not a word was spoken.

The hauteur and vanity displayed here by Elizabeth Woodville marked her life and marred her reign. Her shallow understanding and meddlesome ways made many enemies. Reveling in power, ignorant of the growing enmity, she quickly advanced her relations to high estate. Her father became the High Constable and Treasurer of England; John Woodville, her twenty-year-old brother, married the wealthy seventy-five-year-old Dowager Duchess of Norfolk. The queen's sisters were also well placed: Anne Woodville married the heir of the Earl of Sussex; Eleanor Woodville married the heir of the Earl of Kent; Catherine Woodville married the Duke of Buckingham, the youthful cousin of the king; Jacquette Woodville married Lord Strange; Mary Woodville married the heir of Lord Herbert; Sir Thomas Grey, son to the queen by her first marriage, married Anne Holland, daughter of the powerful Duke of Exeter. Warwick was furious, for through these alliances his power was undermined. In spite of the grace and culture that the Woodvilles brought to court, they were ever viewed as unadulterated meddlers and upstarts. Ways, decided Warwick, must be found to rid England, if not the world, of them.[12]

These tensions at court failed to disturb the calm of the nursery, and the years of Elizabeth's childhood were crammed with attention and affection. More delightful than the dolls and toys were her new sisters who came to stay—to the chagrin of their father. First arrived Mary and a year later Cecily. Each became the other's closest friend. And always there were the servants who existed but to obey, and her uncles George Duke of Clarence and Richard Duke of Gloucester on her father's side, and the dashing Anthony Woodville—Lord Scales—on her mother's, who spun tales of battle and tourneys.

In 1468 her aunt Margaret, the king's sister, provided the most spectacular event in Elizabeth's early years. She married Charles Duke of Burgundy, and the child Elizabeth was held to the window to enjoy the impressive procession as Margaret prepared to leave London. On June 18 dressed in red cloth of gold and waving from her golden litter, Margaret journeyed to St. Paul's Cathedral for prayers for her voyage and marriage. All London, it seemed, turned into the streets, each citizen holding a lighted candle, and the mayor and aldermen in their scarlet robes acting as escort for the bride. At Stratford Priory the king and queen, Clarence, Gloucester, Scales, Warwick, and most of the court rode with Margaret down to Canterbury and the shrine of St. Thomas à Becket. At Margate port they bid her good-bye and she sailed to Sluys.

Elizabeth learned how generous had been the reception of her aunt, of the chivalry of Charles of Burgundy who rode daily to kiss his betrothed, of the wedding, and festival. She heard too of the lavish pageants of celebration, the street processions, the evening masques, the spectacular tree of gold with blossoms of oranges, pears, apples, roses white and red, pomegranates which opened to disgorge their sweets and candies. When Scales returned he told of the great jousts and tournaments, of men in armor racing into each other to snap their spears, of the contests of arms which tested man and horse. He smiled with confidence, knowing that he was the best in the field. Margaret, he felt, would be happy as the Duchess of Burgundy, for her court was a rich and lavish one and a major continental power.[13]

Within the next year Elizabeth herself became an instrument of power. At the age of four she was formally betrothed to George Neville, the nine-year-old nephew and closest male heir of the Earl of Warwick. For the occasion, Neville was created Duke of Bedford and thus a more fitting mate for the princess. Warwick had taken a leaf from the Woodville handbook. Since Edward had no sons, it was possible that Elizabeth might become queen and share the throne with her husband. Warwick, with ever an eye to future power, beamed throughout the pomp of the processions, the sweet music of the minstrels, and the whispered exchange of vows between the children.[14] But the security manifested here contrasted with the confusions of the world beyond the castle walls.

The universe itself seemed disturbed. There were reports of the heavens aflame with three suns, of rains that showered blood, of horsemen in full armor riding through the skies. In one instance St. George, known by his red cross, was seen to lead a vast army overhead.[15] On the ground, this turbulence of the heavens was mirrored. Warwick's anger and ambition fed upon each other as he sought to dethrone the king and place a puppet in his place. He found a willing accomplice in Clarence, the king's brother. Handsome and vain, ambitious and self-centered, more given to posing than making policy, the slow-witted Clarence lacked mental ingenuity. As long as he had handsome clothes, adoration, and the patina of power, he cared little if Warwick did the work of government. The two drew quickly toward an alliance.

While serving as English ambassador to France, Warwick urged the marriage of his eldest daughter, Isabella, to Clarence. Since the bride and groom were within the forbidden familial bond, Warwick secured a papal dispensation. Edward remained unaware of the union, while the French Louis rejoiced in the possibility of greater influence in England. He offered men and supplies if Warwick led an invasion to place Clarence on the throne. Warwick accepted Louis' offer and, with Clarence, fomented uprisings against Edward. Their efforts brought them little success, however. Time and again they and the King of England fielded armies; but Edward, now that he had been aroused from pleasure, was too shrewd a general. Only once, perhaps through overconfidence, did he make a mistake. He ventured too far from London and found himself cut off from its supplies and reinforcements. Near Coventry he was taken prisoner and moved north to Middleham Castle. As word of his capture spread, the south country and London revolted and demanded his release. Edward was allowed to escape, and Warwick and Clarence fled the country to France.[16]

Edward returned to London and his family to the cheers of the citizenry and the relief of the Woodvilles. The seeds of revolt, however, had been widely planted, and there was much discontent. In France Warwick and Clarence were again warmly welcomed. Together with the French king they plotted anew and sought a broader base for support. Residing also in the French court was the wife of the deposed Henry VI, Margaret of Anjou. Unknown to Clarence, Warwick was forced by Louis into alliance with the exiled queen. After much verbal fencing, the two swore allegiance. To seal the pact Margaret allowed her son to marry Warwick's second daughter Anne Neville. Warwick, with the financial backing of Louis, planned a new invasion; only this time the plan was to restore the feeble Henry

VI to the throne, with his wife as regent. Warwick would be at her right hand. Clarence, helpless to interfere, pretended to accept this new alliance on the condition that he or his heirs would succeed the Lancastrian line.

The energy and political skill of Warwick, the power of his wealth and enormous estates, his facile ability to make and break kings, allowed him to match any adversary. Although of only medium height, his courage and appearance commanded respect. He never hesitated to share the dangers and miseries of his men in battle, but with his peers he could be cold and distant, quick to avenge a slight or a wrong. In the field he led with decision and inspired admiration but never devotion or fellowship. Herein lay his weakness. It was only where avarice and ambition beckoned with promises of victory that his men would follow.

Warwick aroused his supporters in England and sailed to meet them. On cue, rebellion flared near York, and Edward's lieutenants were slow to put it down. The king, hesitating to interrupt his hunting pleasures, failed to respond. The days passed and news from abroad was scant; but the news from the north, especially around York, was not encouraging. Edward roused himself, saw his wife and family secured in the Tower, and made a forced march from London to Leicester, Doncaster, and York. By the time he arrived, his enemies were safely behind the Scottish border. The king could do nothing but refresh himself and his men. For weeks he dallied in York while the countryside seethed about him. He did not know that Warwick had already landed at Dartmouth; reinforced his men with Lancastrian supporters; claimed the land for Henry VI, still imprisoned in the Tower; and branded Edward as an usurper:

King Edward . . . is a man contumelious, opprobious, and an injurious person; to them that deserve kindness he showeth unkindness, and them that love him he deadly hateth, now detesting to take any pain for the preferment or maintenance of the public wealth of this realm, but all given to pastime, pleasure, and dalliance; sooner prefering to high estate men descended of low blood and base degree, than men of old and undefiled houses, which have both supported him and the commonwealth of this realm.[17]

When the news of these events arrived, Edward moved with speed toward London. He was too late. The forces of Warwick were already in power. The king reached Doncaster to spend the night in a well-fortified building protected by a drawbridge. But he was not secure. Montague, Warwick's brother and one of Edward's lieutenants, defected and marched to seize the king. The Archbishop of York, another of Warwick's brothers, was less than a day's march away. Outnumbered and with little hope of reinforcement, Edward fled by horseback to Bishop's Lynn, swam the Wash, and on October 3, 1470, commandeered a boat for Holland.

In London, the city was under siege. Warwick and Lancastrian forces in Kent, drunk with the dreams of riches, went mad with power. They beat upon the city walls, stole boats from the docks, and howled along the waterfront. The Mayor of London, a grocer named Richard Lee, rushed from the Guildhall to raise a defense. He was only partially successful. One of Warwick's supporters had irrationally thrown open the Southwark jail, just south of London Bridge. Although he intended to free only imprisoned Lancastrians, he unleashed a brawling mob which ripped through the stores and homes, pillaging, burning, and drinking as it raged. The mayor had time only to secure the gates of London. For the moment London held.

High above the Thames the queen, now eight months pregnant, and her daughters listened to the screaming, crazed mob. Hurriedly she gathered her children and called the mayor before her. Without ceremony, Elizabeth Woodville released the Tower to his control for the better defense of the city. But the mobs and drunken looters pushed into the streets while the mayor led the royal family to their boat. Silently and fearfully they shivered in the barge as grotesque shadows loomed around them and drunken men roamed the shore. Already buildings were silhouetted in smoke and flame, and the curses of the looters shot across the water. Slowly the boat moved through the water until it reached the wharf at Westminster. Then the queen—holding a chest of jewels in her arms—and the daughters—dragging bedsheets stuffed with clothing—scurried through the dark to sanctuary in the Abbey. They, who had a few hours before commanded a kingdom, were grateful for the confining rooms in the abbot's house.[18]

Within hours Warwick's lieutenant Sir Geoffrey Gate led the rebel force into the city. The Tower, under twenty-four-hour guard but without sufficient army to stand, fell to Gate's command. Two days later on October 3, Warwick sent his brother the Archbishop of York to hold the city. He entered the Tower and searched the dungeons for the imprisoned Henry VI. There in a small poorly lighted room, with a caged starling and a dog for his only companions, sat Henry. Although he had long been feeble in both body and mind, his skin held now a prison pallor, his pale eyes lacked concentration, his thinly veined hands hung limply, and his gait was reduced to a slow shamble. He was neither dressed as a prince nor as cleanly kept as he might have been. The archbishop led Henry to the sumptuous rooms recently vacated by the queen. There he was dressed in a blue velvet robe of Edward's and the sleeves hung below his hands.

Three days later Warwick and Clarence entered London. The balconies were draped in streamers of silk and cloth of gold. The martial step of the soldiers matched the thumping of the drums and the serenade of the trumpets. Londoners, always attentive to parades, flocked to the walkways to watch. Warwick, in full armor of Milan steel and seated on a majestic horse, led his retinue: the nobles and gentlemen on horse; the men-at-arms on foot; the retainers in crimson coats designed with Warwick's badge of the ragged staff. Lastly, on a horse shrouded in cloth of gold studded with pearls, rode the pouting Clarence, elegant in crimson velvet, white hose, and tooled Spanish-leather boots with golden spurs. He was not happy, for he had not been the first to enter the city.

The victors dismounted at the Tower and knelt before the soft-spoken Henry robed in Edward's blue gown. Henry, often incapable of making any response, was led to St. Paul's for services of thanksgiving and then to Bishop's Palace. Warwick and Clarence moved into Salisbury's palace. Within the week the rioters in London and its environs were subdued.[19]

News of these events reached those in sanctuary, and they watched from their windows the procession of the street. The five-year-old Elizabeth struggled to comprehend the confusions. Why did her father no longer come to visit? Why did her mother weep and tear her hair? Was it possible that her father was the king and yet not the king? That other men ruled the country? Was the king now the man the servants had whispered of, the man who softly spoke aloud the prayers and poems he composed in his darkened room?

In the rooms of the abbot, there was little to do. The favorite toys had been left behind, and the grounds of Westminster were considered unsafe for the games of the princess and her sisters. Instead they contented themselves with the rooms of sanctuary, studying the illuminations in the books of the abbot's library, practicing their stitches of embroidery, visiting daily the chapel for prayers, and occasionally racing through the hallways of the darkened house. Of course there were no longer throngs of servants who fell upon their knees in service, but it was to Warwick's credit that neither the children nor their mother suffered greater deprivation or public humiliation. In his moment of greatest power, he manifested a humanity little before seen. Other less powerful folk also offered compassion. A local butcher sent half a beef and two muttons every week; Abbot Mylling sent small comforts, such as books and sweets and sometimes cloth; and when the mother's time came, two ladies of quality were allowed to help with the birthing.[20]

On November 3, 1470, after one month in sanctuary, Queen Elizabeth gave birth to a son. Although his grandmother the Duchess of Bedford and his mother's protector Abbot Mylling were godparents, the prince was baptized in the Abbey "like a poor man's child." The news, however, brought hope to the Yorkists, and the apparent poverty of the queen brought sympathy from many commoners. While the baby's eldest sister Elizabeth held the chrism, the child was baptized and named for his father—Edward Prince of England.[21]

The name was a direct affront to those in power and an act of courage on the part of the mother: Henry VI's son and the heir to the throne was also named Edward Prince of England. He and his mother, Margaret of Anjou, had remained in France through the events of October. The delay was typical of Margaret's caution and suspicion. Warwick, after all, had earlier betrayed the Lancastrian throne and forced her present exile. Now that he was again leading Lancastrian armies, he alone might open the way to the throne. She had, therefore, reluctantly accepted the new alliance; but fearing new betrayals she waited in the French court for news of victory.

Margaret's delay proved a fatal decision. The Lancastrian armies lacked a magnetic focal point which either she or her son could have supplied. Warwick, for all his skill, energy, and power, was never able to arouse the loyalties of the common people. Henry VI, pathetic figure that he was, inspired little warmth and less loyalty amongst his subjects. Limp and weary, he was sneeringly called the "sack of wool" or the "shadow on the wall." The Lancastrians thus failed to project a clear image of leadership capable of harnessing the respect, fidelity, or attention of capricious subjects. Henry's government at best was a faltering, shambling one that contrasted sharply with the virile magnificence of the previous reign.

Sycophants and hangers-on crowded into Westminster Palace seeking Henry VI and the wealth he controlled. Henry, a gentle, compassionate, generous man capable of giving away his only cloak, struggled to concentrate on the confused and shoving congregations before him. Among the crowd stood Jasper Tudor and his fourteen-year-old nephew Henry Tudor Earl of Richmond. Having claims to the throne through his mother, Richmond had been a captive at the family estates in Wales throughout Edward's reign. Now that he was free he offered his loyalty to Henry and knelt before him. The king's wandering blue eyes focused long on the kneeling boy, then slowly his mouth opened, and he spoke prophetic words: "Lo, this is he to whom both we and our adversary, having the possession of all things, shall hereafter give room and place." Richmond and his uncle returned to Castle Pembroke in Wales and waited.

The weary and uneasy days in England passed. More heads were axed. John Tiptoft Earl of Worcester, sometimes called "the Butcher of England" because of his habit of impaling victims and replacing their severed heads on the posts protruding from their bodies, was executed at Tower Hill. As he had requested, he was beheaded with three strokes of the ax —one for each member of the Trinity.[22] In London Clarence fretted about his lack of place in the new government. He was sought neither as an important man nor as a claimant of the throne. He increasingly distrusted both Margaret and Warwick and began to fear for his life.

In sanctuary the royal exiles established their routine of daily life. Princess Elizabeth, able to read and write a little English and Latin, added French to these studies. She was taught manners and etiquette, the lives of the saints, and how to play the lute and clavichord. In the evening the mother read to the girls the tales of Chaucer and the chronicles of Froissart; and in time, as despair lightened, she taught her daughters to dance. Elizabeth Woodville believed that their lives would not be spent in exile. When freedom came, she determined, her daughters must be prepared to pick up their lives at court. It was this hope of a return to court, belief in her husband, and joy in her son that sustained the queen in the days of gloom, and in these matters she coached her daughters.

Edward, having hastened to the court of his sister and her husband, Charles of Burgundy, anxiously awaited the attention of the duke and the support he might offer. Daily he solicited the aid and advice of his host. Charles, however, remained elusive, too busy to see the exiled king but alert to the shifts on the political scene. Then politics forced his attention and activity.

Margaret and her son moved toward Rouen and prepared to sail to England. In February Warwick moved to Dover to act as escort. Hoping to distract Charles' attention, France attacked Burgundy. Charles held his frontier, and equipped Edward with an army and sent him against the English. Frequent storms halted all activity on the Channel, and the adversaries fretted away the time and waited for nature to subside. It was not until March 11, 1471, that Edward was able to sail. With him came his brother Gloucester, his brother-in-law Scales, his closest friend Hastings, and a host of Yorkist exiles. They sailed first for Norfolk and found the countryside shuddering in fear of Warwick's well-established authority. With no hope of landing, the ships set sail again and were blown northward. On March 14, out of fear of shipwreck, Edward landed at Ravenspur, just north of the Humber estuary, with five hundred men. Gloucester landed a few miles away with an addi-

tional three hundred men. The following day Scales landed
with two hundred more. None of the aristocracy came out to
welcome the landing armies; but the commoners who continued to hold affection for Edward offered all hospitality in the
little fishing villages of the coast. This simple affection, as op-
posed to aristocratic hostility, was echoed in a popular ballad:

> *Lord, the unkindness was showed to King Edward that day!*
> *At his landing in Holderness he had great pain:*
> *His subjects and people would not him obey.*
> *Of him and his people they had great disdain,*
> *They showed him unkindness, and answered him plain,*
> *As for the King he should not land there for wele**
>
>   *nor woe,*
> *Yet landed that gentle prince, the will of God was so.*

Edward and his followers moved directly toward York, but
opposition to his march appeared only as token resistance. Upon
approaching York, he announced that he came not for the
crown but only for his rightful inheritance as heir to his father.[23] As a gesture of fidelity to Henry VI, Edward wore upon
his head the cap and ostrich feather, the badge of the Prince of
Wales.[24] He rode alone and ahead of his army; and when he
entered the city he often reined his horse to speak to well-
wishers in the street crowds. Even as he moved, the cries of
"Long live the Duke of York" grew and echoed.[25] These as-
surances were indicative of the support Edward found as he
began his move southward to Tadcaster and Wakefield. In this
steady march his armies collected new followers. In areas still
under Warwick's control, the citizenry let Edward pass. His
calculated strategy was working well. The lack of resistance in
northern parts suggested to those further south that the countryside welcomed the invader. Furthermore it was thought folly

---

* good, prosperity

to attack what so many others favored. Steadily Edward marched forward, his armies strengthened, and the people came to believe in his success.[26]

Edward moved toward Coventry where Warwick waited. Edward's army, now swollen by the faithful of the countryside, stood at the Coventry gates. Warwick ignored the challenge and refused to move. Edward then settled his camp in the town of Warwick, an intentional insult to the powerful earl. News came that Edward's brother, lately turned unhappy traitor, was riding in their direction with his army. In short order the two brothers arrayed their respective armies less than half a mile apart, banners were displayed, and trumpets were blown. Silence, broken only by the neighs of the horses and the occasional clang of armor, then settled on the field. The two armies stood and watched each other, waiting for the signal to advance. Suddenly Clarence with his staff and Edward with his lieutenants, each man handsomely armed and horsed, moved toward each other. Gloucester left Edward and rode forward to speak to Clarence; then he rode back to Edward. This was done several times so that the brothers conversed through the third brother. At last Clarence and Edward rode alone towards the center of the field; there they met and embraced. Soon they were joined by Gloucester, Scales, and Hastings. Seeing these gestures, the armies threw down their weapons and raced to embrace each other as the trumpets sounded again, and the minstrels danced about the field. Edward's army was now larger by four thousand men.[27]

Warwick raged at these events but remained within the safety of the walls of Coventry—by so doing, the way to London was left open. On April 7, Edward moved to Daventry, where a miracle took place. It was Palm Sunday and Edward went in procession to the church. There he knelt throughout the service. While the choir chanted its Aves, a cloth was drawn before the cross. Near the cross, in a box nailed shut, was a little image of St. Anne.[28] As the cloth moved over the cross, the box shuddered, and its boards split to reveal to the king a glimpse of the image. Then the boards closed, only to burst open in a mighty effort and reveal the image of the saint to all the people. Edward audibly thanked God and St. Anne for this good sign. And he and his people went away convinced of God's blessing and success in the battle to come.[29]

Edward immediately traveled through Northampton, Dunstable, and St. Albans. Before him rode messengers to the London city fathers with news of his approach and promises to pay his bills. Behind him rode a strong band of archers and spearmen in the event that Warwick decided to follow. Warwick did give chase but always remained a full day behind.

In London the Archbishop of York made frantic efforts toward the defense of the city. He begged for help from the Mayor of London, who took to his bed; the archbishop then challenged the vice-mayor, who fled the country. Finally the archbishop, in order to raise the commoners, paraded the feeble Henry— still in Edward's blue velvet gown—through the streets. Henry's pale, pathetic figure served only to dampen the spirits rather than to stimulate his subjects.[30]

London and its council, in a bloodless coup, turned back to Edward. In quick succession, the council and commoners seized the Tower, held the guns, and subdued the guards of Aldersgate for Edward's entry. Edward arrived the next day "at dinner time," marched directly to St. Paul's and offered his prayers of thanksgiving. From the Archbishop of York, the king received his crown and the possession of Henry VI. The fallen king met Edward's formally extended hand with an attempted embrace and said: "My cousin of York, you are very welcome. I know that in your hands my life will not be in danger." Henry was returned to his single room at the Tower, and Edward hurried to Westminster Palace to which his family had been moved.[31]

His family during these last days had heard conflicting reports of victory and defeat. It seemed as though everyone was either winning or losing. The actions of Clarence, of Warwick, of Edward himself, were not clear. The first clear evidence of the king's success came through Edward's own messenger reporting that yes, he was marching towards them. As Edward entered London, the family moved into familiar quarters at the palace. Immediately the Yorkist laughter and joy chased the Lancastrian gloom from the newly decorated rooms. The romping of the children and the renewed attention of servants vibrated through the chambers. As the king left St. Paul's, the pace of his progress was marked in the palace, for the cries of "A Edward!" "A Edward!" were gathering strength and moving nearer. The trumpets of triumph sounded at the gates, and the king was home in the arms of his family.

For the moment there was quiet only in the private chambers. The tears of the wife were wiped away. The daughters scrambled for places on the father's knees, and the king held in his arms the new son.[32] Words and explanations waited for a calmer time as the family wept and rejoiced. A ballad later described the scene:

> *The King comforted the Queen and other ladies eke.**
> *His sweet baby full tenderly he did kiss.*
> *The young prince he beheld and in his arms did bear.*
> *Thus his bale turned him to bliss.*
> *After sorrow joy, by the course of the world is.*
> *The sight of his babies released part of his woe.*
> *Thus the will of God in everything is do.***

This pleasure of reunion was undercut by insecurity. Warwick remained at large with his army; any day Margaret would land with reinforcements from France. The city of Westminster, if not the palace itself, still contained Lancastrians. Not

* also   ** done

knowing when and how the enemy might attack, Edward insisted that the family go immediately to his mother's home of Baynard's Castle, just west of the city. The move was quickly accomplished; Clarence and Gloucester joined the family for the night. Since it was Holy Thursday, the evening closed with divine service and fervent prayer. Through the next two nights and days, Yorkist adherents appeared for audiences and gave pledges of support.

Saturday, April 13, Edward returned to London, installed his family in the Tower for safety, and hoping to avoid a Lancastrian coup in the capital, took Henry VI with him. In the meantime the army was gathered and the king led the way toward Coventry. Midway between London and Coventry, he met and defeated the advance forces of Warwick. In the evening by a forced march Edward brought his men to Warwick's encampment at Barnet. Throughout the night Warwick's men, unable to believe Edward was so near, overshot the Yorkists. By morning heavy fogs had settled, and between four and five o'clock the trumpets blared through the dawn, and the banners were advanced. So dense was the fog that the armies had difficulty identifying each other, confusing the badges of the various houses. But Edward rode forward with violence, leading his men in the charge. As he hacked to the right and left, he beat and bore down the enemy in his way. The two armies slowly pivoted in the field so that the actual ground changed hands; thus, at one point, Warwick's men fought each other. With screams of treason, the beleaguered group disappeared over the hill. Warwick's army was forced slowly to give way, and the earl hastened to find a more strategic position. Instead of riding into his own ranks, however, he rode into one of Edward's detachments, and was captured, killed, stripped, and left lying on the forest floor.[33]

The entire battle lasted three hours. Since the order to kill the nobles and spare the commoners had not been given, an unusually large death toll, estimated between one and three thousand, resulted at Barnet Field. All but Warwick and his dead brother Montague were buried nearby. For these two noblemen there was further humiliation. Their naked bodies were loaded upon a springless cart and dragged in the procession back to London. The army proceeded directly to St. Paul's, where the bodies were placed on the pavement so that the curious and forlorn might pass by. There the corpses lay for four days, festering in the sun until they were removed for burial at Bisham Abbey. Henry, still wearing the oversized blue velvet gown, rode with his feet tied to the stirrups, and returned to the Tower.[34]

Edward ended his procession of triumph at St. Paul's and offered his prayers of thanksgiving and his banners of victory. Then he quickly turned his mind to matters of state. With Warwick gone, the king assumed more responsibility for government and he suddenly realized he enjoyed it. Uppermost in his scheme was the restoration of peace and prosperity. He wooed the nobles with promises of security and overwhelming power. He encouraged all men to him and won many through his easy sociability; but he kept his eye trained on the west where the Lancastrian supporters had fled.

Margaret of Anjou and the young Edward left France and landed at Weymouth on April 17, 1471. The bad news of defeats and deaths were heaped upon her so that "she like a woman all dismayed for fear fell to the ground, her heart was pierced with sorrow, her speech was in a manner gone, all her spirits were tormented with melancholy."[35] She did not lie long upon the ground. Instead she summoned her followers and moved toward Wales, where Jasper Tudor waited with his army. Her numbers increased rapidly—not enough to besiege London but enough to give her hope.

Edward, now alert to all reports, gathered his army at Windsor and through forced marches sought to intercept Mar-

garet before she reached Jasper Tudor and the armies he commanded. Once again his family stood about him, were lifted
one by one to kiss him good-bye. To his oldest daughter he
was a handsome sight in his gold armor that was cold and
hard to the touch. As he bestrode his horse, the father and king
looked the triumphant warrior, with his golden helmet and
black plumes, his handsome sword and gilt spurs. As the
trumpet blew the call, the royal banner unfurled. Its purple
velvet flashed the gold sun and the white rose in the morning
light. Once again the king pivoted in his saddle, blew kisses to
the ladies of the court, and shouted his challenge to the army.
To the sounds of hooves clattering on the stone and the drone
of feet marching, the army began to move. Each soldier wore
the badge of the white rose and carried a flaming torch; hundreds of priests sang hymns of victory and escorted the army out
of town.

Margaret and her army moved toward Gloucester and
Tewkesbury. On May 3 Edward made contact with his enemy.
Then the two armies rested through the night. Once again at
four in the morning, Edward launched an attack. Margaret, her
daughter-in-law Anne, and the ladies in attendance were
shocked from sleep and forced to dodge the arrows and cannon
fire in order to find safety in a religious house behind the lines.
Once more the battle lasted only a few hours; by the time it
was finished, more thousands were dead—including Margaret's
son the young Edward.[36] Other Lancastrians fled into sanctuary,
hoping to be pardoned by the king; but on the day following,
Gloucester had these men removed and beheaded. Margaret
was brought from sanctuary to become a prisoner.[37] Edward
started to move to subdue Jasper Tudor only to learn that the
Lancastrians had offered peace. The king then turned his army
and its captives toward London.

The city was under siege. The remaining Lancastrians were
making one final attempt under the leadership of the Bastard

Falconbridge. He faced fierce opposition, however, for the defense of the capital had been well planned. The raised draw of London Bridge formed a barricade, but three holes, driven into the bridge, allowed guns to fire from behind it. Guns and gunners also lined the city walls. Barrels of water were placed throughout the city to put out fires. In the Tower the royal family again gathered for safety and watched the attack of the Bastard. He lined his guns on the south bank and on the boats in the river. At his single barrage even the Tower quaked; and when it was over seven hundred men were killed or drowned. Before a second attack could be mounted, news came that Edward was returning to London. Falconbridge dropped the siege and headed for safety.

On May 21 Edward again entered London. The city appeared to be totally his. All Lancastrian badges and banners had disappeared, and no one openly sympathized with the humiliated Margaret as she was paraded through the streets in "a triumphal car,"[38] an object of stones, mud, and verbal abuse. She would remain in captivity for four years, until she was finally ransomed and returned to France. But this day, with all its anguish, meant the apparent end of the House of Lancaster. That evening Henry VI, whether stabbed at his prayers or felled by a paroxysm of despair, was found dead in the Tower.[39] His body, bare-faced upon the bier, was carried to St. Paul's where it bled upon the pavement. This strange fact strengthened the suspicion that he had indeed been murdered. From there he was carried to Chartsey Abbey for burial.[40] The remaining Lancastrian heir, Henry Tudor Earl of Richmond, and his uncle Jasper fled into self-imposed exile at the court of Francis II Duke of Brittany.

Edward subdued his opposers. Some he executed, others he taxed, and the remainder he pardoned. Knowing that increased taxation only hardened his enemies and weakened his friends, Edward determined to make himself and his government self-supporting. He therefore resumed control of nearly all the royal estates; he appointed capable, shrewd men to collect all customs and duties; he even entered the middle-class business of trade. He developed his own merchant ships and loaded them with the best products of the land—wools, cloths, tin, wood, alum, wax, and writing paper. These he sent mainly to Italy and Greece; and as business was transacted and goods exchanged, he was not above haggling over price. Little by little, he achieved enormous wealth and utilized it to the advantage of himself, his family, and his kingdom.

Mindful of the brilliance and magnificence of the Burgundian court, Edward sought to rival, if not surpass, it. The palaces of Westminster and Windsor were refurbished with gilt, oriental rugs, tapestries of rich color and intricate handiwork. The Chapel of St. George at Windsor he rebuilt and filled with gold images of St. George and the Virgin, crosses and crucifixes, basins and candlesticks, hangings rich in white velvet, white and gold damask, blue velvet tissue of gold. He continued the construction begun by Henry VI at Eton and King's College where the chapel, with its delicate fretting and intricate work, continued to stretch to the sky. During the many visits to Cambridge to enjoy the building, Elizabeth Woodville took up the interest of Margaret of Anjou and supported the building and development of Queens' College.[41]

During these years William Caxton, long patronized by Margaret of Burgundy, was encouraged to bring his press to London. He came with letters to her brother the king; and in the yard of Westminster Abbey at the sign of the Red Pale, he set up in 1476 his strange machinery and printed books. Intrigued by the operation, Edward and his daughter Elizabeth went often to the shop and came away with Caxton's work: Chaucer; the tales of King Arthur by Malory; Boethius' *The Consolation of Philosophy; The Mirror of the World;* Higdon's *Polychronican; The Golden Legend; Æsop's Fables; The Sayings of the Philosophers; The History of Troy; The Life of Our*

Lady; and others. In time the father and daughter read them all.[42] In addition Edward added the illuminated texts from abroad, books of hours, the writings of Titus Livius, of Boccaccio and St. Augustine, lives of the saints, and more. These too became part of the library and reading for Elizabeth and her sisters. Even when the family traveled, favorite books were packed in specially built carts so that reading was always possible.[43]

Elizabeth, as the king's daughter growing steadily into girlhood, shared not only these pleasures but also those of the court. On quiet evenings she played at chess and backgammon, danced with her sisters and small brother, sang, and played her lute. More often some festive occasion gave opportunity for pageantry and music, and the minstrels and children of the Chapel Royal played their instruments on "magic islands" or descended from clouds constructed in the great halls. Actors brought to court morality plays and punctuated them with bawdiness. Often the family went into the villages to watch folk festivals, May Day games, and harvest dances.

At Windsor there was always hunting, and Elizabeth and her sisters and parents waited under lodges of green boughs for the release of the hounds. As the three long notes signaled the uncoupling, the family spurred their horses into the fields. Then there would be the ducking of limbs and the racing over fences, as horse and rider responded to the chase.[44] For one who was tired or thirsty, there were throughout the parks of Windsor "vineyards of pleasure" and tiny gardens with fountains running with wine. In the evening after the banquets of fifty dishes and more, after the pageants and games, the king standing above six feet led his daughter in dance.[45]

For special occasions, such as the wedding of Elizabeth's second brother Richard Duke of York when he was three years old, there were tournaments designed to dazzle their beholders. On newly constructed stages Edward, clothed in velvet, the emblem of the Order of the Garter on his leg, a baton of estate in his hand, surrounded by his advisers and family, delighted in the skill of men and beasts. The favorite champion was always Anthony Woodville Lord Scales. Handsome in face, agile in body, quick to shatter a spear or to turn a stroke, he delighted in surprising the king and the court with a dramatic entrance. His attire and that of his retainers ranged from simple monk's robes to exotic armor. By the tourney's end, he was the one presented to his niece Elizabeth of York for the prize and trophies of the day.

There were also more serious occasions in which the princess participated. In 1476 Edward, remembering the humiliation of his father's last hours, the paper crown he was forced to wear before he was beheaded, sought to recompense the dead through reinterment. He therefore had the bodies of his father the Duke of York and his brother Edmund Earl of Rutland carried with great honor and ceremony from their humble graves at Pomfret to the new chapel at Fotheringay near Lincoln. Accompanying them were the leading nobles and ecclesiastics. After the dirges and prayers, the masses for the dead, the hymns of the choir, Elizabeth and her sister Cecily distributed largesse to the crowds. For the family it had been a mournful time, made sadder by the tears of the Duchess of York. And it had been difficult to reconcile the serious service with the joyous cries of the crowds as they scrambled for pennies in the street.[46]

Throughout these events since Warwick's fall, Edward named Clarence's son Edward as Earl of Warwick, demoted young George Bedford, nullified his betrothal to Elizabeth, and thought often of the best marriage he might arrange for his daughter. Opportunity for the most politically advantageous betrothal came in an unexpected way—through the persistent rivalry between France and Burgundy. Urged to battle against the French by his former host and brother-in-law Charles Duke of Burgundy, and not unmindful of Charles' aid in regaining the Yorkist throne, Edward set sail for Calais. The ever-capricious Charles, at the last moment however, refused to commit the promised men and money. But Edward was too politically astute to return home without a victory—any victory. He seized upon France's weakened state, its political unrest, its Italian campaigns, its desire for peace with the English at any price. The English Edward invited the French Louis to parley, and they arranged a most strange and guarded confrontation. The two monarchs met midway on a bridge spanning the river Somme, through two cages "contrived of strong wooden lattice, such as lion's cages are made with, the hole between every bar no wider than to thrust a man's arm. . . ." The two kings embraced cautiously through the wooden grill for fear of assassination. They talked a long time through the bars, and their terms seemed highly successful for England. Edward received the enormous sum of seventy-five thousand crowns and a pension of fifty thousand crowns a year for life. Louis received promises of peace for himself, and the hand of the Princess Elizabeth for the Dauphin.[47]

Great was the reception that greeted the king upon his return home. His subjects from the coast to London stood in the highways with bells and lighted candles; in the capital, butts of wine were rolled into the streets so that the city might toast the king's successes; from balconies and windows, tapestries and banners shimmered in the sun. All England seemed to sport the white rose of York; Edward bathed in the applause and cheers, and quickened the pace of the procession in order to reach Westminster Palace. There he swung his daughter into his arms, called her "Dauphiness" and teased her about her French. She would, he maintained, become the queen of France. She must, he insisted, have new gowns, new laces, new stomachers, new hoods and capes, new caps for her head, new shoes—all in the French style.[48]

For years he harbored the dream of the French marriage, pushed forward his daughter's lessons in the language, schooled her in matters of foreign etiquette. But the years dragged by toward the close of the decade, and Louis paid his debts but talked less of the wedding. Time and again it was postponed, and diplomacy exhausted itself. The wedding never came about.[49]

The French invasion, although seemingly profitable, had been expensive to raise; hence a need for more taxes. This time Edward himself helped with the money gathering. Wooing some citizens with promises and others with fair words, he was not unsuccessful. In one crowded audience an aged, wealthy widow was asked by the king if she were able to contribute to the expense of the wars. She answered: "By my troth . . . for thy lovely countenance thou shalt have even twenty pounds." Edward, expecting half that amount, thanked her, and lovingly kissed her. "Whether the flavor of his breath did so comfort her stomach, or she esteemed the kiss of a king so precious a jewel, she swore incontinently, that he should have twenty pounds more. . . ."[50]

In the days of joy and sorrow the possibilities of renewed Lancastrian risings were never far from the king's thoughts. Henry Tudor Earl of Richmond, the leading male representative of the Lancastrian line, continued to lurk in Brittany, ever vigilant, ever preparing himself for the possibility of wearing the crown. He was still a boy and could afford to wait. Edward, however, was aware of the little band of Lancastrian exiles who continued to plot and dream of conquest, and he did not care to wait for some unforeseen catastrophe. In a gesture which neither took seriously, he offered the hand of Elizabeth to Henry Tudor on the condition that he live in England. Fearing death rather than marriage, the Earl of Richmond escaped from the English ambassadors and took sanctuary.[51]

It was, however, not from abroad that immediate danger

threatened. It was at home. Since the fall of Warwick, Clarence and the king seemed at least outwardly reconciled. They were bound, after all, by a bond of brotherhood and devotion to their mother Cecily Duchess of York. But throughout the years Clarence became increasingly reticent, uttered little in council, and came less frequently to court. He raged and swore in public and private when Edward allowed his brother Gloucester to marry Anne Neville, Warwick's widowed daughter. The marriage meant that Clarence must divide with Gloucester the properties held by their wives—the vast inheritance from Warwick. Furthermore Clarence resented the queen and the Woodville presence. Nor did the queen hold him in liking; he had deserted the king once, and she believed him capable of doing it again. She felt he simply could not be trusted. Perhaps Edward had his doubts too. In any event, Clarence was summoned to the council at Westminster, and Edward railed against his brother "amongst other matters, to inveigh against the conduct of the . . . duke, as being derogatory to the laws of the realm."[52] Clarence was pronounced guilty, removed to imprisonment in the Tower, and later found dead in a butt of malmsey wine.[53]

The death of Clarence, once accomplished, gnawed at the king. He had cut into the flesh of his family and was stained with fratricide; the joy of living fled from life. He continued to hurl himself by day into the work of government, the pleasures of the hunt, the education of his children. By night he caroused —eating, drinking, whoring with his friend Hastings. Gone now was the lean body of youth, wasted by the strains of hardship and pleasure. He became heavy, corpulent, sometimes too easily breathless. Outwardly he seemed robust, but the spirit was out of the man.[54]

In April, 1483, three weeks short of his forty-first birthday, Edward joined a fishing party. In the boat with the damp air around him, he joked and swore, ate and drank, gave himself freely to the pleasures of the excursion. But he caught a chill and was forced to his bed.[55] No one thought him seriously ill, but he felt himself dissolving between the covers, his hold on life slipping away. Ever and again his mind turned to his children, too young to be left alone. He had hoped to see Elizabeth seated on the throne of France, but that proved hopeless. He had wanted to live long enough to see his sons grow to manhood, prepared and ready for rule, but that was now impossible. The princes were still boys. The Prince of Wales, twelve years old, he longed to see, to speak of the problems of power; but the boy was at Ludlow. Somehow the father must provide a strong regency for his children, for only then could the dreams and goals he held for them come true.

Hurriedly, desperately, he called his counselors. Change the will, he said, let Gloucester instead of the queen be regent. Gloucester, ever faithful, ever valiant, was strong enough, courageous enough, bold enough, to hold the throne for the young Edward until he could maintain it himself. Somehow too the factions of court must be removed; his family and that of the queen's must surely rally behind the boy who held the blood of them all. To insure the point, the king called before him Dorset, the queen's son by her first marriage, and Hastings, his own best friend. Edward urged them as representatives of various court factions to reconciliation, to take the initiative to unite political differences to insure harmony and peace. Then he asked, begged them, to embrace. The men, weeping, complied.[56]

Then Edward called his children before him. Elizabeth, holding the nine-year-old Richard Duke of York by the hand, led her sisters Cecily, Margaret, Anne, Catherine, and Bridget into the room. Their father urged them to scholarship, to gentleness, to loyalty to their brother Edward. They must help him to be a good king. They must draw on all their strength to demand the best of themselves, for they were born to serve a nation. Each of the children kissed him for the last time. Somehow he looked less like a king and more like a man weary and worn with life. His strength and stature were gone; his hands, once so strong, now trembled on the cover. It was a dreadful thing to watch a father die.

Edward raised himself again, turned to his advisers, and said: "My children by your diligent oversight and politic persuasion [must] be taught, informed, and instructed, not only in the science liberal, virtues moral, and good literature; but also to be practiced in tricks of martial activity, and diligent exercise. For I have heard clerks say, although I am unlettered, that fortunate is the realm where philosophers reign, or where kings be philosophers and lovers of wisdom. . . . My kingdom also I leave in your governance during the minority of my children, charging you (on your honors, oaths, and fidelity made and sworn to me) so indifferently to order and govern the subjects on the same, both with justice and mercy. . . . Oh, I am so sleepy, that I must make an end. And now before you all I commend my soul to Almighty God my saviour and redeemer, my body to the worms of the earth, my kingdom to the prince my son; and to you my loving friends my heart, my trust, and my whole confidence."[57]

These words stole away his remaining strength, and he slid into his pillows. His eyes continued to watch them all in silent appeal. And as each one in the room joined hands in unity, there was none who refrained from weeping.

2 · THE SISTER OF THE KING

To the queen, resting now from the labor of birth, the death of her father twenty years ago was a vivid and scorching memory. The death itself, a severe psychic blow, had been only the first of a long and bloody series of events difficult to comprehend, impossible to reconcile. As she lay now, lost in the past, she relived the pieces of what she had seen and heard, and sought to understand the motives of men and the horrors they had wrought.

EDWARD IV was dead, and his funeral reflected the vicissitudes of his life. Soon after his death, his body was "laid upon a board all naked, saving he was covered from the navel to the knees." Mayor, aldermen, the lords temporal and spiritual moved before the body in a slow and solemn procession, twelve hours long, to affirm that the king was in truth now dead. The body, wrapped in wax cloth and dressed in a full suit of gold armor, was placed in the silver coffin, the orb and sceptre were settled in the cold hands, the crown was placed on the unmoving brow. For eight days the body so rested in the Chapel of St. Stephen while masses were intoned, prayers offered, and offerings made. He had been a good and

loving prince, and his subjects and family were loath to let
him go. For the last farewell, the king was moved into the Abbey. To pay their respects came bishops and abbots; priests with
their long black flaming candles; knights visored in black mail;
and in a secret place the royal children, now more pitiful for
their black clothes and sorrowing faces. To one side stood the
funeral image of the king, "a personage like to the similitude of
the king in habit royal, crowned with the very crown on his
head, holding in one hand a sceptre and in that other hand a ball
of silver and gilt with a cross pate."[1]

After the services, the cortège moved from the Abbey toward
Windsor. The image of the king preceded his bier, which was
now draped in black velvet and drawn by six black horses.
Knights and esquires in mourning dress rode beside the body,
and the doleful group moved through the spring rains and
muddy roads to Charing Cross, Sion House, Eton, and St.
George's Chapel at Windsor. In the partially completed building which the man had so loved, his body was given to its
marble vault. Standing there at the grave, the chief men of the
household broke their staves and dropped them into the tomb
"in token of being men without a master and out of their
office." The gold armor and the royal banners were hung above
the tomb.[2] Of these sad events the minstrel wrote:

> *O noble Edward, where art thou become,*
> *Which full worthy I have seen going in estate?*
> *Edward the Fourth I mean, with the sun,*
> *The rose, the sun-beam, which was full fortunate.*
> *No earthly prince durst make with him debate.*
> *Art thou agone, and was here yesterday?*
> *All men of England are bound for thee to pray.*[3]

But no member of Edward's family attended these services at
Windsor; though the dead might rest, the living faced new
struggles.[4]

For the children there was great loneliness for the young and vigorous father who was no more. Elizabeth, who inherited his grace, his beauty, and his charm, took on the role of comforter to the younger girls and their brother, the Duke of York. She insisted on the daily routines of prayer and study, and sought to explain to the other children the awesome finality of earthly death and the everlasting quality of spiritual life. If the explanations confused little York, they nevertheless gave his sister solace. Now she had to adjust to new responsibilities—the ordering of the household, the calming of grief among Edward's retainers, the soothing of complaints of the stewards and servants so often made angry by the haughtiness of her mother. The girl assumed the mother's place and became for the family, its friends, and its servants the quiet center to which they all might retreat.

For the dowager queen Elizabeth Woodville anxiety and confusion grew. Alarmed that her husband in his dying hour had replaced her as regent with Gloucester, with whom she shared a mutual loathing, she strove to maintain the regency for herself. She wrote immediately to her son Edward, now the fifth of the name, of his new sorrow and great duty. Acting in his behalf and her own, she sent her son Dorset to the Tower to secure the treasury. This precaution upon a king's death was traditional enough. For greater security, however, the treasury was divided three ways: one part Dorset kept at the Tower; a second part the dowager queen took into her own possession; and the third part she gave to her brother Edward Woodville to hold in the safety of his ships. These actions only renewed the old anti-Woodville feelings. The tensions between the Woodville and court factions had never really died but had, at Edward's command, merely been glossed over by courtesy. Now once again they broke into the open.

While these events were taking place in London, in Wales there was greater activity. Wagons and carts were packed, new livery stitched, the harness polished and fastened, and the banners unfurled at the direction of the young Edward and his council. He had come to Wales when only three years old to make his home in Ludlow Castle, his father's boyhood home and the traditional seat of the heir to the throne.[5] Technically his residency had been to subdue and govern the territory through his ministers. Chief among these was Anthony Earl Rivers,* the handsome, sophisticated Rivers of tournament fame, of the gorgeous dress that hid a knotted hairshirt next to his skin. But all the councilors were Woodvilles or Woodville adherents; Elizabeth Woodville had insisted upon this point, guarding against the day when her son became the king. The plan had worked well; Wales was subdued, the government efficiently maintained.

Under the direction of Rivers and Chamberlain Thomas Vaughan, the Prince of Wales grew in body and mind. The older he became, the more severe the disciplines of his life. Rising at dawn he heard matins in his chamber and mass in his chapel. After breakfast he studied "virtuous learning"—the philosophers, history, languages. At dinner he heard "such noble stories as behooveth to a prince to understand and know." He was returned then to his studies and exercises—wielding the poleax, the dagger and sword; wrestling; climbing; riding with an eye toward future tournaments and jousts.[6] He was so well taught and disciplined that one observer wrote: "In word and deed he gave so many proofs of his liberal education, of polite, nay rather scholarly, attainments far beyond his age . . . his special knowledge of literature, which enabled him to discourse elegantly, to understand fully, and to declaim most excellently from any work whether in verse or prose that came into his hands. . . . He had such dignity in his whole person, and in his face such charm, that however much they might gaze he never wearied the eyes of beholders."[7]

---

* Formerly Anthony Lord Scales. He succeeded to his father's title as Earl Rivers.

Death, however, had broken off the education at Ludlow, and the twelve-year-old prince was called home to be a king. Messages from his mother and his father's friend Hastings encouraged an escort of no more than two thousand men.[8] By mid-April the procession left Ludlow for the two-hundred-mile journey to London. As they moved across the country, men and women turned in their fields to cheer, and the lanes were marked with villagers whose tears of mourning turned to joy at the beauty of the young king. As Edward moved eastward, his uncle Richard Duke of Gloucester and Protector of the Realm rode the two hundred miles southward from his country estate. The two were to meet near London and enter the city together.

Who could define Gloucester's feeling as he left York? Surely his had been the role of the king's younger brother, and he had played the role manfully. He was tried in battle and tested in diplomacy. He had subdued his northern neighbors and won their love. Since he hated the queen and the Woodvilles, he had been to court very little of late; but news of his brother's death had shattered his retreat.[9] Now his was the singular mission to follow his brother's command and to protect the realm and its young prince. His letters to the dowager queen were filled with sympathy, consolation, and promises of fealty to the new king.[10] He had dressed himself and his household in mourning, participated in the memorial services in York, and constrained the northern nobility to the loyalty of Edward V. Now he rode to meet his nephew and his king.

Edward and Rivers were the first to arrive at Stony Stratford, the assigned place of meeting. Since the town was small, the king ordered most of his men to disperse into neighboring villages so that there might be room for his uncle's retinue. Gloucester, however, arrived in Northampton and waited the night. His cousin, the jovial and ebullient Buckingham, hastened from London to meet him. Upon hearing these reports, Rivers saw the king to bed, and accompanied by his nephew

Richard Grey, half-brother to the new king, rode to visit Gloucester.

There in the crowded and darkened inn, the men consoled and comforted each other over heaps of roast beef, chicken, puddings, and ale. Sympathy and the significance of the moment brought the four into unusual conviviality and seeming trust. The talk was for tomorrow, for the king, for the need for faction to be eliminated, for the Woodvilles and the nobility to join in singular allegiance. Edward's throne must be secured, for him, for England, for them all. The light of the evening fire played starkly against the wall, and the light it cast caused grotesque and hovering shadows, while a few miles away the boy king slept.

Rivers and Grey were the first to tire, and at Gloucester's insistence removed themselves to a neighboring inn instead of returning to Stony Stratford. Gloucester and Buckingham talked long into the night, and the conclusions of that evening's conversation challenged the expectations and hopes of men. At dawn, the servants of Rivers and Grey were dismissed and sent away. In their place stood Gloucester's retainers. When the two Woodvilles arose and readied themselves to return to their king, their passage was blocked by armed guards. The two were under house arrest.[11] There was no time for messages or exchanges of thought. By dawn their feet were tied to the stirrups and the movement of their horses was toward a Gloucester stronghold in the north.

Simultaneously, a group of Gloucester's men dashed to Stony Stratford, stormed into the inn where Edward only moments before had been preparing to greet his uncles, seized the attendants, but left the twelve-year-old boy untouched. As he watched with fear and wonder from the window, more horses and riders careened into the yard. Among them was his uncle, somewhat smaller than the others and dwarfed still more by his mourning dress. From the window and the angle it offered, Gloucester's raised shoulder and oversized right arm—the result of intensive physical activity—showed him almost a cripple. The boy king left the window, moved to the gallery, and descended the outer stairs. Gloucester, noting the child's movements, quickly dismounted, bared his head, and knelt upon the cobblestones. In a sudden rush, Buckingham and all the attendants knelt low. The boy stood before them, his eyes searching for his uncle Rivers, for his half-brother Richard Grey. With the realization of their absence, his fear quickened.[12]

Gloucester, perhaps sensing the boy's fear, rose to embrace him, and standing with his oversized arm about the boy's shoulders, the protector caused all present to pledge loyalty to the new sovereign. As cries of "A Edward! A Edward!" died, a herald standing upon the gallery presented the second of Gloucester's announcements, the dismissal of all the king's attendants, of the faithful band of two thousand, of the personal servants, in short, all who had accompanied Edward from Ludlow. All such persons were banished from the presence of the king and ordered upon penalty to return immediately to their homes. Too startled to protest, the king's retainers gave way. They could not reach Edward, standing in the midst of Gloucester's men in the courtyard. But perhaps there was no cause for alarm. Perhaps Gloucester was merely assuming in a literal way the protectorship declared by the late king. Perhaps there was nothing to do now but go home. Indeed Gloucester was showing all honor and humility before the king as the two turned to re-enter the inn. But those kneeling nearby saw the light which glistened on the tear-streaked face of the boy.

The noise in the inn yard increased as the men rose—Gloucester's and Buckingham's men to take arms about the yard, and the king's men to mount their horses, gather their retainers, and move away. Most of them followed Gloucester's suggestion and marched homeward, but several raced along the road southward to London. Hours later they dispersed to inform

the leaders of the king's party of what had happened. One beat
at the gate of Dr. Thomas Rotherham the Archbishop of York
and Chancellor of England. The messenger fell upon his knees
and moaned that Edward V was now a prisoner. The chancellor,
raising the fellow to his feet, answered: ". . . be it as it will,
it will never be so well as we have seen it." Rotherham then
alerted his household, saw that every man was armed, took the
Great Seal in his hands, and with his men about him, sought the
dowager queen.[13]

At Westminster Palace all was frenzy bordering on panic.
The queen wept and swore and sat dumbly upon the rush floor.
The chief steward tried to instill order, and the princesses raced
about the rooms pointing out the furnishings which were to be
moved. For the queen and her children, this midnight news
meant a return to the sanctuary of the Abbey. Elizabeth, as the
oldest child of the family, took charge and ordered everyone,
regardless of rank, to carry the chests, the coffers, the packs,
the fardels into the sanctuary. To hasten the move, walls were
broken down, windows ripped open; all charged back and forth,
sometimes crashing one into another, to send loads sprawling.
And in this confusion, the beggars of the walkways darted in
like so many harpies to snatch away the unguarded parcels.[14]

Amidst the shouting, Rotherham saluted Elizabeth, and the
two returned to the palace and the queen. Disdaining even a
chair, the queen remained among the rushes on the floor. Her
tears traced her face, her hands tore at her hair as she called
aloud the names of Edward, Grey, Rivers—the sons and brother
she felt she would see no more. Her daughter and the archbishop knelt to comfort her. Gradually the anguish and hysteria
subsided. As the archbishop placed in her hands the Great Seal
—without which nothing could legally be done—he tried to
comfort her by expressing his belief that her conclusions were
surely wrong, that Gloucester was merely doing her husband's
bidding, that the young king and her adherents would be safe.

The grieving queen continued to moan that Gloucester "is one of them that laboreth to destroy me and my blood." But to have the Seal was comforting, and the grieving woman stood up, leaned heavily on the arm of her daughter, and bid the archbishop good day. With one final look at Westminister Palace, she crossed the way to the abbot's chambers and sanctuary.

The archbishop returned home. Only hours later Gloucester's liveried men dominated the streets, and the Thames was filled with his boats and men so that no one might pass to the sanctuary or go unsearched. In order to adjust to the changing times, or to be at least prepared for whatever might fall, the archbishop went once again to the sanctuary and took away the Seal.[15]

Elizabeth and her sisters remembered the earlier sanctuary. It had been difficult; the quarters were too small; the confinement, too narrow; the rooms, too dark. Then, however, there had been a dynamic, energetic father who had somehow found freedom and friends, who had sent messages of encouragement, who had promised a quick release. Now who was there to be trusted? Surely their twelve-year-old brother was as helpless as they. Rivers, who might have been the one to bring aid, had disappeared. Some said he was in the north, others that he was dead, but all felt that he would never again come to London. Edward Woodville and his ship heavy with treasure had sought the safety of the sea.[16]

Squeezed once again into the narrow rooms, packing and unpacking clothes and goods to make some semblance of a home, the girls waited. Their mother wept and clasped to her the one remaining son, Richard the nine-year-old Duke of York. Through him, as pathetic as it might seem, there was hope. He was the heir of his brother and as long as he was safe, he protected the king's life. It would be needless to kill the one without the other. News suddenly grew scant. The sanctuary

was so closely guarded that nothing came through but Gloucester's messages of encouragement. There was, he assured
them, no need for sanctuary, no need for fear; he was indeed
bringing the king to London within the week, and he hoped the
queen and the Duke of York would be able to greet them. The
dowager queen had no intention of leaving the sanctuary.

On May 4, the day which had been set for the coronation,
Edward V entered London. Dressed in blue velvet, the golden
boy reined his horse. Next to him rode Gloucester, still in black
mourning, still openly reverent to the king, still loving to the
mayor and aldermen in their scarlet dress. The banners and
trumpets, the men of London, and Gloucester's followers
ushered the king to Bishop's Palace near St. Paul's.[17] Those in
the sanctuary followed their progress through the shouts and
music that accompanied the king and his retinue as they moved
across the city; but they knew there would be no coronation
this day. For a moment there had been fleeting hope that Edward and Gloucester would come directly to the Abbey to
welcome the king's family out of sanctuary. It had been nearly
a year since the mother had seen the son, since the sisters and
their brother had seen the then Prince of Wales. That too had
been an occasion for sorrow rather than joy. The death of the
second daughter Mary, unexpected as it was, had been the last
event to bring the family together. Then the young Edward, as
chief mourner, had accompanied the body, wrapped in its
wax-sheet in a silver coffin, to St. George's Chapel at Windsor.
That sorrow had been replaced by new ones; now as those in
sanctuary listened to the sounds of Edward's procession moving
further away, sorrow gave way to despair.

True it was that Gloucester had made all the lords spiritual
and temporal swear allegiance to Edward V. True too that the
council convened immediately to discuss the date of coronation,
the proper lodgings for the king, and the role of the protector.
According to the terms of Edward IV's will, the protector's

authority was due to cease with Edward V's coronation. At that point, the responsibility for government became that of the king's council. The major issue to be resolved, then, was Gloucester's relation to the rest of the council. Was he, as Dorset maintained, only *primus inter pares*? Or was he, as Buckingham maintained, Protector of the Realm with all the privileges of a king?[18] Of all these events, Gloucester kept the dowager queen informed as he simultaneously pledged good faith, urged her to leave the sanctuary, or at least to send the Duke of York to comfort his brother.[19]

The date of the coronation was set for Tuesday, June 24; the delay was explained as necessary for the elaborate preparations. The place for the king's lodgings was hotly debated; it was felt that the boy needed greater freedom of movement and fewer restrictions than Bishop's Palace demanded. Some of the council insisted that he move to Westminster Palace—a place both fitting and familiar to the king. Some suggested the Hospital of St. John because of its copious apartments. But Buckingham and Gloucester urged the Tower itself as the traditional lodging for a king awaiting his coronation. Therefore during the second week in May, Edward moved into the royal apartments of that stark garrison. The walls afforded him protection, the rooms offered some sense of home and the familiar, and the grounds provided room for horses and dogs, for wrestling and shooting of arrows.

Gloucester, after a brief debate, was installed as Lord Protector by unanimous consent of the council, "with power to order and forbid in every matter, just like another king. . . ."[20] The meetings of the council had gone smoothly, and most felt that the proper decisions had been made. Furthermore, Gloucester seemed willing and able to carry through his office. Thus gradually a sense of calm and well-being began to settle in London, and from there emanated into the countryside. Perhaps these awkward days would bring peace after all. That was the important point.

However, to thinking men loyal to the king, there was growing suspicion and creeping doubt. Why, for instance, were the king's relatives on his mother's side still in prison? Why the pointed display of the seized arms bearing the heraldic devices of the Woodvilles, as though there had been attempts of treason? Most courtiers knew these weapons to be simply caches stowed near London under the directive of Edward IV in the event of new Scottish wars. Why then this intentional disguise of an innocent act?[21] Why the dismissal of those who were known for their loyalty to the late king's family? Why did the dowager queen and her family not join the king at the Tower? Or at least why had there not been correspondence between them? Why, at least, had not appropriate means been taken to assure the preservation of the dignity and safety, the comfort and needs, of the dowager queen and her family?

To those in sanctuary these events only added further anguish. Anyone beyond the walls who attempted to aid them seemed immediately doomed. Gloucester's messages, however, remained assuring. To see the king, the dowager queen had only to leave the sanctuary. To be free, the daughters had only to come to court. As for the young Duke of York, his brother anxiously awaited him in the royal apartments in the Tower. The daughters, like their mother, were frightened by this seeming duplicity and vowed to stay together in sanctuary regardless of the bribes that might be offered. Their safety was a collective one. Comprehension of these events was especially difficult for the Duke of York. Never a robust child, the suddenness of his father's death seemed to tear at his own life. Unlike Edward, who had spent his years alone, Richard had stayed at home, a frequent companion to his father. Now that this major force was wrenched from his heart, the boy sickened. The frantic midnight move, his mother's constant sorrow and woe, the fears of his sisters, the ever-present confusion and insecurity only nettled his spirit. Within days he was ill, and his silent sadness made heavier the dark days of refuge.

May slid into June, and the lengthening ease of the warming days contrasted with the chilling unease of increasing faction. The conspiracy of Gloucester and Buckingham grew. Rarely was the one seen without the other, for access to Gloucester was through his cousin only. Buckingham was fast becoming the second most powerful man in the realm—a place he had long known to be his by descent and by desire. After all, the blood royal in his veins was as pure as that of the kings he had known. Descended from Edward III's youngest son, Thomas Woodstock, it was only an accident of birth which had placed the crown beyond his grasp. Or did it? Others had pushed and shoved to the throne, men of lesser nobility, men tainted by the bastard stain. And surely none could be more charming, more personable, more vivacious, more buoyant than he, Buckingham. He stood now with the man who held the power, and while the two contrasted in manner, personality, and appearance, each served to balance the other's weakness. Bound by ambition and a ringing hatred for the Woodville clan, Gloucester and Buckingham encouraged each other.

Both had reasons to hate the Woodvilles. Gloucester still held the dowager queen responsible for his brother Clarence's death. Buckingham, orphaned as a boy, had become the ward of the queen. Aware of Buckingham's royal descent, conscious of his vast inheritance and holdings, ever anxious to cement members of her family to positions of power, the queen had the boy married to her sister Catherine. Buckingham grew to loathe his wife, the queen, and all her family, their low blood and presumptuous ways. When Lancastrian fortunes seemed high, Buckingham supported Henry VI. When the Yorkists surmounted the wheel, Buckingham proved as agile as the rest. At Edward IV's bidding, he became High Steward of England, and not only contrived the trial of his old compatriot Clarence but also sentenced him to death.

But Gloucester forgave this indiscretion and continued to

give Buckingham his ear and his purse. Buckingham's words fed the protector's ambitions and the money fed his own. Together they would manage the Woodvilles, together they would secure the power. And afterwards, who knew what opportunities might come. Certainly for the moment, opposition was in abeyance. Rivers, Vaughan, and Grey were safely in prisons. The twelve-year-old king was secured in the Tower, unhappy and lonely, perhaps, but that was of little consequence. After all life was difficult, and the boy would be strengthened by adversity. One day he would thank them for it. The dowager queen remained in sanctuary. It was annoying to have her alive at all, but at least she was out of sight, her meddling mouth silenced for the most part. And the daughters—well, they were bright, attractive, and appealing. Marriageable, too. But as long as they were with their mother, locked away in sanctuary, they were harmless enough. One day they might be tempted from their foolish exile-in-residence. And if death pleased to remove the king and his brother, then their charming sister Elizabeth, still a virgin, would inherit the throne. Then the uncle or cousin might take her for his own, share her throne and her bed. But this was the pleasing possibility of the future; there remained more pressing problems of the moment.

Edward Woodville, able admiral and strategist that he was, had fled to Brittany, and placed himself, his ship, and his treasury at the disposal of Henry Tudor Earl of Richmond. Other Yorkists by the hundreds had joined them. Together they plotted, and spawned rumors that invasions would be launched. Additional aid would come from either Burgundy or France. Perhaps from both.

In London Gloucester maintained that Richmond didn't believe he could successfully invade England; but in case he entertained any such foolish notion, precautions must be taken against any help from home. No one, for instance, must see the king, and no one would. He might stir hearts and devotion, he might become the visible rallying point. It was in this vein that Gloucester and Buckingham must have mused as the coronation preparations for Edward V went forward.

But his father's friend Hastings the Lord Chamberlain kept insisting on visiting the young king, inquiring about his health, and interfering and questioning the actions of the protector. Hastings, Edward IV's old procurer and drinking companion, long tolerated by the queen, was now hated by Gloucester. Forgotten were the happy days of companionship when the two had best served Edward IV. Forgotten was the bloody camaraderie of the foggy morning at Barnet when the two fought together for a common cause. Hastings had gained too much power and influence. Had he not in the last years brought about the death of the former king by encouraging his unbounded gluttony and lust? Had he not collected Edward's leavings? Did he not these very nights possess the body of the last royal whore Jane Shore? Might he not, with his laughing ways and flamboyant dress, with his ability for winning friends and arousing discontent, become a focal point of opposition? He not only could, he probably would. In these days of suspicion and capricious fortune, Hastings—now loathed and despised—must die.

But he was not the only one scheduled for elimination. There were others who more and more openly began to question Gloucester's position and government. The opposition, in short, was beginning to find its leadership. In addition to the Lord Chamberlain Hastings, there was John Morton Bishop of Ely, Thomas Rotherham Archbishop of York, and Thomas Lord Stanley.

Morton, best known for his agile mind, his intellect, and his love of learning, had followed Lancastrian hopes to their pitiful conclusion. In and out of prison through the anxious years of Edward IV's early reign, he had at various times followed Margaret of Anjou's bitter exile into France, fought faithfully in her service in both the fields of diplomacy and war. He had marched the long and futile miles to Tewkesbury and become victim of the final defeats. But Edward had recognized the bishop's ambition and abilities and forwarded both, and Morton had served his new king well. Perhaps that loyalty had so grown that he would now serve the boy-king with equal vigor. Perhaps he saw the hopes of restoring once again a Lancastrian Henry to the throne. Perhaps even now he was engaged in forbidden correspondence with the dowager queen, with Richmond, or with both. At any event, he might run counter to the Gloucester protectorate. Morton was marked for extinction.

Rotherham too could not be trusted. Had he not, in his early confusion over the so-called seizure of the king, rushed to Westminster and handed the Great Seal to the queen? True, in a calmer moment he had rushed back to Westminster and regained the Seal. But where did his loyalties lie: with the new king and the new government; or with the Woodvilles and some misunderstood allegiance to the queen? Since Rotherham's actions had been ambiguous and his thoughts unknown, he too was expendable.

Finally there was Thomas Lord Stanley. His long loyalty and service to the House of York was marred, like many others, by certain agile political footwork in the long, hard year of 1470. When Edward IV had disappeared over the Channel taking Yorkist hopes with him, and Warwick and Clarence turned to the Lancastrian forces, Stanley likewise placed his shoulder against the Lancastrian wheel. He too had marched through London, entered the Tower, and led forth into the light of day the pale blinking Henry VI. When Lancastrian hopes proved stillborn, Stanley's indiscretion had been forgiven, and he re-entered Edward's service. He became one of the most powerful and wealthy landholders of the kingdom and gained the title of Steward of the Royal Household. He was so trusted by Edward that the dying king had, in one final gesture, named

Stanley as one of his executors in place of Elizabeth Woodville. Stanley thus became a member of Edward V's council and was seemingly dedicated to the young king. But recently Stanley had married again. The marriage might now raise great political speculation if not real political threat, for the bride was none other than Lady Margaret Beaufort Countess of Richmond and mother of the remaining Lancastrian hope—Henry Tudor Earl of Richmond. Could Stanley with his wealth, his power, his new marital alliance be kept in check? The question was important, and the answer unknown. Stanley too must die.

On Friday, June 13, members of the council gathered in the Tower to discuss the latest developments and plans for the coronation. At nine o'clock Gloucester, still in his mourning robes, appeared. He saluted graciously the men who rose about him, and apologized for oversleeping. As the easy conversation continued, he turned suddenly to Bishop Morton and said: "My lord, you have very good strawberries at your gardens in Holbern, I require you let us have a mess of them." Morton, apparently regretting that he had no finer offering to make, hastened to his feet and immediately dispatched a servant to fetch the berries. With this conversation, Gloucester left the council. The talk returned to the selection of coronation pageants, the invitation lists, the banquet menus, and the order of the processions.

Suddenly Gloucester reappeared, this time with an armed escort. As he entered he began first to mutter and then to declaim about the inadequacies of the dowager queen, Elizabeth Woodville. In one breath he slandered her birth; in the next, he called her a sorceress. And as his voice swelled with anger and hate, he circled about the room challenging the men with his eyes and words. Suddenly he swept down upon Hastings, breathed hard into his face. Gloucester ripped away at his own sleeve, tore it back about his arm and shouted: "Ye shall all see in what wise that sorceress the queen, and that other witch of her council Shore's wife have by their sorcery and witchcraft wasted my body."[22]

The wizened arm shook before Hastings' face as he drew back in astonishment. It was impossible to stand, to answer. The accusations and implications came too fast. Someone was shouting treason. Some jumped up in amazement. An usher pulled open the door, and a body of soldiers roared in, seized Hastings, Rotherham, and Morton. Another soldier slammed his sword at Stanley, who fell under the table and hid beneath its oriental covering. As Hastings, Morton, and Rotherham were dragged from the room, Gloucester stormed out behind them. The chamber was suddenly quiet. The ones left behind stood white and shaken amidst the fallen notes of Edward V's coronation.[23]

For the moment, thoughts took the place of movement. The arm revealed was indeed thinner than the other, as everyone in the room knew. The explanation had always been that the larger arm resulted from overdevelopment, from Gloucester's anxiety to be the best at all physical activity, from his attempts to compensate for his small stature by being better than larger, stronger men. The accusations of witchcraft were obviously nonsense. The idea that Elizabeth Woodville might conjure with Jane Shore boggled all reason—the dowager queen hated the royal whore. They never spoke except with disguised loathing and spite. Besides, the assumption was an impossible one. The queen remained in sanctuary while the whore lived with Hastings.

Stanley slowly emerged from under the table, blood dripping from his head, and the others raised him up. Slowly, somewhat incoherently, he began to talk of his nightmare of the evening before: a boar—Gloucester's heraldic device—raged about the dream, dived into a fathomless pit, and reappeared, lifting the heads of Stanley and Hastings from their bloody shoulders. Escaping into wakefulness, Stanley had sent a servant to Hastings at midnight and invited the Lord Chamberlain to immediate escape. The horses were ready, but Hastings had laughed and returned to the arms of Mistress Shore.[24]

The dream and its instant fulfillment only increased the fear of the moment. Horrendous forces seemed now unleashed. A bloody purge had begun and no man knew where it might lead. The hammering of hearts was suddenly mocked as sounds of scuffling, sounds of marching feet, sounds of a priest's intonement penetrated the chamber. The councilors ran to the window. There in the yard below, soldiers stood about a squared piece of timber. Before it knelt Hastings, his collar now torn away. He seemed to be confessing to the standing priest. Suddenly someone thrust a foot into the prisoner's back. His head slapped against the timber. Before he could move, the axman struck him dead.[25]

In the chamber, Stanley vomited. Sick with fear and disgusted with his weakness, he forced his eyes away from the shame on the floor and looked down to the bloody heap in the yard. His eyes followed the headsman's lifting of the dripping head. But his eyes, not able to tolerate the sight, shifted their gaze to that white spot in the window above the chapel across the way. There in horror and anguish was the ashen face and the widened eyes of the twelve-year-old king. He swooned and dropped from sight.

A guard returned and led Stanley to imprisonment somewhere in the Tower. The sounds of the disappearing footsteps brought the remaining members of the council back to reality. Ashen, shaken, silent, with quickened steps they left the room, the stairs, the hallways. Fearing to be stopped along the way, some of the men all but ran to the gates and the outside freedom.

As they raced to their homes, news of the morning horrors followed. Citizens in knotted, anxious groups appeared on the streets. Some murmured of treason; others, that the boy-king himself was dead. The lanes and roadways became packed with

people. The talk surged with nervousness. The waves of
people bumped the booths and wagons along the streets. The
atmosphere was quickly approaching hysteria when the king's
messengers began to ride through the crowds. Their announcements were fragmentary. There had been a plot against the
government. Hastings, the leader, had been seized, and in the
cause of civil justice and out of fear of renewed war, he had
been executed. The citizens need fear no more. The protector,
through vigilance and perseverance born of his great charge
and love of his people, had seen the danger and amended it.
England could rest. The people must go home. There was now
no danger. Slowly the crowds thinned.[26]

News of these events came in sporadic, confused messages
to those in sanctuary. As the horrors became clear, Elizabeth
Woodville became increasingly sure that she and her family
were now in mortal danger. Hastings, in an earlier context, had
been a hated enemy. The evenings he had led Edward IV to
greater debauchery, the loud hours of carousing, the never-
ending lines of whores and wenches usurping the queen's pil-
low could never be forgiven. But Hastings had worshiped
Edward IV, had answered his needs, had made him laugh
much as she herself had done in those days when she and her
husband were young and in love. Hastings had been faithful.
Whatever else, he was the devoted friend of the father; he
would have proved the devoted servant of the son. In that, he
could have been trusted. Now even this unwanted but needed
ally was gone.

Elizabeth Woodville wept and swore through the day. Bereft
of strength and friends, she turned to her oldest daughter
for comfort and advice. The girl had grown to womanhood,
intelligent and soft-spoken, gracious and sympathetic; she
alone offered the compassion and the quiet contemplation so
necessary to meet these changing events. It was the daughter
Elizabeth who now settled the fears of her younger sisters,

provided the cornerstone of solidarity, challenged despair with hope. And these comforts she brought to the sickroom of the Duke of York. With gentle words and careful nursing, she calmed his fever. In the evenings she and her mother composed letters to Dorset and Edward Woodville, both in exile in Brittany. They alone were free to build an offense, to rally the Yorkists huddled on the shores of France. And if they were to join with the exiled Henry Tudor Earl of Richmond, perhaps they together might raise a meaningful front against Gloucester, might rescue the king, might restore them all to their rightful place.

Elizabeth and her mother smuggled their letters through faithful retainers of the abbot. Whether they reached their destination the women did not know. The writing, however, at least broke the monotony of helplessness, gave a sense of activity to the present, added a dimension of hope to the future. It was better than sitting always at the window, watching the night moths destroy themselves against the pane.

On the morning of June 16 there was increased activity on the river. A great army of men rowed toward Westminster. The clanging of their armor and their boisterous curses split the morning air and brought Elizabeth and her sisters again to the window. At the dock the men disembarked and seemed to separate into two groups. Leading one group was Gloucester, recognizable even from a distance by his crude shape and determined walk. He and his group disappeared into Westminster Palace. The other group, armed with swords and staves and led by the Archbishop of Canterbury, marched toward the Abbey and those in sanctuary. Once there, they beat upon the gates. Horrified by this lack of decorum, this violation of a holy place, the archbishop struggled to restore order; but his cries were drowned by the pounding staves and the shouting men. Realizing the futility of his efforts, he signaled a few of the lords to follow and they entered the building.

Even such a disorderly entry as this had been barely won by
the archbishop. He had urged a secret delegation, a private
meeting with the dowager queen. Gloucester, however, maintained that the Duke of York was being held in sanctuary
against his will. He must be freed. The archbishop maintained
that sanctuary was inviolate under any circumstances. A com-
promise was reached: Gloucester was to wait in the Star Chamber of Westminster Palace while Canterbury went to get the
boy.

The hammering and shouting echoed through the abbot's
chambers. It seemed as though the house itself shook—or was
it the beating hearts of the girls, their mother, their shivering
limbs which made the whole world quake? Feet raced upon
the steps, along the corridors, nearer still until the door flung
back. The abbot entered their chamber and fell upon his knees.
Then he rose to embrace the queen. She must come with him
to the waiting Canterbury. The queen and her family knelt to
receive the abbot's blessing. She rose, kissed her daughters,
wiped away the tears of the little York, and took her eldest
daughter by the hand. Together they descended the stairs. What
need of words? What offer of hope? What awaited them beyond the door? As the queen faltered, the daughter seized the
mother's arm. The abbot opened the door. At the center of the
chamber, Canterbury waited. His anxious eyes traced the lines
of grief in the queen's face, noted the wide-eyed wonder of the
daughter. Clearing his throat, he demanded the surrender of
the boy York. Elizabeth waited at the door, watched her mother
go through and straighten to face the archbishop. Slowly
the old dignity, though some might call it haughtiness, returned. The archbishop maintained that the duke, as the king's
brother, had no need of sanctuary, that there was no reason to
fear, that the boy was not living in the state he deserved. Instead he must attend his brother the king, who had need of
him, who desired his companionship. The queen answered:

> My lord, I say not nay, but that it were very convenient, that this gentleman, whom ye require, were in company of the king his brother; and in good faith, me thinketh it were as great commodity to them both, as for yet a while to be in the custody of their mother, the tender age considered of the elder of them both, but specially the younger, which (besides his infancy, that also needeth good looking to) hath a while been so sore diseased, vexed with sickness, and is so newly rather a little amended, than well recovered, that I dare put no person earthly in trust of his keeping. . . . The law of nature will the mother to keep her child, God's law privilegeth the sanctuary, and the sanctuary my son, since I fear to put him in the protector's hands that hath his brother already, and were (if both failed) inheritor to the crown. The cause of my fear hath no man to do to examine. . . .

The archbishop, noting the queen's increasing anger, uneasy of her growing aspersions against the protector, interrupted. He denied her accusations, reaffirmed that the sole reason for transferring York was for his pleasure and his king's. Furthermore, he pledged his body and soul as security for the boys' safety. The queen, with an air of helplessness, glanced nervously about her. Finally she motioned to Elizabeth to fetch the boy. In moments, the girl returned with York. Taking his hand and placing it in her mother's, the girl turned again toward the door. The queen began once more to speak. Her voice, though controlled, remained charged with emotion:

> My lords and all my lords, I neither am so unwise to mistrust your wits, nor so suspicious to distrust your truths . . . here is this gentleman, whom I doubt not but I could here keep safe, if I would, whatever any man say; and I doubt not also, but there be some abroad so deadly enemies to my blood, they would let it out. We have also ex-

perience that desire of a kingdom knoweth no kindred. The brother hath been the brother's bane; and may the nephews be sure of their uncle? Each of these children is the other's defense while they be asunder, and each of their lives lieth in the other's body. Keep one safe and both be sure, and nothing for them both more perilous than to be both in one place. . . . All this notwithstanding, here I deliver him, to keep, into your hands, of whom I shall ask them both afore God and the world. . . . But only one thing I beseech you, for the trust which his father put in you ever, and for the trust that I put in you now, that as far as ye think I fear too much, be you well ware that you fear not as far too little.

The archbishop promised to return Richard after the coronation, now only eight days away. But his words seemed empty in the emotion of the moment. As the mother knelt to hold the boy, the men shuffled their feet, snorted in discomfort— better to have this awkward moment over and done with. Canterbury continued to speak his promises, his concern. It was, however, the queen's last words to her son that everyone remembered:

Farewell, mine own sweet son. God send you good keeping; let me kiss you yet once ere you go, for God knoweth when we shall kiss together again.[27]

Giving the weeping boy to the Archbishop of Canterbury, the queen tried to control her grief. Failing to do so, she reached for the arms of her daughter, and the two left the room.[28]

The archbishop, also moved, sought to calm the boy. He gathered him for a moment in his arms, gave a silent blessing to the empty door, and turned with his men to depart. After all, he was only doing his duty. As a priest he sought to preserve the security of the sanctuary. As a statesman he hoped to ameliorate the fierce resolution of Gloucester. As a man he could not believe the aspersions and suggestions of the queen. What man could kill a child?

Walking again the lonely steps to the sanctuary of the abbot's chambers, the girl held her mother, and together they sobbed in the darkness of the halls. What could they do, what could they have done, the girl argued against the despair of her mother. Surely Richard would be safe with his brother Edward. At least now the king would not be totally alone. At least they could play in the sunlight of the gardens; that alone would lift York's spirits, make him well again. But as she watched again from the window, the men were leaving Westminster Palace and again taking to their barges. There on the dock stood Gloucester with his arm about his nephew, dark shapes silhouetted against the brilliance of the water. Was this the last of the boy? Were the fears of her mother accurate? Were they all doomed to death? But had there really been choices—were there ever real choices? Men had come and demanded the boy; and regardless of what was said and done, they would take him away. Even now he rode the Thames with his uncle to the Tower. And those he left behind must sit at the window and wait.

The boy was taken to the fortress, and Gloucester returned to his home at Crosby Place to greet another nephew. During the past week, Clarence's son Edward the ten-year-old Earl of Warwick, heir to his father's and mother's vast holdings, cousin to the king and near to his cousin York in succession to the throne, had been ordered to London under guard. He would, at Gloucester's direction, be kept in confinement in the household of the Duchess of Gloucester, the boy's maternal aunt.[29]

Gloucester, no doubt, justified his actions as a means to securing the government for the king. With foolish little boys at his command, with Hastings dead, with Stanley and Rotherham in the Tower, with Morton on his way to imprisonment in Buckingham's Brecknock Castle in Wales, with Edward IV's daughters in sanctuary, with Rivers, Vaughan, and Grey now gathered in the dungeons of northern strongholds, with those penniless exiles huddled on the shores of Brittany, the opposition was quite put down.[30] Or was it? Better to secure once and for all one's position.

The role of a protector was never a happy, never an easy, one. To be a king in all but name was to be no king. It was to be always the object of the ambitious, the bane of the jealous. Remembering the long, angry years of the minority of Henry VI,[31] remembering the difficulties of that other regency, of the suffered responsibilities of that other protector, that other Gloucester—"the Good Duke Humphrey"—who had served so well and so long only to be betrayed and condemned, Gloucester must have wondered if history should be allowed to repeat itself. Once again the king was too young, his years of minority too long. Why allow the continuing faction, why run the chance of another civil war which none could afford, why allow himself to be sacrificed to the rotten ambitions of evil, self-seeking men? He himself was able. He himself had the blood royal in his own veins. He himself was not tainted by low blood, even as the king himself was tainted with what was called that Woodville filth.

Let orders be given. Let Clarence's son have no freedom, no visitors. Let Edward IV's sons quietly disappear, lock them away, and the citizenry would cease to remember the golden hair, the blue eyes, the boyish charm of the young king. Let the vision grow hazy and the ardor dim. The people would forget. What they really wanted was peace, to be left alone without war, to buy and sell and to grow rich. No boy king could bring them peace, and the people would realize that the prosperity they knew came from the protector who loved them all. But until that happy day of recognition, there must be greater security in London. Let, therefore, letters go to the friendly north, relying on the old times of trust, on the old loyalties laid so long ago when Gloucester was actively among them as their lord. Let those armies come to London and bring peace and security with them.[32] In the meantime if various members of his own faction wished to speak in his favor, to speak of his worth and abilities, of his blood and right to the throne— let them.[33]

During the week, the northern armies began to appear in London. On Sunday, June 22, messengers, ostensibly under the banner of the king, circulated about London announcing an important sermon at Paul's Cross by Friar Ralph Shaa, brother to the mayor and famous for his eloquence and knowledge. The predicted large crowd began to shove its way toward Paul's Cross. There was excitement and expectancy in the crowd. Shaa always gave a good sermon; and with the added publicity of royal messengers, the morning promised to be a thrilling one. So anxious was the crowd to hear, that it hushed itself immediately upon Shaa's entrance. His theme for the day was "Bastard slips shall never take deep root." It was a point often heard in the streets these last days, and the crowd, anticipating something of the message to come, shifted uncomfortably. Shaa's stentorian tones rolled across the place. It was easy, he noted, to praise the protector, his grace, his kindness, his character, his features—so like those of his venerable father, the late Duke of York. As the flatteries and descriptions grew, the friar warmed to his topic. How, he asked, could one explain the marked family resemblance between father and son, when the other brothers—Edward and Clarence—had been so dissimilar. The father and one son were both dark of hair and complexion; the others, fair. The only obvious answer came in the shocking word "bastardy." Now it could be revealed for all time that Cecily the Duchess of York had committed adultery while her husband fought in England's several causes. Therefore Edward and Clarence had been no true sons. There remained only one honest son—Gloucester, the only true inheritor of his father's right. Gloucester must be placed upon the throne as God and nature demanded. Furthermore, bastards had begotten bastards. A bastard had held the throne and in death had passed the throne to his bastard son. Yes, continued Shaa, the entire line of the late King Edward IV were bastards all. Now it could and must be told that Edward had been betrothed to another now dead. The betrothal had been consummated; indeed there remained issue from that consummation. Did the audience not remember how Edward's mother the Duchess of York had so strongly urged against his marriage to the Lady Woodville-Grey? The duchess had known of the earlier marriage. Therefore bastards, bastards, nothing but bastards, had been fathered by the bastard Edward. Shaa, his voice filled with emotion, returned to his earlier likening of the good Duke of Gloucester to his dead father York. As he compared them point for point, quality for quality, as he spoke of the line of inheritance and the need, the demand, for the rightful heir to return to the throne, Gloucester and Buckingham suddenly appeared at Paul's Cross.[34]

The strategy was to match the words of Shaa with the appearance of Gloucester so that the moment seemed divinely inspired. It was hoped that the people, caught by the seeming miracle, would hysterically break into calls of "A Richard! A Richard!" However, as Gloucester ascended the nearby balcony, the audience froze in silence and then melted away. The quiet was awesome. Shaa himself hurried from the pulpit, slipped away to his home, and kept himself "out of sight like an owl."[35]

The long fever of the last two months had finally surfaced in the pustules of slander and corruption. The lines of Edward and Clarence were to be smeared with the taint of bastardy. To some the release of Gloucester's political poison brought relief. A boy king always meant faction, strife, and war. A strong man on the throne might bring peace. But to others the aspersions of bastardy marked one further stage in the dreaded events.

In the sanctuary, the queen was moved to hysteria. The daughters were moved to grief and disgust. Elizabeth, ever the favorite of her father, was moved to rare anger as she considered the implications of what men said of her father. How dare they name him bastard; how dare they challenge his birth, his marriage, his children as his heirs. Surely there had been bastards enough by Edward, and they had been loved by the father, been recognized by him. But the line had been clear. Edward had enjoyed his bastards, but he had expected his lawful children to inherit the rights and prerogatives of their estate. How dare Gloucester challenge his mother's virtue, his brother's word, his nephew's throne. And the boys—what of Edward and York? What was happening to them? Did they know their rights were being eaten away by the lies and ambitions of loathsome men who tempted God's law? They were bright boys, intelligent boys, born to lead men and nations. Surely they must know their inheritance was being stolen. Surely they must know their lives were threatened. But they were boys, only boys, and they were locked in the Tower away from all who might succor them. Where now was their uncle Anthony Rivers? Did he know they all must die for Gloucester? Where was Dorset? Were their letters getting through? Could he and Richmond unite before they all must die?

All this was wishful thinking as the week spun frantically from event to event. On Monday Buckingham assembled a group of nobles and prelates in a meeting preliminary to the gathering of Parliament on the following day. Before the hushed congregation, Buckingham summarized Shaa's allegations of the day before. First he recalled Edward's notorious promiscuity, how he had forsaken his first wife for the adulterous affair with Elizabeth Woodville, how he had begotten upon her bastards. Then he recalled the infidelity of Edward's mother, how she had betrayed the virtuous York, how York had left only one son—the most excellent prince, the Lord

Protector. The words flowed so eloquently "without any impediment of spitting or other countenance" that the audience long marveled at the well ordering of his words if not his thoughts.[36] In his closing statement, Buckingham urged the men before him unanimously to acclaim Gloucester as King Richard III. The room remained hushed and mute. Buckingham again urged the point. Again he was answered only by silence. Finally the recorder read the appeal, and this time some of Gloucester's apprentices standing at the back of the hall cheered. Buckingham smiled and noted it was a goodly reply.[37]

To those in prison, these events meant death. To Anthony Rivers, Thomas Vaughan, and Richard Grey came the news that they were to die on the morrow, Wednesday, June 25, 1483. The order had been issued by the Lord Protector. The condemned, the order continued, were to have confessors and anything else they might desire. Rivers, as a man of letters, had many times before turned to writing as a means of ordering his thoughts, of controlling his emotions.[38] On this final night, he wrote his will, expressed the hope that his debts be paid to the living and that his bequests to the Church be honored for the sake of his soul. He noted too some business he had transacted, perhaps unfairly, and instructed that such matters be reviewed and righted. In closing, he named his executors, petitioned the protector to carry through the directions of the will, and requested that his body be buried next to his nephew Lord Richard Grey.[39] Having willed away that part which was assignable, Rivers sat through the night composing a ballad that became his farewell to life:

Somewhat musing
And more mourning,
In remembering
   Th'unsteadfastness;
This world being

Of such wheeling,
Me contrarying,
  What may I guess?

I fear, doubtless,
Remediless
Is now to seize
  My woeful chance;
For unkindness,
Withoutenless,
And no redress,
  Me doth advance.

With displeasure,
To my grievance,
And no surance
  Of remedy;
Lo, in this trance,
Now in substance,
Such is my dance,
  Willing to die.

Methinks truly
Bounden am I,
And that greatly,
  To be content;
Seeing plainly
Fortune doth wry
All contrary
  From mine intent.

My life was lent
Me to one intent,
It is nigh spent.
  Welcome Fortune!

But I ne went*
Thus to be shent**
But she it meant:
Such is her won.***[40]

In the morning the prisoners were gathered together. Rivers was brought from Sheriff-Hutton; Richard Grey, from Middleham Castle. They joined Thomas Vaughan, already at Pomfret. In the meantime one of Gloucester's northern armies, under the direction of Sir Richard Ratcliff, had arrived at the castle. Under his command and without any form of trial, the three men were beheaded. But the hairshirt that Rivers wore throughout his life and to his death was hung on the walls of a church in Doncaster and became a holy relic.[41]

In London a few hours later, Parliament assembled at Westminster.[42] Nearly all members of the House of Lords were in attendance, while the thin ranks of the House of Commons were fattened by London citizenry. The meeting, originally called as a preliminary to Edward V's coronation, had few illusions. By now the thread of development was well delineated, although no one except Buckingham probably knew of the executions of the morning. But many on their way to the session had seen the mustered armies of some four thousand men dressed in their best leather coats and helmets in Moore Field.[43] The Lords whispered among themselves. The Commons stretched and peered around each other trying to catch here and there a phrase. After the opening ceremonies and prayers for divine guidance, a roll of parchment was read aloud. There in the presence of the assembled Lords, the Mayor of London, and the Commons, the now familiar tale was retold. It reviewed the claims of the Lord Protector, it challenged the preference of the sons of Edward IV. In conclusion, the lengthy petition

---

* never thought   ** ruined   *** custom

stated that Gloucester was "the undoubted son and heir of Richard late Duke of York . . . wherefore . . . we humbly desire, pray, and require your said noble Grace, that, according to this election of us the three estates of this land, as by your true inheritance, ye will accept and take upon you the said crown and Royal Dignity. . . ."[44]

Whatever thoughts passed for those hiding a few yards away in sanctuary, what prayers were offered for the boys in the Tower, will never be known. They remained unspoken. Whatever the motivation—fear of the assembled armies, hopelessness at the prospect of interrupting these awesome events, ambition for more money and power—the assembly unanimously signed the petition.

The deed was done. Elizabeth and her sisters, watching again from the windows of sanctuary, had seen the throng gather, had seen the men on foot and horseback, the men in barges, the shoving, jostling crowd which elbowed its way toward the Parliament Chamber. In the silence left behind the crowd, in the silence of sanctuary, in the silence of the watchers at the window, hopelessness descended. What now could be done for themselves, for their brothers? Were they only like the night moths, beating toward the light and hitting against the pane? Was their only purpose to live unseen, unnoticed, unfulfilled, while men signed away their fortunes and honor, and perhaps life itself?

The next day, Thursday, June 26, 1483, the decision of Parliament was to be implemented. In the morning, a great convocation of members of the Houses of Lords and Commons, retainers, hangers-on, and the idly curious rode, walked, jostled their way to Baynard's Castle, home of the Duchess of York and Gloucester's current residence. Gloucester had removed himself from direct contact with, if not control over, the events of the week. The crowd, in boisterous pleading, demanded his appearance. Slowly, with seeming reluctance, Gloucester appeared on the battlements. He gestured with warmth and humility. He smiled in recognition at certain faces in the crowd. He nodded toward Buckingham. The royal cousin rose once more to speak. He began in loud and steady tones to read the proclamation of the day before. Gloucester moved to protest, but Buckingham read on with increasing fervor. Gloucester had no choice but to accept the call of his cousin, his countrymen, even God himself. Thus with all humility, the Lord Protector faced the crowd, the lines of concern etching his face. He thanked those gathered, protested briefly, and then concluded: "Sith [since] we perceive well that all the realm is so set, whereof we be very sorry that they will not suffer in any wise King Edward's line to govern them, . . . and we well also perceive, that no man is there, to whom the crown can by just title appertain, as to our selves, . . . we be content and agree favorably to incline to your petition and request, and here we take upon us the royal state. . . ."[45]

The crowd immediately shouted its gratitude by naming him King Richard III. Gloucester descended the battlement, mounted his horse, and moved with Buckingham to the head of the procession. Riding in royal magnificence, Gloucester saluted, waved, and nodded his way toward Westminster Hall. Once there, he moved directly to the marble chair of the King's Bench. As he seated himself, the gesture alone stated that the protector had formally assumed the royal prerogative. It was now as the king that he spoke, urging justice and impartiality for all. To prove the point he ordered that a minor Woodville adherent be freed, and made him Justice of the Peace for Kent. Richard III then rose to enter the Abbey to offer prayers of thanksgiving at the shrine of Edward the Confessor. From this day he would date his reign and so end that of his twelve-year-old nephew Edward V, who had reigned scarcely two months and eleven days.[46]

To those in sanctuary, riveted to the window, there was no

doubt now of the meaning of the moment. Gloucester was riding to and from Westminster to the accompaniment of trumpets and banners and hundreds of marching men; he was receiving the plaudits reserved for conquering heroes and kings. Today Gloucester had become both; and as he rode from the Abbey, he was literally bypassing them all.

3 · THE NIECE TO THE KING

I N the days which followed, conciliatory messages from Gloucester came frequently to Elizabeth Woodville. He insisted he meant no harm to her or her daughters; he was merely assuming his rightful responsibility for the crown —a crown which under God's law must pass through the true, not the bastard, line of descent. He was ready to receive her and her family if only they would leave their shameful, needless exile and come to court. In the meantime, he strengthened the vigilant guard about the sanctuary and kept soldiers along the streets and waterfront—some even in boats about the Westminster frontage. Consequently fewer friendly messages reached the deposed queen and her daughters, and they knew only that Dorset and Richmond were in Brittany planning an invasion, and that there were designs for immediate uprisings to release the prisoners of the Tower. But from the boys themselves, Edward V and the Duke of York, there was no news at all.

In the first days of July the ringing of hammers, the songs of workmen, the occasional curses in the street drifted to the windows of the sanctuary. Sickened now with fear and hopelessness, paled by the days in darkened halls, the princesses watched the building of the scaffolding for the crowds, the hanging of arms and brilliant cloths in the surrounding streets, all part of the preparations being made for Gloucester's coronation set for July 6, 1483. How easily in the stitched banners the E's for Edward had been changed to R's for Richard; and because the planning for Edward V's coronation had been so thorough, that of Gloucester's could take place immediately.

On July 4 increased activity on the river reflected preparations for Gloucester's arrival at the Tower. Occasionally the music of the royal barge drifted toward the sanctuary, but the events themselves went unseen by the exiles. The daughters of Edward IV could only imagine the scenes taking place downstream. Gloucester, calling himself once and for all time King Richard III, would land with his wife Queen Anne at the Queen's Stairs next to the wharf at the Tower of London. Together they would be saluted by mayor, aldermen, sheriffs, constables, and commoners and welcomed ashore. Together they would proceed to the Tower, hear the cheers of acclamation, bathe in the glow of well-being, of a victory finally won. They would enter the royal quarters in the White Tower and for the next two days spend their hours in retreat and contemplate the awful duties they were now to assume. So acted all monarchs prior to their coronations.[1] But were there no doubts, no private fears, no hesitation about the deeds which must be done if the usurpation were to succeed, no thought of the rightful king, Edward V, or of his brother, both behind the Tower walls. Surely if any humanity remained, Richard III hid certain fears and doubts. Surely he had bad dreams.

And what of Queen Anne herself? She too had known great adversity, had twice ridden Fortune's wheel full circle. As a child she had been the adored of her father Richard Neville Earl of Warwick. She had witnessed his triumphs, had enjoyed the delights of Edward IV's court, had followed the Lancastrian dream to France when Warwick became a turncoat. Indeed she had become Warwick's pledge of fidelity and been forced to marry the exiled Prince of Wales—Edward, that unhappy son of Henry VI. Together with her husband and mother-in-law Margaret of Anjou, she had suffered the hardship of battle and of nighttime flight through muddy roads and darkened forests. She too had been awakened that bloody dawn at Tewkesbury, had fled with Margaret to sanctuary, had known a husband's loss, had wept for his torn and humiliated body, had prayed for his soul. After her own capture, Clarence, her brother-in-law, had stripped her of all identity and tried to whisk her into obscurity. Disinherited, branded as a traitor, nameless and unknown, dressed in rags, forced to work the kitchens and empty the slops in mighty homes, she had survived for five years. She did not know that Gloucester had loved her, had sought for years to find her, to marry her, and to bring her and her fortune home. His search and persistence explained her numerous and sudden moves—Clarence had refused to have her discovered. He had enjoyed the inheritance of his wife Isabella, Warwick's other daughter, and had feared the necessity of dividing that vast inheritance if Anne were ever found.[2]

But Gloucester had located her, had seen her safely to the sanctuary at St. Martin's, had argued with his brother Edward IV to act as mediator in the matter of Anne's inheritance. Finally the king agreed. Clarence was forced to a grudging division of lands—only after he was allowed the lion's share. Anne had married Gloucester and moved with him to his northern estates. But her health was broken after the years of deprivation, and numerous miscarriages further undermined her strength. Hope as she might, only one son now survived, Edward, named for his uncle the king. She had enjoyed the north, the freedom from court, the open greenness of the rolling lands, the friendliness of its people. With poor health as an excuse, she rarely came to court. Now she was the court, she was the Queen of England, and she must have wondered how it all could be. Perhaps she didn't realize as she left the royal barge, that somewhere in the keep of Wakefield Tower in silent watch stood young Edward V and his brother York.[3]

On July 5, Richard held court within the Tower. There amidst the assembled lords he created John Lord Howard as Duke of Norfolk, his son Sir Thomas Howard as Earl of Surrey, William Lord Berkely as Earl of Nottingham, and Frances Lord Lovell as Viscount Lovell. With further fanfare, Thomas Lord Stanley was delivered from the keep of the Tower and restored to favor; he became the new Steward of the Household. Thomas Rotherham Archbishop of York was likewise freed from the Tower and returned to his ecclesiastical see. Later in the day Richard presented to the assemblage his ten-year-old son Edward newly created Prince of Wales. His investiture would come later. In the evening, the king named seventeen Knights of the Bath.[4] True, this designation of new titles was part of coronation-eve ritual; but it also offered an opportunity to allay grievances, underscore new alliances, stress new loyalties against the day when revolt or war might threaten.

But here within the royal apartments of the Tower harmony and growing excitement for the coronation set the tone. The morning of July 6 brought a brilliant day. With banners flying, drums beating, trumpets sounding, feet marching, Richard and Anne were brought early from the Tower to Whitehall where they rested. The day would be a full one that would mark the most brilliant coronation ever witnessed at the Abbey. From Whitehall they moved in triumph to Westminster. And if occasionally there were solemn faces in the crowd, they were overshadowed by the cheering throng along the way. Nowhere was it more somber than in the chambers of the exiles in Westminster. The dowager queen Elizabeth refused to watch, but the girls could not keep themselves from the windows. Perhaps some friend might see them and remember.

Below, Richard and Anne went first to the King's Bench and

assumed again the royal authority; from there they walked barefoot, as a sign of humility, into the shrine of St. Edward. With them came the trumpets; the heralds of arms wearing upon their rich coats the insignia of the new king; the priests in their fine surplices; the abbots and bishops in rich copes, with their crosiers in their hands; the Bishop of Rochester carrying the cross before the Archbishop of Canterbury, who would do the anointing; the Earl of Bedford with the holy relic of St. Edward's staff. Following closely came the Earl of Northumberland holding the pointless sword of mercy; Thomas Lord Stanley with the mace of the constableship, a purely honorary designation; the Earl of Kent with the pointed naked sword signifying temporality; Francis Lord Lovell carrying in his left hand a sword signifying justice to the clergy; the Duke of Suffolk with the sceptre of peace; the Earl of Lincoln with the orb and cross of monarchy; the Earl of Surrey with the sword of estate. Together walked the Garter King at Arms, the Mayor of London with his mace, and a gentleman of the Privy Chamber.

Next came the Duke of Norfolk bearing in his hands the king's crown, then the king himself in his robes of purple velvet, a canopy, borne by four barons of the Cinque Ports, over his head. With him were the bishops of Bath and Durham, and behind him, carrying his train, walked the Duke of Buckingham—himself magnificent in robes of blue velvet embroidered with golden wheels. Next to Richard, Buckingham was the most glittering figure in the procession. Behind Buckingham were the earls and barons who escorted the queen. The Earl of Huntington carried the queen's sceptre; Viscount Lisle, the rod with the dove; the Earl of Wiltshire, the queen's crown. The queen herself was robed not unlike the king, and with her walked two bishops and barons of the Cinque Ports who suspended a canopy above her head. Behind the queen, lifting her train, was Stanley's wife, the Lady Margaret Beaufort Countess of Richmond and mother of Henry Tudor, exiled in Brittany.

Closing the procession were numerous countesses, baronesses, ladies, and gentlewomen, each moving in stately measure through the aisles into their seats.

After the songs and prayers, the king and queen moved to the high altar, removed their outer robes, and were anointed. Having thus observed further postures of humility and received many blessings, they were dressed in cloth of gold, returned to their seats and crowned by the Archbishop of Canterbury. After receiving the orb, the sceptres, the swords, they heard mass and shared the Host between them. They moved then to the tomb of St. Edward. Here after more prayer and greater silence, Richard left upon the shrine St. Edward's crown. The procession re-formed and left the Abbey for Westminster Palace, where the festivals lasted long into the night. The dishes were of gold and silver, and no one but Norfolk, Stanley, Surrey, Hopton the Treasurer, and Percy the Controller could serve the king and queen. After the second course, the king's champion Sir Robert Dimmocke rode his handsomely trapped horse into the hall and challenged any who failed to recognize Richard as lawful king. To strengthen his challenge, he threw down his gauntlet. No one picked it up. Three times in different parts of the hall Dimmocke raised his call, and three times he was greeted with cheers for the new king. Thus the challenger went unchallenged, drank some wine from a golden cup, dashed the undrunk wine to the floor, kept the cup as payment, and rode from the hall. Ushers offered largesse to the company; the king and queen personally offered cups of gold to their most powerful adherents. These activities over, time was well into the night, but Richard rose to thank and to admonish his supporters, to send them home with directions to keep the peace and to order justice. With these words he ceremonially began his reign.[5]

Now that the crown was his, Richard sought to hold it securely, and there were matters which demanded immediate

attention. Where possible he offered pardons and reprieves. To
appease the Lancastrians, he caused the body of Henry VI to
be removed from the obscurity of a tomb at Chertsey Abbey to
honored interment at Windsor.[6] Richard's enemies scoffed at his
good intentions and saw the removal of Henry's body as merely
an attempt to destroy the growing veneration, the developing
cults, and the rumor of miracles which had become associated
with his tomb.[7] To appease the Yorkists, Richard promised
pardon to those who had fled abroad and a return of their
confiscated lands, possessions, and monies.

To those who had threatened Richard's royal person, however, justice would be swift. To Hastings' mistress, Jane Shore
of London, there would be no mercy. Honestly born and well
befriended, married too soon to a man she could never love,
beloved instead for her merry ways and quick wit by King
Edward IV, and after his death inherited first by Dorset and
then by Hastings, Jane Shore was condemned to public humiliation and lasting poverty. By means of Sir Thomas Howard,
Richard ordered her imprisonment and the confiscation of all
her worldly goods. In a cell filled with rank straw and vermin,
she lay in filth and rags until sent to open penance one Sunday. Kirtled, barefoot, and carrying a lighted candle in her
hand, she walked before the cross in a procession through the
streets. Although the tears in her eyes would not be stayed,
the blush of her cheeks could not be hidden, she carried herself in calm dignity. And there was sympathy for her as the
crowd murmured that this base humiliation outweighed the
crime. From that time on she was forced to beg of those she
had earlier helped into the court, and her days of hard poverty
would be long.[8]

For those who had supposedly urged Jane Shore to treason
against the protector now king, justice and mercy were mixed.
Hastings, of course, had died swiftly, but honor had been shown
his body. In fulfillment of King Edward IV's dying request

that he and Hastings might rest near each other at Windsor, Richard ordered the removal of Hastings' body from the Tower chapel of St. Peter ad Vincula to St. George's Chapel. Furthermore Richard granted to Hastings' widow Katherine the custody of all the castles and lands formally held by her husband, together with all powers in those areas and the guardianship of her son Edward, Hastings' sole heir.[9] To give a woman such power over so great wealth was unusual, and there were many who thought the gesture unnecessary but generous.

Of the other alleged conspirators, Rotherham was safe again in his ecclesiastical duties. Thomas Lord Stanley, freed, and honored with his wife through positions of significance at the coronation, was returned to his own estates. But he came freely to court in his new position as High Steward. The Bishop of Ely John Morton continued a captive at Buckingham's castle in Wales.

The rest of the group were unreachable. The dowager queen Elizabeth and her daughters seemed absolutely uncompromising. They ignored all petitions to leave the sanctuary, they found no assurance in promises. But as long as they remained in sanctuary, one knew for certain where the ladies were; and with vigilant guards, one knew with some assurance what the ladies were doing. To storm the sanctuary was unthinkable, so they were allowed to remain there. As far as the princes in the Tower were concerned, however, that was another matter. While the brothers lived, they would serve as a focal point for the opposition. Yorkists at home and abroad would keep alive the hope of freeing the king, would see it as a divine duty to restore to the throne the rightful head of state. The problem would grow with time. Once Edward reached manhood, he could encourage and authorize rebellion. Already rumors came from the south: there were plans afoot to free the king and his brother and to help his sisters escape abroad.[10]

Leaving Buckingham in control of London, filling his purse

with gold and his ambition with power, Richard with his wife
and son set out on a progress through the north. They traveled
to Windsor, Oxford, Coventry. By mid-August the family
reached York and a warm reception. In many ways Richard
was home in the lands he loved and among the people he
knew. To show his feelings and to share his sense of well-being,
he ordered a second coronation at York Minster on August 19.
There amid pomp and pageantry, he again received the crown.
This time, however, the service was extended to include the
investiture of his son Edward as Prince of Wales. The boy was
so frail that he had been carried in a litter to York. Now in the
cathedral, weighted by his robes and weakened by illness, he
found it difficult to stand and nearly impossible to support his
coronet or to hold the insignia of the golden wand.[11] On this
same day Richard's natural son John the Bastard, now named
John of Gloucester, still in his teens, became the Captain of
Calais.[12]

Meanwhile in London, to ward off any chance of escape and
to discourage any attempts at rescue, the area about the Westminster sanctuary was looking more and more like a fortress.
Men of known strictness were chosen to increase the guard.
Their captain John Nesfield set a watch upon all doors, pas-
sageways, and inlets of the river so that no one came or went
without permission.[13]

Buckingham, as Constable of the Tower, increased the security there: no one was to see the young king or his brother.
They were never seen again. Their disappearance in the hot
August of 1483 was a mystery and remains so. In July, Edward V, his brother York, and his sisters had been formally
declared by Parliament to be bastards. They thereby lost all
property, all rights of inheritance, all titles, even their sur-
names. The boys continued to be kept in the Tower, however,
and were moved frequently from apartment to apartment—
each more secure than the last and each more severe. Finally

they were placed in Wakefield Tower with its unadorned grey stone walls, its bare floors, and its small high windows through which the air scarcely panted in the summer of 1483.[14] Occasionally the boys could shoot their bows and race and wrestle in the Tower gardens; but as one by one their servants were dismissed, the visits to the gardens became less frequent. By July there were few servants and no visits to the playground. By mid-July the last of the personal servants were relieved of their services to "Edward bastard, late called Edward V."[15] In their stead, hostile guards stood watch and grudgingly brought food or emptied the slops. Dr. Argentine, Edward's physician, and the last to see the boys, marked their increasing pallor and listened to their anguish. But what solace, what consolation, could soften the realities? Edward advised his brother to prepare for death; and so with daily confession and penance, they readied themselves for the slaughter. In spite of being young boys reaching for manhood, growing tall and lean, they spent the days and nights of youth kneeling upon the stone floor and praying for their souls. On his last visit, Dr. Argentine embraced the princes, and Edward now the Bastard noted that death itself was not much farther away.[16]

Within days stories began to circulate amongst whispering congregations that the princes were dead. Some believed that Buckingham, out of false loyalty to Richard or out of his own ambitions to open his way to the crown, had murdered them. Surely as Constable of the Tower with the keys and power in his possession, he had ample opportunity to do so. Others rejected this story; if they sympathized with Richard, they maintained that he had spirited the boys to some northern stronghold beyond any attempts of Yorkist revolt. Still others maintained, perhaps out of hatred for the king, that he had murdered the princes by smothering them between feather beds, or by stuffing them in butts of malmsey to drown as did their uncle Clarence; still others talked of poison.[17] But whenever men congregated and conjectured of these events, there were always some who wept and lamented.[18] Even to France, the rumors spread. There, for either political or true purposes, the deaths of the princes were placed upon Richard's head. Masselin, the famed historian, ecclesiastic, and orator, exhorted the Etats Généraux:

> If I were determined to recall special proofs of your loyalty to your prince and the treachery of others . . . it will be enough to cite as an example our neighbors, the English. Look, I pray you, at the events which have happened in that land since the death of King Edward. Reflect how his children, already big and courageous, have been killed with impunity, and the crown transferred to their murderer by the favor of the people.[19]

Years later when Henry VII became king, a new story—or at least one more detailed—came to light. Sir James Tirrell was brought to trial for the murders of Edward and York. Tirrell related how, at the instigation of Richard, one John Green had taken orders to Sir Robert Brackenbury, who was in charge at the Tower. The order had demanded the immediate murder of the princes. Brackenbury had refused. Tirrell himself had then gone to the Tower and gained possession of the keys. He employed two executioners, Miles Forest and John Dighton. The next night the two, armed with the injunction to spill no blood, entered the chamber of the sleeping princes. With decision and silence they quickly wrapped the bedclothes tightly about the boys. Pillows and feather mattresses were then heaped upon the struggling forms, but the bedclothes held them fast. Finally the heap upon the bed ceased to move. The bodies were uncovered and straightened. Tirrell came in to examine them. Yes, they were dead, there was no breath. Quickly he ordered a burial at the foot of some stone steps under a heap of stones.[20] The murderers disappeared and with them the knowledge of the burial spot. No bodies had been found in Henry's attempts to recover them; nor in the years before did Richard, obviously aware of the rumors, make any attempt to solve the mystery, to answer his accusers, or to place the guilt upon Buckingham or someone else.[21]

Thus no one was ever sure of what really happened. There was only the vivid fact that the princes were never found. To those in sanctuary that was reality enough. The rumors fixed themselves like lice and found ready carriers into the lonely rooms of the exiles. After the experiences of Edward's imprisonment, York's seizure, Hastings' death, Jane Shore's exposure, Morton's capture, and Richard's coronation, the deaths of the princes were not unexpected. The rumors were accepted as truth. Elizabeth and her sisters gulped their sobs; their reddened and swollen eyes refused to focus, but the girls' attention was directed to their mother. Upon hearing the awful news, Elizabeth Woodville had screeched and fallen prone upon the floor. Elizabeth and Cecily had tried to lift her, had tried to revive the prostrate form. As the mother fought against consciousness, her hands tore at her hair, beat upon her breasts. She gasped the names of her sons, called upon God's vengeance, cursed herself for capitulating to false promises, for believing in broken dreams. All the while Elizabeth and Cecily offered comfort, but the dowager queen could not listen. A few hours later, the sobs weakened with exhaustion. Elizabeth sat upon the floor and held her mother in her arms. Cecily wept, Margaret and Catherine stood embracing each other and stared vainly toward the Tower. In the corner, Bridget the devout whispered her beads and prayed.[22]

In their sadness and grief, the girls did not know that many shared their sorrow. The princesses and their mother were only the center of despair. From them, there emanated into the streets of London, into the countryside itself, waves of emotion and growing dissension. Once the shock of horror passed,

Yorkists became more determined than ever to free the princesses, to establish the eldest daughter Elizabeth upon the throne. If that were impossible, the least that must be done was to effect an escape, to have the daughters of Edward IV cross the seas in disguise. On the continent they would be safe living in the court of their aunt Margaret Duchess of Burgundy. Such designs were shared by those who had earlier supported Richard as the Protector of the Realm, even by those who had explained away the usurpation through fear of the long years of minority. Few, regardless of allegiance, however, could stomach the assassination of boys. The murmurs of fragmented statements slowly began to solidify into vague plans.[23]

The planning spread into Wales. There Buckingham fretted and mused. He had all but placed the crown upon Richard's head, and what had he for it—vast holdings in Wales.[24] There he was virtually a suzerain with almost total power, but what of it? London was the true seat of power. There he could bring his titles, including that of Constable and Great Chamberlain of England, but few men. Only recently he had claimed family lands in Hereford, and Richard had refused. No reason, no explanation, only a refusal.[25] The reasons were clear enough; Richard would risk no powerful agent near him. Buckingham could not be a king, but he could create them—that he had proved. Why not create another? Why not build upon growing frustrations, elevate another to the throne, and this time solidify his position behind it?

In the evenings he began in a circuitous way to speak his mind to his prisoner John Morton Bishop of Ely. Morton, old and devoted Lancastrian that he was, had long harbored the hope that a Lancastrian might again hold the English throne. The chief claimant, if not the only one, was Henry Tudor Earl of Richmond banished now some twelve years. If Richard were to be put down, he must be replaced. Elizabeth of York was now heiress to her father's throne. Bright, attractive, personable she might be, but a lone woman as ruler was unthinkable. Morton thus proposed a marriage between the two claimants. The marriage itself would unite the old rivalries of Lancaster and York, and civil war would at last end. Together Elizabeth and Henry might found a new dynasty.[26]

Buckingham agreed and indicated that the suggestion was not an entirely new one. Only recently, as he traveled between Worcester and Bridgnorth, he had met upon the highway Richmond's mother, Margaret Beaufort, the wife of Thomas Lord Stanley. The two had talked, and the mother had solicited Buckingham's aid in restoring her son to favor. She hoped Richard might allow Richmond's return to England. To show good favor and obedience to the House of York, she added, Richmond was willing to marry without dowry Elizabeth of York.[27]

The longer Buckingham and Morton exchanged ideas, the more feasible seemed the possibilities of revolt. Already the citizens of London, Kent, Sussex, Hampshire, Dorsetshire, Somersetshire, Wiltshire, Berkshire, and other southern counties were speaking openly of the overthrow of Richard.[28] Morton sent immediately to Stanley's household in Lancashire for one Sir Reginald Bray, known for his devotion to Margaret and loyalty to the Lancastrians.[29]

Within a few days Bray arrived. Having talked with the Countess of Richmond, he knew of her conversation with Buckingham. What he did not realize was Buckingham's firm commitment to raising the country against Richard III. He also brought a suggestion from the countess. Why not send her physician Dr. Lewis into the sanctuary to test Elizabeth and her mother's reaction to the plans? Lewis had had occasion, as a doctor of medicine, to visit the prisoners. As a messenger he would be above suspicion. Buckingham and Morton agreed and hastily dispatched Bray. In turn Margaret revealed the plan to the doctor and sent him to London.[30]

Although Lewis of necessity met with Captain Nesfield, he was allowed entrance to the sanctuary. He went directly to the dowager queen. Shortly the two were joined by Elizabeth of York. Lewis revealed his plan: "If you could now agree and invent the mean how to couple your eldest daughter with the young Earl of Richmond in matrimony, no doubt the usurper of the realm should be shortly deposed, and your heir again to her right restored."[31] Elizabeth Woodville became ecstatic at this proposal. Relief from the dreadful sanctuary was again possible. A return to comfort and dignity surpassed all expectation. Of course, she maintained, she willingly consented.

Throughout the discourse between Lewis and her mother, Elizabeth remained silent. All her life she had known that her marriage must be a political union.[32] First it had been little George Bedford to strengthen her father's alliance with Warwick; later it had been the Dauphin to strengthen her father's alliance with France. Now it was to be the foremost rival of her house. At least, he had never shed the blood of her family; he had never had the chance. In reality there was no choice. If ever she or her family were to leave these doleful rooms, she alone could set them free. She must marry Richmond. And if she did in truth become the queen, might she not then be able to offer the comforts of security to her mother and sisters who had suffered so much for so long. The tragedy was that this one last hope had come so late—too late to save her brothers. Or maybe the rumors were just that—perhaps her brothers lived and she might yet save them. Yes, she would marry Richmond. She would write him now, her mother would write, and together they would pledge a troth.[33]

Lewis was delighted and dashed back to Margaret with the news. Every day thereafter through late September he carried messages between the women. He told Elizabeth how Margaret, knowing of Richard's increased watchfulness, had avoided all risk of error by sending two trusted messengers to Richmond by separate routes—Hugh Conway, who left from Lancashire, and Thomas Rammer who traveled from Kent to Calais. Unknown to all parties at the time was the fact that both messengers were so successful that each reached Richmond in Brittany less than an hour apart.

Lewis told of Buckingham's betrayal and impatience, of his letter of September 24 to Richmond. That letter, sent in the name of Yorkists and Lancastrians, invited Richmond to share the crown with Elizabeth. The uprising was set, the letter continued, for St. Luke's Day, October 18. Buckingham maintained that he himself would raise the standard in Wales and that other supporters throughout the south and west would seize the field that day and make possible Richmond's landing upon the coast.[34] Lewis then spoke of the progress at home. He described how Margaret was raising money and forces in England. In her position of power and influence as Sir Thomas' wife she easily met those who could offer support. As she secretly gathered her strength, she sent great amounts of money to her son to equip his soldiers. The plans were going well, prospects of victory seemed certain, and Richard remained on his progress.

As the green of summer burned into the autumn, Lewis told how Buckingham readied his forces and prepared to march through the Forest of Dean. He would cross the Severn River near Gloucester and join large armies of Welsh and western families. What Lewis did not know was that Buckingham had indeed marched; but as he approached the Severn, rains fell for ten days. While Buckingham waited, the waters rose; it was impossible to cross. The floods rolled back and over the banks; it swirled into the fields and took away the crops; it drowned men in their beds and washed children from their cradles. Buckingham waited and his men grew discontented. Wet, cold, hungry, without adequate clothing, and infirm of purpose, they worried for themselves and the families left behind. In scores they deserted. Thus in a short time, Buckingham stood alone upon the swollen banks of the Severn. His power had fled, his support was gone, and shortly—as soon as Richard heard of the revolt—the Chancellor of England would be outside the law and every man's prize. Rather than face the humility of capture, he chose to flee.[35]

His plan had been reasonable enough. An old friend and retainer, Ralph Bannister,[36] lived near Shrewsbury. There one might hide, have opportunity to weigh the disaster, perhaps even raise another force. Barring that, there was always escape to Brittany and the Earl of Richmond. Richard III, in the meantime, gained word of the attempted uprising. He quickly closed the ports; and for the capture of Buckingham, the king offered rewards: ". . . if he were a bondsman he should be enfranchised and set at liberty; if he were of free blood he should have a general pardon and be remunerate with a thousand pounds."[37]

Buckingham reached Bannister's home and was well received. He felt confident and secure; all he needed was time to evaluate the calamity. Besides, Bannister was a trusted friend. And so Bannister remained until he heard of Richard's rewards—the general pardon and the thousand pounds. That was enough to ease his old age, to provide good marriages for his children—would any man do less? In haste and secret he sent to John Mitton, the sheriff of Shropshire, the news of Buckingham's arrival. Mitton gathered his men and without warning bore down upon the hideaway. There was no need of lengthy search, Buckingham was found walking in the garden. With no trial and no questions, Buckingham was tied to his horse, his feet to the stirrups, and the excited band rode off to Salisbury where Richard kept his household.[38]

At Salisbury, Richard refused to see his former friend. Instead, groups of councilors interrogated Buckingham, who finally admitted his entire guilt, named those who were fellow conspirators, and begged for mercy. Above all, he maintained his desire to see the king, to beg of him reprieve. The councilors, fearing further betrayal, fearing that Buckingham might stick Richard to the heart, refused. Buckingham insisted, perhaps hoping that his earlier support would help him now, that his old charm could arouse Richard. His pleas went unheeded. On the morning of November 2, he—without trial—knelt and sobbed in the marketplace as his collar was torn away and his head struck off. For his part in the capture, Ralph Bannister was granted the manor of Ealding in Kent.[39]

With the other members of the conspiracy, Fortune was more generous. Morton had effected escape from Brecknock. Through stealth and swiftness born of necessity, he made his way across England, stopped briefly at Ely and pocketed hidden monies. With the help of friends he reached the coast, boarded a ship, and reached the shores of France unscathed. Disguising himself, he moved into Flanders seeking to unite all Lancastrians and exiled Yorkists in Richmond's name.[40] For the next year and a half he remained in Flanders busily and eagerly writing letters and making plans. In short order, John Morton Bishop of Ely became a center for lost and lonely men of many factions. Regardless of their particular dreams or ambitions, he managed to unite them in the single cause of Richmond.

Meanwhile in England, Parliament met and attainted those persons, ninety-six in all, who had encouraged the rebellion. Jasper Tudor and Henry Earl of Richmond were included in the list. As for Lady Margaret Beaufort, members of all parties were amazed at the leniency with which she was treated. True, it was stated by Parliament, that she "of late conspired, confedered, and committed high treason in divers and sundry wises, and in especial in sending messages, writings, and tokens to the said Henry (the King's great rebel and traitor) desiring, procuring and stirring him by the same to come into this Realm, and make war against our Sovereign Lord."[41] For punishment she was placed in the keeping of her husband, Thomas Lord Stanley. He was charged to hold her in some secret place at home, without any servant or company, so that henceforth any communication with Richmond, his friends, or confederates would be impossible. In addition all her lands and properties were confiscated and given to her husband for his lifetime.[42]

As to other participants in the uprising, Richard followed the policy of his brother: seek out and destroy the leaders but leave the commoners unharassed. For the leaders, where possible, there was execution; for the commoners there were no sentences, no fines, no taxation—just the encouragement to take up again their peaceful existences.

Throughout the uprising, Richmond attempted to coordinate his preparations with those being made in England. With the help of Morton, he raised several thousand men—for the most part Bretons. Following the advice of Sir Edward Woodville—the dowager queen's brother and one of the best admirals alive—Richmond supplied his ships, boarded his men, and set sail for England October 12, 1484. The wind was fair, their hopes were high, and the venture charged with confidence begotten of ambition and surety of purpose. Then nature again intervened. On the second day out, the fair winds turned to raging tempests, the seas whipped and swirled the ships in diverse directions, some toward Normandy, others toward Brittany. Richmond's ship alone maintained a semblance of true course, and he was blown toward England. By noon the next day, his ship anchored off Poole in Dorset. From the ship it was easily discerned that the banks were lined with men. Were they Buckingham's men? Richard's? Richmond ignored the cheers and held his men on board. Caution was of the essence. He ordered a small boat ashore. It was welcomed with more cheers. The word was that these look-out forces were waiting to lead the way to Buckingham's main army, just below the hill. In reality they were Richard's men waiting to capture the invaders. Suspicious of the flattery and sensing the trap, Richmond ordered his ship to sea once more. He returned to Normandy and sent immediately to the French King Charles VIII for safe passage into Brittany. Charles not only granted the passage but also sent monies to cover the costs and equipment of the journey.

After resting his men for three days, Richmond returned to Brittany. There he was greeted with stories of the flood of the Severn, now called Buckingham's "Great Water," and the news of Buckingham's death. Thus ended any immediate hope of a successful invasion. Gradually, however, the parties of the other ships found their way again into Brittany; their ranks swelled daily with newcomers from England. In short order, hope, renewed by greater firmness of conviction and a sense of imminent victory, roused the men to celebration. Richmond's headquarters shifted to Rennes, and on Christmas Day with jubilation and rejoicing, the exiles moved in procession to the cathedral. There each man pledged to the other renewed trust. Suddenly the crowd hushed. Richmond himself had risen to speak. Before the assembly, he vowed to return victoriously to England, and most importantly, to marry the Princess Elizabeth of York, daughter of Edward IV. While the shouts of "A Henry! A Henry!" slammed against the cathedral ceiling, one by one his followers pledged loyalty to him as though he were already the crowned king.[43] Together they planned and waited.

With invasion and war seemingly averted, Richard III took precautions against future attempts at rebellion. He at once reinstituted a practice first utilized by Edward IV by stationing a single horseman every twenty miles along major roadways. Each man upon command would ride with utmost speed to the next point twenty miles away. In this way, a letter could be carried from hand to hand two hundred miles within two days.[44] Secondly, in those counties bordering the sea, he ordered beacons built atop every hill or high place. Within these towers great lanterns were placed. At any sign of invasion, the lanterns could be lit and the warning flashed a great distance away. Villages and towns could then be aroused, and messengers sent to the inland areas. In this manner the country could be quickly alerted and prepared to defend itself against any invader.[45] Finally Richard commissioned numerous spies in Brittany to report all the activities of the Earl of Richmond.[46]

For the next months England settled into an uneasy peace under the rule of its thirty-one-year-old king, Richard III. Despite his own political and personal cares, he held a magnificent Christmas court to give the appearance that all was well. As long as Richmond remained safely abroad, the king could not relax. In addition, a concern which touched him more closely for the moment was the failing health of his young son. The Prince of Wales had been too ill to accompany his mother from Middleham Castle to London. But the festivities, the music and pageants, the minstrels and dancing, held intact the façade of prosperity.

There were, however, no Christmas festivities in the sanctuary of Westminster—only solemn services of repeated prayers and whispered hopes. Hope was fainter now. The defeat of the revolt became the defeat of the last dreams for the dowager queen. The despair which she harbored and her constant lament for sons and brothers dead leadened the air and made darker the grey days of December and the somber halls of existence. Too many deaths were heaped upon the daughters, too much horror and sadness shuttered youthful minds. The voice of the handsome father, the echoes of a brother's boyish laughter, the warmth of golden courts, the wind in the face of a morning's hunt—in short, all that represented life and living seemed to be frozen imaginings in this chill of winter days. Now only through the kindness of the monks was there wood to burn, food to eat. There were fewer friends and less news. Perhaps it was true that Henry Tudor still ranged abroad, that hundreds of Yorkists surrounded him and awaited the call to battle and home. But those were thoughts possible to men who moved about in the open air, who walked beneath a sky, who smelled the earth and shared its plentitude. In sanctuary, the girls could only turn inward on themselves. The streets below, now memorized, held no more surprises. Only God seized and held their thoughts; and already one of the daughters, Bridget, had sworn—if ever free to choose—to spend her life as a Bride of Christ.

By the end of January, Parliament confirmed its earlier action and declared the children of Edward IV bastards and confiscated all their properties. This final resounding disclaimer might have pierced more deeply had not graver sorrows already been suffered. What, after all, did labels matter now? Perhaps, argued the dowager queen, it would be well to accept Richard's letters of petition and promise. Only recently letters came which attempted to exonerate him from questionable deeds; at least he was trying, seeking to make amends. He offered, for instance, safety for her daughters and promises of promotion for her son Lord Thomas Marquis of Dorset.[47] Could more be lost than had been lost? Might it not be more reasonable to return to court? At least one would be out of the wretched chambers of sanctuary. At least at court there was always the possibility of intrigue. There, considering the caprice of Fortune, the wheel might turn again to advantage.

Furthermore, the early evidence of Richard's reign indicated that he intended to establish a government of fairness and justice. He set about reestablishing economic controls, insuring free titles to lands bought and sold, insisting that any lawsuit be brought within five years or become null and void; he insisted that no king had the right to demand money directly of his countrymen, and in so doing, reinforced Parliament's right to levy taxes and designate the uses to which the monies would be put. The king insisted that jurors in the courts be qualified and impartial men, that defendants be allowed the right to bail, and that no goods be confiscated until after a verdict of guilty. He attempted to control the outrageous piracies on the seas, and did so with some success. On land and sea, he had defeated the Scots and brought them to truce. For his most common subjects, he became accessible and concerned, paying from his own treasury, for instance, the creditors of the dead Buckingham.

Perhaps Richard sought to ease a heavily laden conscience, to exercise the justice and mercy which had failed him as protector. Perhaps he felt he could best honor the memory and work of his brother Edward IV by reinstituting Edward's policies. Perhaps he merely wanted to be a good king.

Finally on March 1, 1484, Richard appeared before his summoned Parliament and made a most remarkable public statement:

. . . I, Richard, by Grace of God King of England and of France, and Lord of Ireland, in the presence of you, my Lords spiritual and temporal, and you Mayor and Aldermen of my City of London, promise and swear *verbo regio* upon these holy Evangelies of God by me personally touched, that if the daughters of Dame Elizabeth Grey, late calling herself Queen of England, that is to wit Elizabeth, Cecily, Anne, Catherine, and Bridget, will come unto me out of sanctuary of Westminster and be guided, and ruled, and demeaned after me, than I shall see that they shall be in surety of their lives, and also not suffer any manner hurt by any manner person or persons to them or any of them or their bodies and persons, to be done by way of ravishment or defouling contrary to their wills, nor them or any of them imprison within the Tower of London or other prison; but that I shall put them in honest places of good name and fame, and them honestly and courteously shall see to be found and entreated, and to have all things requisite and necessary for their exhibition and findings as my kinswomen, and that I shall marry such of them as now be marriageable to Gentlemen born, and everyone of them give in marriage lands and tenements to the yearly value of two hundred marks for term of their lives; and in likewise to the other daughters when they come to lawful age of marriage if they live. And such gentlemen as shall hap to marry with them I shall straightly charge, from time to time, lovingly to love and entreat them as their wives and my kinswomen, as they will avoid and eschue my displeasure.

And over this that I shall yearly from henceforth content and pay, or cause to be contented and paid, for the exhibition and finding of the said Dame Elizabeth Grey during her natural life at four terms of the year, that is to wit as *pasche,* midsummer, Michaelmas, and Christmas, to John Nesfield, one of the squires for my body, for his finding, to attend upon her, the sum of DCC marks of lawful money of England, by even portions; and moreover I promise to them, that if any surmise of evil report be made to me of them, or any of them, by any person or persons, that then I shall not give thereunto faith nor credence, nor therefore put them to any manner punishment, before that they or any of them so accused may be at their lawful defense and answer. In witness whereof to this writing of my Oath and Promise aforesaid, in your said presences made, I have set my sign manual the 1st day of March the first year of my reign.[48]

In this statement Richard said things no king had ever said and made promises no king had ever made. Elizabeth Woodville capitulated. Whatever her daughters, and especially her eldest, thought about the removal, they would not say. During their ten months of vacillating emotions, they had vowed to remain together, and so they would remain.

In the middle of March, Elizabeth Woodville and her daughters earnestly thanked the monks for their kindness and charity. They embraced the abbot John Eastney, and stepped into the sunlight. Waiting for them was an escort of nobles and a few familiar faces. The morning was cold and brisk, and a sense of solemnity prevailed—no rejoicing or cries of well-wishers. Those who had entered as princesses of the realm, sisters of a king, now emerged as simple gentlewomen,[49] bereft of name and heritage, ignorant of what they might expect. The women entered the litters provided them, and the small procession moved quickly and without ceremony to Westminster Palace. There Richard III waited; he embraced each niece and quietly acknowledged the presence of their mother, who had forced herself to kneel before the king. But words were few. What was there to say to the man who had reduced them all to bastardy and dishonor? How grateful must one be for the months of confusion, the anguish of not knowing, the disappearance of brothers? Now the king seemed anxious to compensate them for their losses, as though that were possible. And yet in order to survive, how much should one dwell in the past? One must cope with the present if there were to be any expectation of the future. So they entered the palace with all courtesy and great seriousness. It was a strange and subdued homecoming.

Elizabeth Woodville, unable to endure another on her throne, soon petitioned release from attendance at court and a separate residence. Both points were granted, and she remained under the less strict guard of John Nesfield, Captain of the Watch at Westminster. Her daughters must rely on themselves for whatever they might accomplish, and they settled into the household of Queen Anne.[50]

When Elizabeth of York first saw the queen again, she scarcely knew her, so wasted was she by the dread tuberculosis. The same disease had devoured her sister Isabella, and Anne believed that she too must soon die. Already her doctors had pronounced her too weak to engage in much court activity or to share Richard's bed. As Elizabeth and her sisters joined the ladies of the court in the chambers of the queen, their heaviness of spirit grew heavier as they listened to Anne's wracked cough and choked breathing. The evenings at court were more sub-dued now, and together the ladies read aloud and played quiet games of chess and backgammon.

With the matter of the exiles in sanctuary over, but ever aware of the possibility of renewed invasion—especially as spring approached and the weather cleared—Richard moved his court to Nottingham Castle. It was better situated to answer attacks from many directions. After only a few weeks there, he received news worse than invasion or Elizabeth of York's pos-sible escape and marriage to Henry Tudor. Richard's only son Edward, the twelve-year-old Prince of Wales in whom rested all hopes of dynasty, was dead at Middleham Castle. Long had he been weak and sickly, but so had the father in his youth. To-gether the father and mother had consoled themselves with that fact: once the boy ceased to grow, his strength would re-turn. God could not be so cruel as to award an empty crown.

Now there was no more consolation, no more wishful think-ing. The boy was dead, and his parents plunged into grief and despair. No prayers of priests, no words of friends, no comfort of a vague heavenly reunion eased their sorrow. Their anguish bordered on madness, and the mourning court waited for the sorrow to exhaust itself.[51] With the grief, however, went the last vitality of the court. For Richard and Anne, recovering slowly from their loss, all meaning of life was gone. The festivals might be renewed, war itself might be waged, but life was now a gesture, a ceremony which waited conclusion in the grave. Richard would wait five months before naming another heir, his nephew John Earl of Lincoln.[52]

In Brittany, there was now heightened impatience to seize a destiny and, hopefully, a crown. Henry Tudor Earl of Richmond paced the corridors of the estate of Duke Francis near Vannes, and neither he nor the duke felt himself to be in sure control of his destiny. For Richmond there was always the knowledge that he was a man in exile, a valuable item on the political market. He could be traded, imprisoned, or even killed for a price. He was dependent on others for ships, arms, supplies, men, loyalty, life itself. Though weary of the waiting game, he had grown expert at it. He was quick to understand a pause, a glance, a hesitation, and he had developed a wary sixth sense which could instantly mobilize him into defensive posture. For Duke Francis there was a more insidious plight. He need fear few men about him or ponder the question of loyalties; instead he was betrayed within, and his reason struggled against insanity. At times he lost.

During one such bout, his treasurer Pierre Landois privately pursued a permanent peace with England. He was sick of lost sea battles, so costly to maintain and so demoralizing to continue. From England came a ready response. Peace was possible, the price being only the secure and lasting imprisonment of the Earl of Richmond. Landois acquiesced and primed his trap. Somehow Bishop John Morton, still encouraging invasion from his residence in Flanders, heard of the Richard-Landois pact. Morton quickly sent Christopher Urswick to warn Richmond in Vannes of what was taking place.

The news of the plot came not unexpectedly; indeed, plans had already been laid for just such a contingency. Consequently, Jasper Tudor, Richmond's faithful uncle, announced he was off to visit Duke Francis. He openly discussed his alleged plans in the streets, bid his friends good-bye, and set off. He and his men's pace was at first slow, but once near the border of France, they suddenly turned south and galloped into Anjou. Two days after his uncle's departure from Vannes, Richmond, with five servants, also left the city, calling out to his many followers that he was taking a morning's ride. Once beyond the city, however, he abruptly turned into a wood, changed clothes with his page, and rode hard toward the French border. One hour after he crossed into Anjou, Landois' men raced to the frontier. With the escape went all hope of a treaty with Richard III.

Francis recovered his reason long enough to chastise Landois and to allow the remaining English in Brittany to seek their leader in France. Having received from the king promise of safe passage through France, Richmond was on his way to Charles VIII. Much of the year would find the exile either at court or in Rouen. Wherever he went, however, he talked of men and supplies, of arming soldiers and rigging ships. Now, backed by French monies and interests, especially those of Charles' sister Anne of Valois, invasion again seemed the reasonable course. But to one who had waited so long, there was no need to hurry, no need to risk another disaster. Time was with him and would signal when ripe.

There was news from England that the country was being primed to disinherit the usurper. In spite of Richard's best efforts and efficient and effective government, he seemed unable to touch the hearts of his countrymen. Small in stature, dark of complexion, liberal of heart but introspective of nature, he could not spark the trust in men's souls. Edward IV had been able to secure affection with a smile, a gesture, a hand on a shoulder. Richard could not. Perhaps he was still governed by hovering images of the past, of his recent acquisition of the throne, of a certain disdain for frivolity and easy familiarity. Whatever the reason, the security of his throne began shifting under him.[53]

In July, 1484, an insignificant gentleman, William Collingborn of Wiltshire, nailed to the door of St. Paul's a sordid little rhyme:

The Rat, the Cat, the Lovell our dog
Rule all England under the Hog.

While demeaning the king through his heraldic device of the boar, Collingborn also attacked Richard's chief councilors,

Richard Ratcliff, William Catesby, and Francis Lovell. He was arrested, and during the ensuing trial, it was soon realized that Collingborn, in addition to being libelous, was also an agent of the Earl of Richmond. The abortive poet was condemned to death on Tower Hill. First hanged, but cut down alive, he watched as his stomach was slit and his entrails spilled into the fire. As the butcher groped again within the victim's bowels, Collingborn moaned: "O Lord Jesus, yet more trouble." Finally his body was quartered and hung about the Tower and its bridge.[54] When Richard saw the bloody remains, he asked that they be removed and buried.[55]

In the fall, dreaded news compounded itself. Queen Anne's health was visibly failing. Her chest and lungs were wracked with coughing, and no physician could promise relief. The daughters of Edward IV offered their prayers and comfort, and saw no joy in the agonies before them. Anne, the kind and generous, had welcomed them into her court and heart, identifying with them in shared grief and continuing sorrow.[56] For Richard, hardship was heaped now upon hardship. News had arrived that John de Vere Earl of Oxford had defected. He had placed men, money, and material at Richmond's disposal, and most importantly, he had offered himself. The blow was more grievous in that Oxford was one of the best and most tried of the English field commanders.

At Christmas, Richard held his court at the Palace of Westminster. Perhaps he realized this to be his last great festival— with his heir dead, his wife dying, his friends deserting—this Feast of the Nativity became ultimately his gesture of defiance. Almost daily there was music and gaity, masquing and pageants, dancing and song. Throughout these occasions he honored his niece Elizabeth of York as never before and caused her to be dressed in robes of the design and color like those of the queen. Let the court murmur and wonder as they might. Regardless of what he tried to do, men would talk and twist his designs. He enjoyed the girl. She was charming of face, her movements and the cast of expression brought flashes of her father—the brother Richard had adored. The law, his law, might proclaim her "Gentlewoman," but the blood of kings coursed through her veins. Her look alone bespoke royalty. Let her lead the dancing, become the center of attention. Life had already been too crass for one so young, so lovely.[57]

His obvious delight in the girl and his marked attentions toward her throughout the Christmas festival quickly gave rise to rumors. Richard, it was said, designed to marry his niece, he hungered to be again free to marry. With Anne so ill, he would be a widower soon enough. Elizabeth, on the other hand, was much beloved by the commoners, for she was her father's daughter. She was also his heir—a point which Richmond had a year ago admitted during his Christmas prayers and oaths at Rennes. Perhaps Richard had begun to reason that Elizabeth offered the security no one else could. As queen she would hold the love of her subjects—his subjects. The throne would be hers by right of inheritance, and the marriage would frustrate Richmond's plans and undercut his Yorkist appeal. Finally, Elizabeth would bear sons, and together she and the king would renew a dynasty.[58] There was, of course, the problem of the right to marry one's niece, but a papal bull could no doubt be secured.

Elizabeth was appalled. It was one thing to pay homage to the king, to dance at his parties, to become a showpiece of his generosity. Those were duties of a subject who had, under the present law, no rights. The king and Parliament had seen to that. She lived with her sisters at court; she lived anywhere, for that matter, only at the will of the king. Whatever she did, she did so that she, her sisters, and her mother, might in some small way call their days their own. However, it was a different matter to marry an uncle, to incite the wrath of God through an incestuous union. Moreover it was unthinkable to consider a union with the man who had usurped her brother's throne and now wore his crown.[59]

The awful suggestions grew as the queen's health diminished. Through February and March she scarcely left her chambers. By March 16, the day of the sun's eclipse, she was dead. Elizabeth assisted in the preparations for Anne's burial, she participated in the masses for the good queen's soul, but she was denied attendance at the public funeral at St. Peter's Church in Westminster.[60]

With the queen now removed, open speculation churned through the court and into the streets. The vulgar sniggered that Elizabeth had already entered Richard's bed, had borne him a child. Others ignored these low insinuations and begrudged their possibility. By April, Richard was forced to convene his council. There in the great hall of the Hospital of St. John, before the Mayor of London, the aldermen, many lords and other members of the nobility, Richard appeared with great discontent and displeasure. He maintained that he had never conceived so unrighteous an idea as that of marrying his niece. Did not those men about him know of the sorrow of losing a wife, a wife that one had loved? Turning boldly to his audience he charged and admonished them all to cease the untrue stories on "peril of his indignation." Henceforward, he continued, all who either fostered or entertained such tales would find themselves in prison until the originators were produced.[61] Out of deference to his followers in the north and anxious as well that the widely told tales would be believed, Richard forwarded his statement of defense to the city of York.[62]

Henry Tudor, when he heard of the rumored marriage of Elizabeth and Richard III, was infuriated. She, by her own hand and the word of her mother, had been pledged to him, had given ballast to Yorkist plans, had strengthened the political hand of the Lancastrians. It had been difficult enough to stomach Elizabeth Woodville's deliverance of her daughters into Richard's trust. It had been nearly impossible to understand the dowager queen's duplicity in encouraging Dorset to leave France and return to the English court. It had been mere luck that the French had cooperated quickly enough to interrupt Dorset's escape.[63] But this marriage was the final stroke. Let the Yorkists damn themselves in their own double dealings. There were brides aplenty who would serve as a fitting consort. In the rage of ravaged hope, Richmond sent messengers to his old companion at Pembroke Castle, Sir Walter Herbert. Herbert's sister Mary had been a childhood playmate; she too was of aristocratic blood. She was invited to become Richmond's consort. But the messengers were intercepted in England by Richard's agents.[64]

Elizabeth, in the meantime, was removed from court. In order to give substance to the king's disclaimers and to eliminate further cause for discussion, Elizabeth of York was sent to the Lancashire estate of Thomas Lord Stanley and his wife Lady Margaret Beaufort Countess of Richmond.

Throughout the days of seclusion Elizabeth and Stanley conferred. No, it had never been a possibility that she would marry Richard. She was pledged to Richmond. Was it not time now to encourage Richmond's return to England, to take her and the crown? Stanley refused any part in such planning. Already he had heard too much from his wife of Richmond's return. The realities of ruin had been too close when Margaret Beaufort had been stripped of property. Still there were the old whispers that Edward IV had once, when his daughter was a tiny girl, lifted her onto his lap and spoken the words which afterwards became the heart of a ballad:

> *For there shall never be son of my body begotten,*
>   *That shall be crowned after me,*
> *But you shall be Queen and wear the crown,*
>   *So doth express the prophecy.*[65]

It was not long, however, before the system of Margaret's couriers worked its way into Elizabeth's chamber. At last she could write to Richmond himself, disclaim the discrediting statements, and reaffirm her oath of allegiance. Upon receipt of this word from his mother, Richmond stopped all attempts at arranging another marriage. He was to have, after all, the foremost prize of the Yorkist line. By summer he would be ready to try for the crown again. At Harfleur his ships were being rigged, in Rouen his soldiers were building supplies of arms and equipment.

Richard through his agents kept abreast of these developments. He knew of Richmond's intent, his every preparation; but try as the agents might, they could not detect the precise place of Richmond's planned invasion. Richard could do no more than concentrate his plans for defense at Nottingham; from there he might easily move in any direction. Carefully he checked his alliances, searching each man's eye if he could not pry open his heart. He urged his nobles, Stanley, Norfolk, Northumberland, Lovell, and others to be ready to march on twenty-four hours' notice. Especially in his mind were his old northern friends of Yorkshire; of them Richard requested constant awareness and readiness. These men, the comrades of his youth, he knew would respond to his appeals, and to them he sent his dearest hostage, Elizabeth of York. Feeling that Stanley's estate might eventually prove too accessible to Richmond's reach, the king sent his niece north to Sheriff-Hutton, the well-fortified castle near York. There she was to remain under close but honorable confinement until the end of August, sometimes sharing the company of her cousin and fellow prisoner, the Earl of Warwick, the slow-witted son of the Duke of Clarence. Once again it was a period of waiting. Elizabeth and Warwick in Sheriff-Hutton, Richard III in Nottingham Castle, and Richmond in Rouen. For the winners there would be thrones and life, for the losers there could be only death. A weariness settled over the land in the warm days of July. There had been too many wars, too many rivers of blood, too much horror of betrayals and beheadings, too much repudiation of the throne.

And there must be more to come. As the days of July heated into August, there was a tension in the air which did not dissolve in thunderstorms.

The lightning crashed beyond the sea, and Richmond hoisted sail at Harfleur on August 7, 1485. Backed by a fair wind, he was shortly to land at Milford Haven in Wales. He had returned to the land of his fathers, the country of his boyhood. Wales had been a conscious choice; it was home. As the earl stepped ashore, he ended his fourteen years of exile, and kneeling upon the ground he prayed: *"Judica me Deus, et decerne causam meam. . . ."* After finishing his prayer, he prostrated himself upon the ground and kissed it. As he rose, he crossed himself, and then seized his white banner with the red dragon of Cadwallader—his legendary ancestor and the hero of Wales —and loudly proclaimed to his followers to set forward in the name of God and St. George.[66]

Scarcely had the army of five thousand Bretons and exiles formed when there unexpectedly appeared the chieftain of the country about Milford Haven—Rap ap Thomas. Although it was assumed that Thomas, as a Welshman, would readily join this invasion of his countryman, he stood armed, in a posture of defense. Behind him were ranked his followers. Richmond advanced, saluted his countryman. He needed help in entering this land. Would Thomas come with him, share in this search for a crown? Thomas hedged; he was bound by oath to Richard III to admit no enemy except over his body. John Morgan, later Bishop of St. David's, offered a ready response: let Thomas lie upon the ground and let Richmond step over him. That seemed too humiliating, but a solution was reached: Thomas would stand under the bridge and allow Richmond's passage over the bridge, and consequently, over Thomas' body.[67]

Richmond now began his march toward the Severn. This time there were no rain, no floods, but the expected hordes of supporting Welshmen failed to leave their homes and follow the champion. Only a few straggled into the ranks; others stood in their fields or hid behind rocks and watched the army march by. No one, however, attempted interference, and so the army moved toward Shrewsbury. At Nottingham, Richard heard of the advancing force, astounded that Richmond had come unimpeded through the land. The king alerted his commanders— John Duke of Norfolk, Henry Earl of Northumberland, Thomas Earl of Surrey, and others—"willing them to muster and view all their servants and tenants, and to elect and choose the most courageous and active persons of the whole number, and with them to repair to his presence with all speed and diligence." Thomas Lord Stanley, in attendance upon the king, requested permission to go home to Lancashire as his estates demanded attention. The request was granted upon the condition that he leave his son Sir Thomas Strange as hostage. Stanley consented and bid his son farewell; Strange remained under close watch.[68]

Why Richard III allowed his chief supporter, the husband of the invader's mother, to leave in this supreme hour of peril no one would ever understand. Surely the king was as familiar as anyone with Stanley's political agility; the memory of the Hastings' insurrection was still fresh, not to mention the old treasonous alliance with Warwick. Was Richard seeking vainly for the element of loyalty and trust? Was he leaving his fate to Fortune? Was he in reality baiting the hook for his own demise? Was he courting death and relief from conscience-riddled days and dream-wracked nights?

The questions remained unanswered. Richard gathered his force, and riding upon his white courser with wings of horsemen ranging to the right and left, he led the way to Leicester. Richmond continued his uninterrupted march through the country to Lichfield and Tamworth. Riding for a time behind his men, the earl became separated in the dark from the main force. Fearing betrayal and ignorant of his true position, he ordered the remaining twenty light horsemen to silence. Huddled in the darkness, fearing almost to breathe, they waited for dawn. Richard spent the night in the White Boar Inn.[69] In the morning his scouts spoke of Richmond's army, still too far for instant battle. He rode forth, surrounded by his lords and nobles, including Norfolk and Northumberland his best commanders, with great pomp, wearing the crown upon his head. Richard then encamped near the Abbey of Merival, eight miles from Leicester. Now there was no need of dispatch, of haste. The battle would come when it would come. Here there was no joy, no excitement in the coming events—only a heavy weariness of spirit. Fate might not be stayed; neither could it be hurried.

Richmond had rejoined his army. In the evening he learned that his stepfather Stanley was encamped with three or four thousand men near Aderston. The invader rode to meet his father. The two talked in the local inn. Stanley's brother, Sir William Stanley—himself leading some twenty-five hundred men—joined them. The Stanleys were evasive. They were, after all, sworn adherents of Richard's cause. The boy Strange remained in Richard's camp. Tonight there were to be no decisions, no conclusions. And Richmond left them knowing no more than when he entered the room. Returning to his men, however, he learned that many of the king's forces were deserting to the Lancastrian side. That was the single good sign of the night.[70]

In the morning Richard shifted his men to Bosworth, pitching his camp on the hill called Anne Beame, stretching his vanguard of horsemen and footmen "in a marvellous length" across the hill. In the forefront he placed his archers under the command of Norfolk, Surrey, and his son.[71] Richmond arrayed his troops directly across the way. The two armies thus faced each other, now separated by the space of a few miles. Between them and to the side, the Stanley brothers led their armies into the position of spectators. Day turned into night. In neither camp was there much conversation, only the murmurs necessary to cover the practical duties of eating and preparing armor. Most sat in the darkness and watched the flickering fires of other camps.

On the morning of August 22, Richard announced to his friends that the night had been fretful, that he had had haunting dreams. His "countenance which, always attenuated, was on this occasion more livid and ghastly than usual." He would eat no breakfast. He could hear no mass since there were no chaplains in the camp.[72] Instead he went straight to the task of checking his lines, of encouraging his men, but lacking "the alacrity and mirth of mind and of countenance as he was accustomed to do before he came toward the battle."[73] The dark shades of the night before would not be lifted.

Richmond awoke early, breakfasted, heard mass, and dressed himself in armor. Orders were given for his men to do the same. A message was sent to Thomas Lord Stanley requiring him to bring his army into the camp and to help place the soldiers along the line of defense. Ambiguously, Stanley answered that Richmond should put his own men in good order, that he would be joined "in time convenient." Richmond had no choice but to wonder, to be anxious, and to put his men in order. In the front, he placed his archers under the command of the Earl of Oxford, to the right were footmen and horsemen under the captaincy of Sir Gilbert Talbott; to the left was a similar host under Sir John Savage. In all Richmond commanded five thousand men. Richard commanded nearly twice that number— about nine thousand. The Stanleys, watching from the sidelines, held between them more than six thousand men.[74]

Except for the differing costumes of each house, the white coats of Savage's men, the blazons of the boar, the rose, the red dragon of Cadwallader, among others, the soldiers of all three armies looked much the same. All were armed with swords, staves, or bows—thick, massive, heavy to wield. The common soldiers in their heavy padded tunics moved more easily than their wealthier comrades in breastplates or the noblemen in full armor. Few had any knowledge of gunpowder; those who did feared it, realizing that guns more often than not exploded, killing or wounding the gunner rather than the enemy. Cannon had been left in London, for in this countryside there were no fortresses to be blown apart, no walls to tear down.[75]

Richard rose to arouse his men, his crown flashing upon his helmet, his visor up. He looked upon his warriors and realized that the men of York had not arrived. He did not know that they were now on the road to him, but that they would not come, could not arrive in time. Nevertheless this was the day of battle, he must somehow encourage his men, renew their spirit, awaken their fighting hearts. He began to speak of his throne, his inheritance, of the significance of the day's victory. It was, he maintained, a battle which would change the English world, and ". . . to whichever side the victory might be granted, would prove the utter destruction of the kingdom of England . . . it was his intention, if he should prove the conqueror, to crush all the supporters of the opposite faction; while . . . he predicted that his adversary would do the same. . . ."[76]

The speech did little to change the waning spirits of his men. The matters of which their king had talked touched their souls, and the changes of which he spoke held the foreboding of the unknown. It did not help that today there would be no quarter; although King Edward IV had usually ordered that the defeated common soldier be spared. Today each man must strive to kill, to take no prisoners. And in spite of the morning glare, the glory had gone out of war. They tended their arms and stared into the morning sun. Somewhere behind the light the enemy waited.

Richmond, climbing a small hill so that all might see and

hear, began his challenge. He spoke of the justness of his cause
which now challenged that tyrant, that homicide, that murderer
who robbed a throne, who bastardized its rightful claimants,
who defamed his mother, and sought to dishonor his niece.
Henry Tudor then proceeded to recall God's care in the escape
from the numerous deceits in Brittany, the dangers of the seas;
how God himself had led the way to this place to hunt the boar.
Furthermore, his men must remember "that this victory is not
gotten with the multitude of minds. The smaller that our number is, the more glory is to us if we vanquish; if we be overcome,
yet no laud is to be attributed, to the victors, considering that
ten men fought against one. . . . And now advance forward
true men against traitors, pitiful persons against murderers,
true inheritors against usurpers, the scourges of God against
tyrants. . . . This is the day of gain, and this is the time of loss,
get this day victory and be conquerors, and lose the day's battle and be villains, and therefore in the name of God and St.
George let every man courageously advance forth his standard."[77]

As though an unseen signal had sounded, men of all parties
moved into action, buckling harness and helmets. Soldiers
flexed their swords, archers bent their bows and dressed the
feathers of their arrows. The trumpets blasted the morning air,
and the soldiers answered with ringing cries; on both sides the
archers let fly their piercing arrows, and the armies stilled and
waited for the deadly shower. Once past, those not skewered to
the ground roared forward into hand-to-hand combat, hacking
and slamming their way into the enemy ranks. Men fell, split
from temple to crotch; others, limbless, writhed about the field.
Shrill screams of horses heralded men's deaths and their own.
Bowels spewed across the now-red fields, hooves trampled retch-
ing men into the ground. Blood squirted through the eye slits
of vizors, through holes in flesh, and blazoned its way into
heraldic designs.[78]

On Richmond's side, Oxford held his men closely about his standard; stray no further than ten feet had been the command. His men thus banded into a tight wedge which slowly hacked and ate and finally devoured the ranks of Norfolk. Norfolk stood firmly though his army could not, and he died in the service of his king. Behind him stood Northumberland, who tentatively stirred, had second thoughts, and held his men in passive resistance.

Stanley and his brother continued to hold their men from battle. Richard commanded the Stanleys' instant attendance on pain of Strange's life. Stanley answered that he had other sons. The king was enraged, ordered Strange's immediate execution. His councilors demurred—why not let the battle victory also settle Strange's death? Richard, too weary to argue, allowed the order to be overruled.

On opposite hillsides, Richard and Richmond waited, each surrounded by a private guard, each searching for the other through the confusion. In the final analysis the fight was theirs, and only one could ride in victory that day. There in the morning mists, strangely detached from the horrid gore about them, shivered the banner of the red dragon and the banner of the white boar. Beneath the standards, the armored leaders waited. Richard was the first to sight his opponent. The king then looked quickly to those friends about him. Few though they were, there was instant communication. No need for words. Here they stood waiting for the moment to ride to life or death. The king nodded, slammed shut his vizor, goaded his horse to fury. His men galloped with him. Past the lines of battle, shooting directly before William Stanley's army, Richard kicked and urged his white courser forward. Through the slits in his helmet he stared at only one target, that mounted form under the banner of the red dragon. Into the midst of the waiting host, he hurled himself slashing with his battle sword to the right, to the left.

The Tudor seemed to hesitate. Richard pushed on, and his deadly sword crashed down into the neck of Richmond's standard bearer Sir William Brandon. As his blood soaked the earth, the standard slipped to the ground. For a moment Richmond sat only a sword's point away. Then suddenly from all sides came piercing thrusts into Richard's armor. Sir William Stanley's men had entered into battle against their king, and their stabs and slashes hacked at his body. As the helmet was ripped away, the crown atop it rolled loose and down the hill. In moments his body was stripped of its magnificent armor and lay naked, bleeding upon the earth. Men mocked and scorned and spit upon his flesh, a halter was tied about his neck, and his body was flung across the horse of a servant.[79]

The cry went up. The king was dead—long live the king! Soldiers dropped their arms. Thomas Stanley, his fresh troops just entering the battle, ended all the skirmishes of Richard's forces. After an hour and a half the battle was over.[80] Richmond moved again to the hilltop, and in view of his entire army he knelt once more and offered thanks and praise to God for the victory of the day. The men now massed on the plains of Bosworth Field answered with cries of "A Henry! A Henry!" Toward the victor walked the Stanleys, Sir William holding Richard's crown, which had been found hanging on a thorn bush. He handed the crown to his brother. Thomas Stanley advanced and briefly knelt before Richmond. He then arose and announced that he acted now as in ancient times when kings were elected by the voice of the people. Amidst the shouts of the surrounding soldiers, Stanley placed the crown on the head of King Henry VII.[81]

Here on the barrenness of Bosworth Field no more could be done. Henry dispatched messengers to his mother to tell of his victory, and to Elizabeth of York, now waiting at Sheriff-Hutton, to remove herself with a company of noblemen and honorable ladies and make goodly procession under the protection of

Sir Robert Willoughby to London and her mother.[82] Then the king, now at the head of his swollen army and wearing his crown, ordered the trumpets to precede him, and he marched forward to Leicester. In the rear of the procession, the naked body of King Richard III still dripped its gore upon the flanks of the horse. Sitting before him in the saddle was his pursuivant of arms, a novice herald, derisively called *Blanche Sanglier,* or "the White Boar." As the train moved across the bridge of Leicester, the head of the dead king thumped a steady rhythm against the stone walls, but no one minded. Now there was a new king, a new power which moved the procession and held the city in awe. While the dead Richard was stretched by the city gates for two full days so that all might gawk at his despoiled body, few remembered that he had reigned two years, two months, and two days. Finally the body was offered to the men of Grey Friars Church, who buried it. For years there would be talk of a tomb. Henry even offered to buy it himself, although he never did.[83]

FEBRUARY 9, 1503

IN *the darkness of the room, illuminated only by the glowing*
fire, the shapes of Margaret Beaufort and Alice Massey
the midwife moved silently. The queen turned, shifted
on her pillows, drifted in and out of consciousness, accepting
both equally and without struggle. The small body of the
baby kicked at her wrappings, stretched, and slept. Only the
tiny face peeked out of the blankets, one white mark in the
grey light.

The queen's chaplain and the Lady Catherine, sister to the
queen, entered the chamber. Withdrawing with Margaret Beau-
fort to the far end of the room, the three exchanged whispers
and looked toward the bed. Then they approached the queen
to pray at her side. The women knelt and the priest prayed.
The words, barely audible, spun their rhythmic spell—nomine
Pater—sanctus—Maria—spiritus. They rose and took the child
away; she would be christened and named Catherine. The
stepping feet, the rustling clothes, the voices, even the warm
spot beside the queen left the room. All was quiet now, save the
drifting of tapestries caught by the draft against the stone walls.
The patterns of the hangings slipped in and out of the dark.
Silence . . . drifting silence and shifting shadows.

Far away there were more sounds—men's voices: "Your Grace"; "Good health"; Your Grace . . . ," sounds of loving voices. But the door closed and only one entered. He moved quickly to the bed, touched the covers, straightened them; touched his wife's face, her eyes, her lips—pale and feverish. The yellow hair was spread across the pillows, her neck was sweating in spite of the morning's chill.

Slowly, gradually, nearer still—his face swam into her vision. It was a good face, marked by years of labor, but the chin and cheekbones were still strong—they bespoke his strength. How sad to see him worn so quickly by time and care—prematurely old, with his hair, once so thick and dark, now thin and white; his smile, so flashing that day they met, now dimmed by darkened teeth. Eight times he had come like this, to sit at her bed, to lift her body next to his, to share the joy of birth too often coupled with the sadness of death. These moments of quiet waiting for the newly christened infant to return were among their rarest moments together, for they belonged wholly to them and to each other. How happy was the morning when they were both young and proud at the birth of Arthur who combined the roses white and red. How open the world had seemed, how brilliant the morning and the songs of courtiers. But it was all a long time ago, and the innocence of that September morning had been blasted by grief, by death.

Now there was little need for speech. They knew each other, had shared a life together. And they could sit now in quiet, scarcely touching, and understand. The past had been full, perhaps the future would be equally so.

4 · THE CONSORT TO THE KING

To Henry Tudor—riding in triumph and victory into Leicester, pausing at the city gates to be welcomed by the mayor and city fathers, turning to view his proud army, acknowledging the familiar faces from exile, extending pardon to the soldiers of the other faction—the day of August 22, 1485, was sweet indeed. But would the savor of this moment, of the days to come as king, be sufficient to neutralize the fourteen years of bitter and wandering exile? Had there been too many treacheries in the past, too many narrow escapes from dungeons and death, too many challenges to his time and throne to allow tranquility of mind and perserverance of peace? Life for him had always been insecure.

His father Edmund Tudor, half-brother to King Henry VI,[1] had died two months before the son's birth. His mother Margaret Beaufort, not quite fourteen, found refuge with her brother-in-law Jasper Tudor Earl of Pembroke; her son was born January 28, 1457, at Pembroke Castle in Wales. While the civil wars raged in the center of England, Jasper, as the leading Lancastrian in Wales, managed the defense and control of his holdings while the nephew grew into boyhood. By 1468, however, Yorkist power pushed through the Lancastrian defenses; Jasper fled into exile. Margaret Beaufort and her eleven-year-old son became prisoners in their former home. Life was honorable enough. Their Yorkist protector William Lord Herbert was anxious about the well-being of the boy, continued his education in books, manners, sports, and even considered marrying his own daughter to the young Earl of Richmond. The marriage plans ended, however, when Sir William was killed by local insurgents led by Robin of Redesdale.[2]

By 1470 the Lancastrians, thanks to Warwick, were again in command. Henry VI was brought back to his throne, and Henry Tudor and his mother were free. Home from the new wars came Jasper Tudor filled with the confidence of victory, happy to stride his own lands in peace. But his loyalties were firmly with the king, and he was anxious to present his nephew to the throne. Together they rode the hard journey to London, together they joined happy throngs in Westminster Palace, together they knelt before the king. But it had been the pale, thinly boned boy of thirteen who alone received the blessing and the prophecy of the king: the kneeling boy would one day rule them all.

The words then had brought the blush of pride and embarrassment, and the flattery of many men. The words then only served to focus on a well-known point—Henry Tudor Earl of Richmond stood in the Lancastrian line third to the throne behind the king and his son Edward Prince of Wales. True, Richmond's claim was somewhat delicately founded—not through the traditional male line, but through his mother. And the line itself carried the taint of bastardy. Margaret Beaufort, like Henry VI and Edward IV, claimed descent from Edward III. Henry VI and Margaret were descended from one son, John of Gaunt Duke of Lancaster; Edward IV was descended from a younger son, Edward of Langley Duke of York. The problem, however, was that John of Gaunt had married three times and had sons by two wives: the first wife, Blanche of Lancaster, produced the legitimate heir from whom Henry VI descended;

ELIZABETH OF YORK.
Courtesy of the National Portrait Gallery, London.

ELIZABETH WOODVILLE-GREY,
CONSORT OF EDWARD IV.

Courtesy of the President and Fellows of Queens' College, Cambridge.

KING EDWARD IV.

Courtesy of the National Portrait Gallery, London.

KING HENRY VI.
Courtesy of the National Portrait Gallery, London.

KING RICHARD III.
Courtesy of the National Portrait Gallery, London.

KING HENRY VII.
Courtesy of the National Portrait Gallery, London.

MARGARET BEAUFORT COUNTESS
OF RICHMOND AND DERBY.
*Tomb by Torrigiano. Courtesy of the Dean and Chapter of
Westminster Abbey.*

MARGARET BEAUFORT
Courtesy of the National Portrait Gallery, London.

ELIZABETH OF YORK.
Funeral effigy. Courtesy of the Dean and Chapter of
Westminster Abbey.

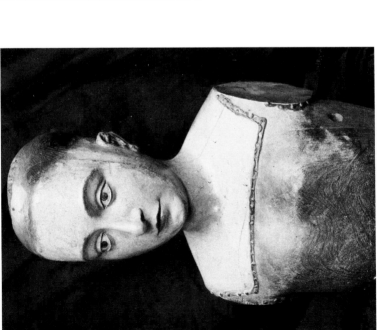

KING HENRY VII.
Funeral effigy. Courtesy of the Dean and Chapter of
Westminster Abbey.

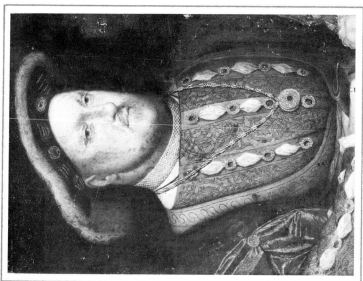

KING HENRY VIII.
Courtesy of the National Portrait Gallery, London.

KING HENRY VIII AS THE DUKE OF YORK.
Courtesy of the Bibliothèque Mejanes, Aix-en-Provence.

PRINCE ARTHUR.
Courtesy of H. M. The Queen from the collection at Windsor.

KING HENRY VII AND ELIZABETH
OF YORK

Tomb by Torrigiano. Courtesy of the Dean and Chapter of
Westminster Abbey.

the third wife, Catherine Swynford, Lancaster belatedly married after she had produced numerous offspring. The marriage brought legitimacy, for Lancaster forced the issue through.[3] But the line had never really cleared its name, and its right to the throne was open to question—a point which Edward IV and Richard III never allowed anyone to forget.

Henry Tudor, resting now in Leicester, would make the world forget the bastardy of his great-grandfather John de Beaufort and remember the prophecy of the sainted Henry VI. Had not God himself preserved a precarious life in a sickly boy, the dangers of exile in a homeless youth, to bring him to this day and to present to him through trial by combat the laurel crown of victory? Had not God himself fulfilled the ancient prophecy of Cadwallader that his line of Welshmen would again reign? Had not God himself made possible this day and sanctified this new king? Henry Tudor would make the world understand that these things were so.

Here at Leicester the king was reunited with the mother he had not seen for fourteen years. She was smaller than he had remembered, more delicate of stature and face. But he knew that her blood, her will, her patience, and her wit and wisdom, combined with the ingenuity and skill of John Morton Bishop of Ely had been the determining factor in making possible the victories of Bosworth Field. The king would restore his mother to her former possessions and heritage; he would keep her near him for the rest of his life. As for John Morton, he must be called home, elevated to an archbishopric, perhaps even made Lord Chancellor of the realm. These things would be done in due course.

Now there were more pressing problems. First he must make his way to London—slowly, with dignity, with confidence, with mercy, and with justice. None must be unduly punished. No one must be aroused to decry this day of triumph. He would not sweep through as a conquering warlord, but proceed

as one returning home. He would arouse no fear, encourage
no anger, allow no vindictiveness. He wanted his people to
welcome him into their homes and hearts, and he in turn
would love them as a father and make them safe.

During the slow progress to London, the people did come
to greet him—drawn perhaps by hope that the wars might now
end. The king, after all, had sworn marriage to the beloved
daughter of Edward IV, Elizabeth of York. If there were no
great throngs of cheering thousands, there were many who assembled by the roadsides, saluted him as king, filled the length
of his journey with tables heavy with food and goblets over-
flowing with drink. There were none who openly challenged
his way.[4]

The king came to London on September 3, 1485. There in
Shoreditch stood the mayor, the aldermen, the sheriffs all
dressed in violet, the people themselves in their best attire—
each trying to press before the other to see the king, to kiss his
hand. The king returned their greetings, acknowledged the
pledges of loyalty and the cries of welcome.[5] He proceeded then
in great pomp through the city to St. Paul's Church. There he
offered the banners of victory: the banner of St. George, the
red cross on a field of white; the banner of Cadwallader, the
red dragon on a field of white and green; and the banner of
the ancient Tudors, the dun cow on a field of yellow.[6] Amidst
the prayers, the orisons, and the thanksgivings of victory, the
king knelt to offer his private prayers. It was a gesture which
marked his life, for he was genuinely pious.

During these services, the crowds in the streets of London
thickened and spoke openly, many joyously, of the new monarch
and his promised bride. Although she was rarely seen, she was
much beloved already for her father's sake and for the memory
of happier days. Some claimed that she was already in London; a few maintained the Lady Elizabeth was now preparing
for her wedding; others were skeptical that the marriage would
ever take place.

The lady herself was journeying toward London. The months of confinement at Sheriff-Hutton had not been nearly so barren as those months at the Abbey. At least in Yorkshire the gardens had been open to her, the fields and parks offered opportunity to ride, to gallop against the wind. The place itself, with its eight mighty towers of stone, its magnificent hangings and hallways, its stately stairways—perhaps the handsomest in the land—had been huge and lonely; but the servants and keepers had not been unkind.[7] Often she had walked the halls and grounds with her cousin, the pathetic Earl of Warwick. Protected by innocence of mind and lack of memory, he failed to realize his own deprivation and lack of privilege. The two cousins spent most of their time in silent companionship.

News of Henry's victory had ridden swiftly north to the castle of Sheriff-Hutton. What did it really mean to Elizabeth? Did it mean freedom, did it mean a husband, a family, and a crown? Or was this one more ruse? Would Henry be willing to share his crown? Could he know that she held for herself no political ambitions, that policy failed to interest her, that power drew no fascination from one who had been whirled so viciously about Fortune's wheel? All she wanted was security of body, peace of mind. All she wanted was to see her sisters safe, her mother at ease, to see peace maintained, and justice mingled with mercy. Could these things be possible in a world so fickle, or was this victory of Henry's one more aching blow to the family hopes?

Sir Robert Willoughby and his escort clattered through the gatehouse into the courtyard, and dismounted with agility born of excitement. Would the Lady Elizabeth receive them? Had she a choice? Footsteps raced along the corridors—pages completely undone by the news of defeats and victories. Voices of servants, pitched too high but caught by the aura of changing events, chittered past. Sir Robert, ushered into the room, bowed low and came forward to kiss Elizabeth's extended hand. Would the lady prepare to ride to London as her king had bade her

to do? The journey would be slow, not unduly tiring. The king
would reach the city before them. No, he would not meet her
or welcome her to the city. Her entry was not to be marked—
with dignity and solemnity, but without pomp, without ceremony. She would proceed directly to her mother, now at Westminster Palace. Later the king would send for her. Of the wedding nothing was said.

The next day the procession formed itself and moved towards London. From a closed litter Elizabeth watched and
welcomed the numerous matrons and ladies of gentle birth on
horseback who became her escort. She knew that somewhere
in the caravan under close but unobtrusive guard rode the
fifteen-year-old Edward Earl of Warwick. Did they again ride
to a common fate; would they ever again pass through this open
countryside?[8]

In London, Henry VII rested and celebrated among the
comforts of Bishop's Palace, and throughout the city the very
atmosphere seemed to lighten. For many it was a time of joy,
of pageants and plays, music and festival.[9] God be praised—
the heavy, troublesome reign of the dark Richard III was over.
Perhaps the violence and strife were finally past. Perhaps dignity and respect could again be joined to the throne. Perhaps
the hovering spirit of the dead boy king would rest and allow
the grimy guilt to settle. All things were possible now—especially since the king had promised, indeed had sworn in his
exile, to marry the Princess Elizabeth. She was, after all, her
father's heir; she was in fact the white rose of York—pure,
untouched. And as though to welcome the new day with its
hope, the people sang:

> *This day, day dawes**
> *this gentle day, day dawes,*
> *and I must home gone.*

---

* dawns

In glorious garden green,
saw I sitting a comely queen;
among the flowers that fresh been,
She gathered a flower and sat between.
   The lily-white rose me thought I saw,
   The lily-white rose me thought I saw,
      and ever she sang:
This day, day dawes
this gentle day, day dawes,
   and I must home gone.[10]

Some still claimed that hers was the better right, that she was the true monarch, that the crown belonged to her alone. These grumblings, however, were scattered only amongst those who fastened themselves to dying Yorkist dreams. For most of England, it would be enough if the two factions joined in marriage—that in itself would bring peace, and that was cause for celebration. London hung out her banners, cleaned her streets, paid her pipers and trumpeters, and drank and danced.

The frolic and celebration were crudely broken off in late September by a new and unknown plague—the sweating sickness. This insidious enemy, striking from within, hit swiftly; and many who comfortably dined at noon were dead by supper. The victims, seized with violent fits of sweating, suffered great pains in their heads and stomachs; if they endured for twenty-four hours the victims survived. Many, however, found it impossible to sustain the heat and ripped away their clothing, others sought to soak themselves in cold water; but all who did so perished. Within days two mayors of London and six aldermen died, together with some thirty thousand citizens rich and poor alike.[11] The survivors wondered what the plague meant, and the commoners concluded: "It was a token that the king should reign in labor, because his reign began with a sickness of sweat."[12]

By the end of October the plague disappeared and preparations for Henry's coronation drew to conclusion. Having visited
with the Archbishop of Canterbury at Lambeth Palace during
the late days of October, Henry crossed London Bridge and, like
many kings before him, went into the Tower to ready his heart
and mind for the coronation itself. There he made twelve
knights banneret and created three peerages: his uncle Jasper
Tudor, for his protection during the long years of minority and
his sharing of Henry's exile, became Duke of Bedford; his stepfather Thomas Lord Stanley, for his help at Bosworth Field,
became the Earl of Derby and High Constable of England;
and Sir Edward Courtenay, for his loyalty, service, and supplies, became the Earl of Devon.[13] Sir William Stanley received
the gold chain as the King's Chamberlain; Reginald Bray received knighthood, became Treasurer of England and a member of the Privy Council; Christopher Urswick became Dean
of York Minster; and John Morton Bishop of Ely, who was
called home from Flanders, would soon become the Archbishop of Canterbury and the Lord Chamberlain of England.[14]

On October 30, coronation day, the king created a personal
guard of fifty yeomen, sturdy men armed with staves and bows,
dressed in scarlet and gold. Their function, unprecedented in
England but patterned after the French court, was ostensibly
to exalt the throne, to surround the king on public occasions,
to make him seem more remote and distanced from the crowd.
In reality the yeomen of the guard stood ready to protect the
person of the king in these unsettled times.[15]

From the windows of Westminster Palace, Elizabeth of York
watched as the king was rowed by barge to Westminster Abbey. All morning she waited there, hoping like thousands of
others to have sight of the new monarch. But for her there was
additional meaning. The wedding had been postponed, plans
for her coronation delayed, and she wondered now, as the music
of the trumpets came down the Thames, if either event would

ever take place.[16] Today amidst the hangings of white cloth of gold, blue cloth of gold, green cloth of gold and red-velvet roses and dragons, fringes and tassels of gold and silk, the man dressed in his purple velvet robes would be anointed and crowned King Henry, the seventh of the name.[17] Why, she wondered, was he so insistent that his must be the power— alone. Why this need for the single coronation to underscore the fact? She herself had seen enough of power, had watched it waste her mother and gather more enemies than friends. She had seen power devour Margaret of Anjou and drive her homeless, childless, into exile. She had seen power twist her uncle Richard from a kind and gentle man into a usurper of little children. And he had been butchered for it. Let the kings have their power, their parliaments, their crowns. She would not interfere. Indeed she could not. She knew that Henry Tudor had had choices regarding his right to the crown: by his Lan- castrian descent, which might raise the problem of the bastard stain; by the title of the sword of conquest, which might in- vite others to the same deed; and thirdly, by the right of his betrothed Elizabeth of York as the heiress of King Edward IV, which might suggest merely the crown matrimonial, valuable only during the life of the queen.[18] He had rejected all three possibilities. He would have the crown as his own in his own right by the real fact that he possessed the crown. He sum- moned Parliament on November 7 to verify the point:

> Be it ordeigned, established, and enacted by this present Parliament, that the inheritance of the crown of this realm of England, and also of France, with all the preeminence, and dignity royal, to the same appertaining, all other sei- gnories to the king belonging beyond the sea, with the ap- purtenances thereto in any wise due or appertaining, shall rest, remain, and abide, in the most royal person of our now sovereign lord King Henry, the Seventh, and in the

heirs of his body lawfully coming, perpetually, with the grace of God so to endure, and in none other.[19]

The crown was granted to the king simply because he held it. In addition he insisted upon dating his reign from August 21, 1485, one day prior to the battle of Bosworth Field. In so doing, Parliament was able to attaint all those who fought for King Richard III as traitors to the present king. In accordance with this act Norfolk, Surrey, Lovell, Walter Devereaux, Robert Harrington, Robert Brackenberry, William Catesby, Humphrey Stafford, and a dozen or so more were deprived of their rights and privileges, and considered outside the law. All others were to be pardoned, provided they submitted themselves within forty days and acknowledged Henry VII as king. Upon hearing this news, many came out of sanctuary, had their civil rights restored, and renewed their lives. But many Englishmen of both parties begrudged this twisting of history: "Oh God! what assurance, from this time forth, are our kings to have, that in the day of battle, they will not be deprived of the as- sistance of even their own subjects, when summoned at the dread mandate of their sovereign? for, a thing that has been witnessed, it is far from improbable, that, deserted by their ad- herents, they may find themselves bereft of inheritance, posses- sions, and even life itself."[20]

In addition, all acts of attainder passed during the reign of Richard III were removed. In particular the king's mother, Margaret Beaufort, possessed again her rights and properties; Elizabeth Woodville resumed her title of dowager queen, with the rights and certain properties appertaining; her daughters lost the name of bastard and resumed their royal prerogative as daughters of their father. This act merely restated what the daughters knew and believed. They were the daughters of a king and that fact had sustained them in the days of exile, the moments of lost hope. But did the act have meaning? They still remained at Westminster Palace. To be sure, it was comfortable.

There were clothes, food, and old familiar servants, who continued in devotion; and the notorious guard had been lifted. Was this, however, no more than honorable exile? How free was the family of Edward IV? They might have the freedom of the chambers of the palace, but not of the gardens and the streets.

Parliament continued to sit through the days of November with still no mention of the marriage. Instead the members busied their minds with matters of the king's household, payments and procedures, minor trivia to those waiting for settlement of larger matters. The king remained silent. And the anxiety in the mind of Elizabeth of York and her family became like that of many of the lords and commons.

So much tranquility of the kingdom rested on this marriage into the rival house, so much loyalty to the crown rested on Henry's accepting Elizabeth of York as consort. Rumors were already afloat that he was jealous of his betrothed's rights to the crown, that he refused to expose the weakness of his own grasp to her superior claim. Some even suggested that the king no longer intended to marry Elizabeth, that he would choose instead a consort whom he might raise to favor rather than accepting Elizabeth as an equal.

These rumors seeped into Westminster, and the princess knew no more. Was the illusion of prosperity giving way again to the reality of deposed and crippled power? Would peace of body and soul never come? She was nineteen years old, and she felt her life wasting away in confinement. These years of shock, sorrow, and deprivation, and the uncertainty and anguish, ate into her consciousness while she prayed for relief. Was it even possible to repel any longer the feeling of despair? Her weariness of spirit became a silent retreat, for she could not, would not, vent her feelings as did her mother who fretted and cursed the day she had ever sanctioned the marriage.

Fortunately for the girl and her family, Parliament seized

the initiative. On December 10, 1485, Thomas Lovell, Speaker, offered in the House of Lords a request to the king from the House of Commons. The speaker urged that since the crown was settled on the king, would he not then fulfill his bond and take the Princess Elizabeth to wife. With these words, all the lords spiritual and temporal rose from their seats. Standing with bowed heads before the throne, they repeated the request. The king admitted his desire to do all that might bring peace to the kingdom. He would marry the Lady Elizabeth.[21]

The news raced to the palace. Elizabeth Woodville was enraptured. True, she argued, the wedding was long overdue, but at last they would move back to court, they would have fine clothes and jewels, be able to make appointments, and reward old friends. She could not understand the daughter who stood by the window and gazed at the Abbey. This daughter was to be a queen; could she not understand that exalted role, the power it contained? The girl turned to watch her sisters embrace for joy. But again what meaning was there for her? Yesterday she had been the Lady Elizabeth, today she was to be a queen, a wife, a mother if God so willed. And what these things meant, really meant, to her life, she did not know. She only knew that from this day her life would be totally changed.

The marriage took place January 18, 1486, and London went hysterical with joy. It was the occasion of the first public appearance of the Lady Elizabeth since the death of her father. There were many who remembered him with great affection and extended that love to his daughter. She felt the warmth of their emotion well about her, heard the fervent cries of "Elizabeth! Elizabeth!" That day, dressed in her white cloth-of-gold tissue with gold netting and pearls in her hair, she knew herself to be beautiful, to be the golden princess. It was the day for which she had been born—to be the symbol of the hopes and dreams, the glory of a nation. As the cries of joy and welcome reached out, she gathered in her arms the white roses of paper and silk heaped within her litter, and with them gathered the love of a people. She promised herself never to betray it.

Did Henry, riding so proudly beside her, begrudge his wife this open display of devotion from his subjects? Did he notice that the cheers for her outweighed those for him? Was he indeed jealous of her, her popularity, and this great emotion she elicited with a smile?[22] Or was it enough to know that he had made these moments possible, that he was in truth responsible for this marriage? Did he realize that his subjects were grateful for his letting it all happen? Did he appreciate that the pageants and their roses of white and red were intertwined for him too? Did he feel in his heart that as the barrels of beer opened in the streets, the Londoners drank and danced to his happiness also? Could he believe that he had brought again the happiest days England had known since Edward's easy familiarity? These things he must understand. He must grow confident in himself, in his crown, and in his queen. He must believe as did the common folk that "peace was thought to descend out of heaven unto England, considering that the lines of Lancaster and York . . . were now brought into one . . . and connexed together. . . ."[23]

No one questioned the fact that the necessary papal bulls allowing the marriage had not yet arrived. Since the wedding had been so eagerly pressed, a temporary dispensation had been obtained for the bride and groom who were within the bonds of kinship. It was not until June that the full dispensation from Pope Innocent VIII arrived.

Their marriage was, in truth, a political one born of necessity and popular demand. For the peace of the country, to harness both Yorkists and Lancastrian loyalties, the king and queen had little choice but to marry. In many ways the union had long been inevitable. From the early negotiations of Edward IV, bogus though they might have been, through the long years of plotting and maneuvering in separate exiles, emerging against all odds as the inheritors of their respective houses, Henry and Elizabeth moved steadily towards each other. Now that they were joined together, they would rarely be apart for the rest of their lives—unless necessity wedged between them.

So it happened in the months of January and February, often accompanied by one mother-in-law or the other, the king and queen came to know each other as they moved easily from residence to residence—Westminster, the Tower, Greenwich, and Sheen being the favorites. The eternal peregrinations were necessary to allow the houses to rest and recuperate from the hordes of people, courtiers, servants, and hangers-on who followed the court wherever it went. Most often they traveled the Thames by barge, preferring its comfortable mobility to the twisted joggings over muddy roads.

Unfortunately the harmony found in the royal household was not matched in all of England. The north country especially, still smarting from the defeat of Richard III, still harboring Yorkist sentiments, disenchanted over Henry's delay in allowing his queen's coronation, continued to resent the fact that an upstart of bastard descent sat upon the throne. Knowing of the discontent, and well aware of the power of the mere presence of a sovereign, Henry decided on immediate progress into the north. He hoped to smother the embers of rebellion before they enflamed the countryside. Not knowing what to expect, unsure of the reception he might receive, suspecting that his wife might already be pregnant, he left his bride of two months in the safety and comforts of London.

She herself had offered his stirrup cup as he mounted and prepared to ride. His tall thin body sat well upon the horse, and with the purple mantle flowing below the saddle he looked every inch a king. She knew the pace of the journey would be purposely slow, befitting a monarch visiting for the first time many of the towns and cities of his realm. He wished to see and be seen. In March, 1486, he moved through Waltham, Cambridge, Huntingdon, Stamford, to Lincoln for Easter celebrations. There on Maundy Thursday he gave alms and washed the feet of twenty-nine poor men, one for every year of his life. Good Friday, a day of fasting, humiliation, and prayer, concluded with the giving of large sums of money to the poor, to the poor friars, to the prisoners, and to the inhabitants of the lepers' houses. After keeping strictly the religious observances of Holy Week, he continued his progress, bypassing Newark, where there was evidence of the plague. He wrote the queen often of the sights he saw, of how the mayor of Nottingham and his councilors, dressed in scarlet robes and mounted on horseback, had escorted him over the bridge of the Trent, through the city, and into the castle. There he rested before continuing to Doncaster, Pomfret, and York.

At Tadcastle, Henry prepared for his entrance into the former stronghold of Richard III. Surrounded by the leading men of the nation, Sir Thomas Stanley, Sir William Stanley, John Morton Bishop of Ely, the Earl of Oxford and numerous others, the king mounted. He had dressed himself in a robe of cloth of gold furred with ermine, and his pages and members of his household in golden work. At the entrance of the bridge, the sheriffs of York rode forth in greeting and escorted him into the city. Three miles outside York waited the mayor, aldermen, and a host of citizens. The procession lengthened as it was joined by friars and representatives of the churches and convents. Along the way great numbers of men, women, and children cried: "King Henry! King Henry! Our Lord preserve that sweet and well-favored face."

At the city gates and through the streets, magnificent pageants were presented: "Solomon" stood amidst ships symbolizing the landing at Milford Haven; "King David" held the naked sword of justice; and the "Blessed Virgin" stepped forth to entertain the king. Their themes were the same—York had never raised its sword against the king (its soldiers had been on the road to Bosworth while the battle was taking place) and the city asked for mercy:

It is known in Truth of great Experience
For your Blood, this City never made Digression,
As recordeth by the great Hurt for Blood of your Excellence.
Wherefore the rather I pray for Compassion,
And to mind how this City of old and pure Affection,
Gladdeth and enjoyeth your Highness, and Coming,
With whole Consent, Knowing you their Sovereign and King.

The city was hung with tapestries, and from the galleries and balconies were tossed down great quantities of wafers and tiny cakes stamped with the cross, white roses and red, "for joy and rejoicing of the king's coming."[24] From this incident and many like it, men concluded that the king's "victory gave him the knee of submission, [and] . . . marriage with the Lady Elizabeth gave him the heart; so that both knee and heart did truly bow before him."[25]

This conclusion, however, was a false one. Henry went about his round of prayers, masses, and banquets, but he barely escaped being kidnapped while celebrating the feast of St. George at York. Richard III's old companions, Lovell and the brothers Humphrey and Thomas Stafford, raised men and tried to seize the city of York and the king. Hearing of these plans, the king, though unprepared for battle, sent his uncle Jasper Duke of Bedford to meet the enemy. Strengthened by a weapon more powerful than arms, the duke proclaimed pardon to rebels who would leave the field. The Lovell and Stafford armies dissolved.[26] Lovell, more frightened than ever, fled England to Flanders for refuge with Margaret Dowager Duchess of Burgundy and sister to Edward IV. The Stafford brothers were caught. Humphrey was taken to London and hanged at Tyburn; his younger brother Thomas, believed too much under the influence of Humphrey, was pardoned.[27]

The king resumed his progress and was welcomed at Worcester by more pageants. One, dominated by a figure of Henry VI, "sober and sad," urged the king: "To be mine Heir, use well my Governance/Pride with Mercy, have always in thy Cure,/ For by Meekness thou shalt longest endure." On Trinity Sunday after high mass and in the presence of the sovereign, the Bishop of Worcester concluded his sermon with a reading of the pope's bull of confirmation concerning the marriage of the king and queen:

> . . . Understanding of the long and grievous variance, contentions, and debates that have been in this Realm of England between the house of the Duchy of Lancaster on the one party, and the house of the Duchy of York on that other party. Willing all such divisions following to be put apart by Council and consent of his College of Cardinals approveth, confirmeth, and establisheth the matrimony and conjunction made between our sovereign lord King Henry the seventh of the house of Lancaster of that one party, and the noble Princess Elizabeth of the house of York of that other, with all their Issue born between the same.
>
> And in likewise his holiness confirmeth, establisheth, and approveth the right and title to the Crown of England of the said our sovereign lord Henry the Seventh, and the heirs of his body lawfully begotten to him. . . .
>
> Furthermore he approveth, confirmeth, and declareth that if it please God that the said Elizabeth which, God forbid, should decease without issue between our sovereign lord and her of their bodies born than such Issue as between him and her whom after that God shall join him to shall be had and born heritors to the same crown and realm of England. . . .[28]

A copy of the bull was presented also to the queen, and it held no surprises. Her purpose from birth had been to supply the needed alliance through marriage. She may have been a princess, may have carried the blood royal in her veins, but she was to be bought and sold to the most important bidder. In the long run, that had happened. The King of England won the bid. And now, although uncrowned, she was queen by blood, by law of man and God. Even so she was in this papal bull a mere commodity. Her function was to provide an heir, give that heir brothers and sisters for more marriage alliances. If these things she could not do, if she died trying, another would take her place. And she wondered about her role as brood mare to a kingdom, if not to the world. If this was her purpose in life, and so she had been taught, she would fulfill that function. Even now that babe for whom men clamored kicked in her womb. She would give them sons, she would give them daughters, she would provide issue for alliances, even if it killed her. For a moment she could not keep from bitterness.

Henry continued his progress. He wrote how each reception became warmer than the last. Rebellion now must surely be over, for his people of Hereford, Gloucester, and Bristol cheered and lined his path. He described how they dressed their streets in pageants of welcome; how they blessed his presence and gave him gifts. The poverty of Bristol, however, bothered him. The people had outdone themselves with generosity although they could ill afford it. He told them he would ease their pain if he could, see that their shipyards were busied, that they reactivated their merchant fleets. He would be true to his word, declared the mayor, for no king had shown such interest for a hundred years.[29]

From Bristol, Henry returned to Sheen and his wife and mother. It was time for celebration: the progress had been successful; rebellion had been thwarted; and the queen most surely would offer in the fall an heir to the throne. Margaret Beaufort busied herself with preparations against the coming of the prince; she thought her daughter-in-law too young, too inexperienced, to handle such affairs. Thus the king's mother devised detailed plans for the lying-in ceremony, the furnishings of the queen's chamber, the cradle, the christening, the nursing of the prince.[30] She was anxious to put her ideas into operation, and she and Henry discussed where the child should be born.

The king and his mother were not only pious, they were also superstitious. Margaret Beaufort was given to visions; her earliest dated from age nine, when she was torn between the possibilities of two suitors. Fortunately an angel had appeared in the middle of the night and named Edmund Tudor as God's choice.[31] Henry, on the other hand, was convinced he was the fulfillment of the dream of Cadwallader 797 years ago—the promise of the angel that the English would be displaced from power and that the line of early Britons preserved through the Welsh would again maintain the crown.[32] The king did all things possible to convince others that he was correct in tracing his lineage to the greatest of all English kings—Arthur himself.[33] To further this end, he and his mother maintained that the child would be born in the city of Winchester, ancient seat of British kings and a legendary home of Arthur.

Elizabeth mulled over these situations and liked them little. She could understand her husband's devotion to his mother— he owed her his life and crown—but she resented the wholesale control that Margaret exercised over the court.[34] The woman was so strong-willed that she made disagreement impossible. With her surety of purpose, Margaret Beaufort made an excellent saint, but a difficult human being. It was irksome, for instance, the way she always wept and sobbed on any happy occasion for fear of the adversities which might follow.[35] Somehow, however, they must learn to live together in domestic peace; and occasionally Margaret must surely have to visit her own estates and husband Thomas Stanley. In the meantime let her fuss about the nursery.

The child was born September 20, 1486, eight months after the wedding. In spite of his premature entry, he was a healthy baby of fair complexion and large bones. The people drank and cheered and sang:

> *"I love the rose both red and white"*
> *"Is that your pure perfect appetite?"*
> *"To hear talk of them is my delight!"*
> *"Joyed may we be,*
> *Our prince to see,*
> *And roses three!"*[36]

Messengers galloped to all parts of the realm with the happy news, and wherever they went bonfires were lighted in the streets and butts of wine opened in the crossroads. In the Cathedral of Winchester, grand preparations for the christening itself went forward. Special platforms were built; a square stage, draped in red worsted and reached by seven steps, supported the baptismal font of silver gilt, itself lined with fine linen. Over the font a canopy, richly fringed, hung from a large gilt ball; and the walls of the cathedral were draped with tapestries.

The procession formed in the Prior's Great Hall, the queen's Great Chamber. The Earl of Essex held the salt and carried the towel about his neck. Lord Neville, son of the Earl of Westmoreland, carried the taper. Lord Strange, son of Thomas Stanley, carried a pair of gilt basins with a towel folded upon them. As they moved toward the church, they were joined and preceded by the king's henchmen, squires, gentlemen, and yeomen of the crown, two by two together, each bearing an unlighted torch. Then followed the King of Arms; the Sergeants of Arms; Thomas Lord Stanley, the Earl of Derby; and Lord Maltravers. Afterwards came the salt, taper, and basins borne by Essex, Neville, and Strange; Lady Anne, sister to the queen, bore the chrism, and knights bearing their staves of office walked at her side. After them walked the queen's eldest sister, Cecily, carrying in her arms the prince, who was wrapped in a mantle of crimson cloth of gold furred with ermine. The child's train was carried by the wife of Thomas Grey Marquis of Dorset and Sir John Chepe. Edward Lord Woodville, uncle to the queen, with Sir John of Arundel and Lord La Warre supported the canopy.

The procession waited three hours for the Earl of Oxford, godfather, to arrive. Caught by the suddenness of the prince's birth, Oxford was hurriedly making the journey from his own estate in the west. The service would go on without him. In his stead Derby and Maltravers stood as godfathers and accompanied the dowager queen Elizabeth Woodville to the font where the baby was christened Arthur.[37] The torches were lighted, the officers of arms put on their coats, hymns burst forth, and Oxford breathlessly entered the cathedral. He watched as the dowager queen laid the child on the altar; there the baby lay throughout the ceremony, the reading of the gospel, and the singing of *Veni Creator Spiritus* by the chapel choir. Then with the taper preceding him, Prince Arthur was dedicated to God at the shrine of St. Swithin. Oxford approached the baby and took him upon his right arm, and he was confirmed by the Bishop of Exeter. The audience and choir joyfully sang the *Te Deum Laudemus.*

The heralds with their sounding trumpets and the yeomen with their flaming candles brought the baby home to his chamber. There Lady Cecily laid the child in his mother's arms, and he again received the blessing of God, the Blessed Virgin, St. George, his mother and father, and the gifts of his godparents: from his godmother, a cup of gold; from Oxford, a pair of gilt basins; from Derby, a saltcellar of gold; from Maltravers, a coffer of gold.[38] But as the mother looked down upon the child, her own victory and fulfillment of duty were overshadowed by his presence. If God willed that he live, he would be king. And she could only pray that Henry would live long enough for the prince to grow to manhood before the heavy charge of kingship was laid upon him. Already this tiny babe wrapped in crimson meant peace and victory for them all. He was the majesty of England even though he was only one day old.

Arthur was taken away to his nursery. He would be fed and rocked by three nurses—each already having sworn to watch his health and guard his life. Whenever he ate, a physician waited in attendance to supervise the feeding; whenever he cried, yeomen and squires—each also having sworn their oaths of allegiance—reached out to rock the cradle.[39] These were the directives of his grandmother.

Meanwhile, believing that this hasty birth and its glorious celebration spoke of God's blessing upon the land, the common folk joined in the thanksgiving and sang the royal family overland to Sheen and down the river to Greenwich:

> *"I love, I love, and whom love ye?*
> *I love a flower of fresh beauty"*
> *"I love another as well as ye."*
>   *"Then shall be proved here anon,*
>   *if we three can agree in one."*
>
>   .   .   .   .
>
> *"Now have we loved, and love will we*
> *This fair fresh flower, full of beauty;*
> *Most worthy it is, as thinketh me,*
>   *Then may be proved here anon*
>   *That we three be agreed in one."*[40]

Greenwich, that home on the banks of the Thames, with its green parks and open vistas, the sounds of lapping river and crying gulls, had been since childhood a favorite residence of the queen. It would come to mean as much to her children. Isolated from the noise and smells of London, life was simpler here, the ceremony of court lessened, the political intrigues distanced, and the outside world far away. Here, in quiet and relative privacy, the family could come to know each other better; and the grandmothers, Margaret Beaufort and Elizabeth Woodville, could argue over the treatment and nursing of the prince. Henry and Elizabeth could ride to the hounds, stroll in their parks, enjoy the luxuries of peace and security so long and so often denied them.

Suddenly it was Christmas, and Christmas at court was always gala. Henry saw to that. He spared no expense in the rich feasts, offering as many as sixty dishes of confections in addition to the other courses at the banquets, at which six hundred people or more were entertained.[41] Men might call him penurious, but they were wrong. True, he kept close accounts, avoided needless spending and careless extravagance. The household expenses might seem close at times, and the queen might be forced to turn the hems of her garments. But these were matters of reasonable frugality, and both of them realized the political necessity and the charismatic effect of royal magnificence and display. So they dressed themselves in their purple velvets, their clothes of gold tissue, their ermine and sable, their jewels and golden crowns and collars which dazzled in the light. They surrounded themselves with scarlet-coated henchmen, pipes and trumpets, and the music of the minstrels.

On each of the twelve days of Christmas, the monarchs themselves distributed to their courtiers and servingmen the largesse and bounty of the throne. Each day the gifts of money, goblets, cups, dishes, capes, and cloaks, grew more lavish—all to celebrate and honor the greater gift of God. The religious services themselves, in their faithful observance, moved with increasing spectacle to that most glorious night of all—Twelfth Night, the feast of the Epiphany. There would be the sudden burst of lights in the chapel and afterwards the pageants of holy subjects—the Coming of the Magi or the Visit of the Shepherds. Afterwards the Lord of Misrule might dress Patch, the queen's jester, in mockery of some foreign court, present the traveling troupes of jugglers and acrobats, invite performances by the local dog acts or the music of the villagers. Dancing too was part of the festival, and king and queen, lord and lady, courtier and mistress moved palm to palm in stately measure. For the court of Henry and Elizabeth became a warm and happy court, and its brilliance and security permeated into the countryside and warmed its heart.[42]

In Canterbury there was especial pleasure. In the early days of January, John Morton, the former Bishop of Ely, became the Archbishop of Canterbury. The bells of the city rang as he walked toward the cathedral. Upon entering the church, he knelt and wept. No man had done more to restore the House of Lancaster and to join it with the House of York; now he enjoyed the results of his labor.[43]

Many, however, fretted at these demonstrations of Lancastrian prosperity. Francis Lovell, who had fled to Flanders after his abortive rebellion, found a ready ally in his aunt Margaret of Burgundy. Together they fed upon hate and vague hope. They spawned Yorkist plots and utilized all rumors. To engage support, they wondered openly why Henry seemed so loathe, so slow, to hold the coronation of his wife. Why was Warwick, the son of the late Clarence, held in close confinement? Wasn't Henry plotting the death of the boy? And with the birth of Prince Arthur, there would be no end of upstart Tudors, claimants to a crown. It would be best to renew the wars before Henry became more firmly seated on his throne.

In Oxford, a curious charade developed that was well suited to the purposes of Yorkist propaganda. An obscure priest—one Richard Simon—took his brightest pupil, Lambert Simnel, tutored him in civil manners, princely behavior, and good literature, and encouraged him to impersonate the dead Richard

Duke of York, brother to the queen. Rumor soon had it, however, that the Earl of Warwick was dead. For whatever reason, Simon had his boy switch impersonations and pretend to be the Earl of Warwick, newly escaped from the Tower. To gain time for their machinations, Simon and Simnel traveled into Ireland, a stronghold of Yorkist sympathies. There the boy was welcomed with little question and apparently few doubts as the Earl of Warwick, son of the Duke of Clarence, and rightful inheritor of the crown of Edward IV. On May 24, 1487, with a diadem borrowed from a statue of the Virgin, the ten-year-old boy was crowned in Christ Church Cathedral in Dublin as King Edward VI.

In the meantime John de la Pole, Earl of Lincoln and designated heir of Richard III, had escaped to Lovell in Flanders and brought word that Warwick had escaped to Ireland. Backed by the money and influence of Margaret of Burgundy, the two men engaged an army of two thousand experienced German soldiers under the command of Martin Swart. They sailed to Ireland and landed May 5.

Henry, not ignorant of these affairs, ordered the beacons watched along the coast and caused Warwick to be paraded through the streets of London to converse with those who had known him.[44] In addition he ordered his uncle the Duke of Bedford and the trusted Earl of Oxford to gather forces and prepare for an invasion from both Flanders and Ireland. The king, understanding that rebellion was best thwarted by the royal presence, prepared for a progress. He traveled quickly into Essex, Suffolk, Norwich, to Coventry where on St. George's day, Morton read again the papal bull recognizing Henry and Elizabeth's rights to the crown, and cursed with bell, book, and candle "all those who did anything contrary to their right and titles."

By early June the Irish-German forces were in England. Henry sent word that all who would lay down their arms and come to him would be pardoned. Not unaware of the need to keep the countryside neutral, he issued strong commands to his own army:

> The King our Sovereign Lord straightly charges and commands that no manner of man, of whatsoever state, degree, or condition he be, rob nor spoil any church, . . . nor yet rob nor spoil any manner man or woman, upon pain of death. Also, that no manner of persons, whatsoever they be, make no quarrel to any man, nor seize, nor vex, nor trouble any man, by body or goods, for any offense, or by color of any offense heretofore done or committed against the Royal Majesty of the King our said Sovereign Lord, without his authority and especial commandment given unto him or them that so do in that behalf, upon pain of death. Also, that no manner of person nor persons whatsoever they be, ravish no religious woman, nor man's wife, daughter, maiden, nor no man's nor woman's servant, or take or presume to take any manner of victual, horsemeat, nor man's meat, without paying therefor the reasonable price thereof assessed by the clerk of the market, or other King's officers therefore ordained, upon pain of death.

The queen, the prince, and members of the royal household joined the king at Coventry. There they maintained their court, enjoyed the pageants of welcome, indulged their subjects with spectacle and the royal presence. To those who watched, life must seem to continue unruffled by rumor, unchallenged by rebellion. Never for a moment did the queen believe that Lambert Simnel was her brother. She knew he could not be Warwick. Her mother might cherish a hope that the son was alive and masquerading as Warwick. Her mother might relish the place at court so firmly held by Margaret Beaufort as mother to the king, might dream of the long years of the boy's minority and a regent's power. But Elizabeth of York never believed these foolish dreams. Why cherish a hope for which there was no substance? Why breathe life into bodies long gone? The dead deserved their rest and the living must accept the life God gave them. For her part, she moved freely about the country to give a sense of security to the countryside and strength to her husband's position.[45]

Lambert Simnel's supporters landed in Lancashire, marched down into Yorkshire and gained the support of only one major family, that of Thomas Broughton. Lovell, Lincoln, and the rest were amazed at how their armies dwindled while Henry's began to swell. Still the invaders came. Henry sent his family to the safety of Greenwich, and moved his army northward to Nottingham. There word came that the newly redeemed Thomas Marquis of Dorset was racing toward the king to reaffirm his loyalty. Not sure of Dorset's intent, the king ordered Oxford to interrupt the exile's journey, to convey him to the Tower "to try his truth and prove his patience." The king added that if Dorset were truly loyal, he would willingly undergo this slight reproof—Dorset had no opportunity to reply.[46]

It was time for confrontation. Henry marched his men westward in search of a fitting battle site. The army settled near Newark. The archers were placed, the horsemen, the several guards were newly strengthened by the arrival of the men of Derby and Strange. The opposing army moved into position, but they were poorly armed, and the Irishmen were half naked, few having as much as a leather shirt for protection. At nine the next morning, June 16, 1487, the armies moved slowly towards each other. They met a mile or so from Newark at the little town of Stoke. The battle itself lasted a mere three hours, but the slaughter was great. Lincoln, Broughton, Swart, and the Irish leaders were killed. Lovell disappeared into the river Trent. The soldiers themselves were hacked to pulp, and few lived to return to Ireland. The priest Simon was captured and committed to life imprisonment. The pretender Lambert Simnel was, in one of Henry's most shrewd maneuvers, pardoned and placed in the royal kitchen and ordered to turn the roasting spit. In that posture many saw him, and so he continued his life in the king's household, working himself from position to position until finally he became the king's falconer.[47]

Henry resumed his progress with the express purpose of discouraging local rebellion. At Lincoln he offered thanksgiving for his victories and traveled north to Pontrefact, York, Durham, Newcastle. On the lesser offenders he imposed fines; on the greater, death. Throughout these northern searches, however, it was to Henry's enduring credit that he pardoned more than he persecuted. Concerned not only with the immediate rebellion, his mind searched also for the kingdom's future security. Therefore from Newcastle he sent an embassy to James III of Scotland to renew the pledges of peace between their two countries. To cement further their relations, Henry offered a triple marriage alliance: the hand of the queen's sister Catherine to James' second son; another sister, unnamed, to the heir apparent of the Scottish throne, the Duke of Rothesay; the third marriage would be of the dowager queen Elizabeth Woodville to the Scottish king himself.[48] None of these marriages ever came about because James soon died, but their intention was rightly placed.[49]

Throughout these events, much confusion centered on the dowager queen. Ever a flighty woman too given to meddling, still surrounded by many who begrudged her sudden rise to fortune through marriage, she had been inadvertently connected with the recent plottings of Simnel, Lovell, and Lincoln. Her worst crime, if any, had been indiscretion, her careless conversation to any who might listen; for there were moments when she loathed the prosperity of the king and the maneuverings of his mother. Often she encouraged her daughter to seize control of the household away from the mother-in-law. Granted there were too many women in control, and Elizabeth Woodville still demanded the center of attention. Henry, however, wearied of her machinations and sought grounds to send her permanently from court. Nursing the old insult, the king ordered conviction, and the dowager queen was forced to forfeit her newly restored possessions and holdings on the grounds that "she had voluntarily submitted herself and her daughters wholly to the hands of King Richard, contrary to her promise . . . in the beginning of the conspiracy made against King Richard. . . ."[50] Realizing that her daughter could do nothing to aid her in these matters, Elizabeth Woodville left the court and moved to the Abbey of Bermondsey in Southwark. It was a house to which she had given much attention and support while she had been Queen of England, and with her gifts during that time had gone the stipulation that royal apartments were to be kept there in the event she should ever desire them. Now they were a welcome refuge.

The king, having given his mother-in-law's confiscated properties to his wife, provided a pension of four thousand pounds a year for the dowager. That sum, coupled with those sent by the queen, allowed Elizabeth Woodville to live in comfort without splendor. Visits from her daughters came regularly, although the mother preferred no longer to attend court.[51]

Having completed his progress by autumn, the king entered London much in the manner of a conquering hero. The greetings of the mayor and aldermen were more effusive than those after Bosworth Field. The banners about the buildings hung in greater profusion, the citizens lining the streets cheered with greater enthusiasm. In some imperceptible way, the battle at Stoke had cemented Henry's grasp on the crown. Now that he had married, had provided the kingdom with an heir, his reign developed a certain respectability and a security all its own. And in its reception London showed itself grateful.

To enjoy the pageantry, without actually joining in it, the queen and her mother-in-law came by barge from Greenwich. From a private house near Bishop's Gate, they watched the fair sight of the king's triumphal procession to St. Paul's to offer the banners of victory. The family could do no more than acknowledge each other's presence, for today the king belonged to his subjects. The wife and mother watched him pass and then took their barge again to Greenwich. The private welcome would have to wait.[52] That evening at Greenwich the king told of his entry into St. Paul's and described how a boy dressed as an angel was let down from the ceiling to cense the king. It had been a dramatic moment, but now he wished to speak of matters more important—the coronation of the queen.

Whether he at last felt it politically feasible to enlist Yorkist sentiments by crowning the heiress of their house, whether he had satisfied his own fear concerning his wife's political aspirations, or whether he simply now felt secure in his own right to the throne, no one would ever know. Henry, however, oversaw each detail of the coronation and spared no expense in ordering the spectacle and the most elaborate event England might ever witness.

Six days before the coronation, invitations and directives regarding participation in the services went to all the nobles of the realm. On Friday, November 23, two days before the coronation, Elizabeth, her mother-in-law, and many ladies of noble estate sailed in their barges from Greenwich. They were accompanied by numerous other barges, decorated with banners, streamers of silk embroidered with badges and emblems of the crafts and guilds. One barge in particular, The Bachelor's Barge, outshown all the rest—it was fashioned like a great red dragon and belched its flames into the Thames. On every side and in every barge there were figures of repute, the mayor and aldermen, members of the nobility, guildsmen, and lawyers. And the music of the minstrels, clarions, and trumpets escorted the floating procession to the Tower wharf. There waited the king and his attendants. As the queen landed she was royally welcomed by her subjects and embraced by the king. "A very good sight, and right joyeous and comfortable to behold." Together they entered their apartments at the Tower; awaiting them were gentlemen who were created Knights of the Bath. Throughout the day and well into the evening, banqueting, masquing, and festival filled the hours.

On Saturday morning the queen was provided with privacy and seclusion in order, as tradition dictated, to contemplate the moment of coronation to come. After dinner, with the aid of her ladies and sisters, Elizabeth was richly dressed in a gown of white cloth of gold; a mantle of the same fabric, but furred with ermine, was fastened before her breasts with laces "curiously wrought" of gold and silk, tasseled with knots of gold. Her hair, pulled back but hanging straight well below her knees, was sparingly covered by a net woven of gold threads. Upon her head was a golden circlet richly garnished with precious stones.

Accompanied by many people and great pomp, Elizabeth entered her specially prepared litter. It too was covered in cloth-of-gold damask and filled with down pillows of the same fabric. The procession moved from the Tower through the city to Westminster. All the streets she passed through were newly swept and dressed with tapestries and banners of velvet and silk. Along the route stood the guilds of London, every man dressed in the livery of his craft. From the rooftops and windows, thousands edged each other for better views, to hear the songs of the children—some dressed like angels, others, like virgins—as the queen passed by.

Mounted on handsome horses were Jasper Tudor the Duke of Bedford; John de Vere the Earl of Oxford; Thomas Stanley the Earl of Derby, now the High Constable of England; the Mayor of London; and two Esquires of Honor handsomely dressed in gowns of crimson velvet with hats of red cloth of gold edged with ermine. Following closely rode the Duke of Suffolk, the Garter King of Arms, heralds and pursuivants and the newly created Knights of the Bath. Each man was dressed richly and preceded by his banner of estate. To hold back the press of the viewers and to clear the passage, many officers of the marshal—dressed in red gowns and carrying in their hands mighty staves—walked with the procession.

Above the queen and her litter was a pall of cloth of gold sustained by four gilt staves carried by four Knights of the Body. So arduous was their work that the men were forced to rotate their task every few blocks. Immediately following the litter was Sir Roger Cotton, Master of the Queen's Horse. He led her horse of estate, which was dressed with a woman's saddle covered in red cloth-of-gold tissue. Next followed the henchmen, or pages, each on his well-garnished horse, showing white roses and suns richly embroidered. Then came numerous chairs carrying the ladies of distinction, the Lady Cecily, the Duchess of Bedford, the Duchess of Suffolk, and the Duchess of Norfolk. Six baronesses followed in matching dresses of crimson velvet, each lady mounted upon her horse, each horse decked in cloth embroidered with more white roses and emblems of the sun.

Sunday, November 25, St. Katherine's Day, was the day of coronation. This time the queen was clothed in a gown and mantle of purple velvet. On her hair was a circlet of gold garnished with pearls and precious stones. With Lady Cecily carrying the train, Elizabeth moved from Westminster Palace to Westminster Hall and waited under the cloth of estate while the procession ordered itself. Esquires, knights, heralds, and barons, each man dressed according to his estate, moved between the sergeants at arms who held back the shoving throng. Afterwards came the lords spiritual, bishops, abbots, the monks of Westminster, the Archbishop of York. The mayor and aldermen followed with the Earl of Arundel, who carried the ivory staff supporting the dove. The Duke of Suffolk bore the sceptre. Bedford carried the crown. Next with the queen came the bishops of Ely and Winchester followed by the Lady Cecily holding the train, the duchesses in scarlet carrying coronets of gold studded with stones and pearls.

The procession moved with stately pomp into the Abbey. When, however, the queen moved out of sight, the sergeants at arms were forced to give way and the crowds of watchers, eager to have the coronation carpet—a traditional gift to the commoners—crushed forward into the procession. The cloth upon which the queen had walked was quickly snatched into pieces; the procession of duchesses was scattered, their dresses rumpled, and their tempers frayed, but the holders of the ragged trophies were slain on the spot. The procession reordered itself, and the coronation went forward.

Elizabeth moved through the west door, through the choir toward the pulpit, to the royal seat itself, dressed in cloth of gold and cushioned. John Morton Archbishop of Canterbury celebrated the mass. The queen then came forward to the high altar, prostrated herself upon the carpet, and Morton prayed over her. She rose and opened her gown so that she might be anointed on the breast and the head: *"In nomine Patris et Filii et Spiritus prosit tibi bec unctio."* That done, the queen fastened her garments as the archbishop blessed her ring. He placed it on the fourth finger of her right hand, then took the crown, blessed it, and set it on her head. Placing the sceptre in her right hand and the rod in her left, he offered the prayer, *Omnipotens Domine.* Elizabeth returned to her seat royal for the prayers and the *Agnus Dei*; Morton, interspersing his prayers with blessings, listened as she answered Amen to each part. The pax, a tablet decorated with holy images, then was brought to the queen, and she kissed it; again she moved to the altar and again prostrated herself upon the ground for her confession. Morton offered absolution; and the queen, raising herself somewhat from the floor, received the sacrament. She was escorted to her chair and waited while the mass concluded. Afterwards, in procession, she moved to the shrine of St. Edward and placed her crown upon his altar.

Far above these activities stood a latticed stage between the pulpit and high altar. From here the king and his mother, with a small court of their own, watched the coronation. Etiquette prevented the king from openly attending the services. Surely the services here were far more extravagant than those held for himself in troubled times. But looking down upon the crowning of his wife, the king enjoyed a certain pride, for he had made all these things possible—the lavish magnificence, the display, and—at his own pleasure—the elevation of the House of York.

Below the procession reversed itself and escorted the queen to Westminster Palace. The queen, passing through the White Hall, entered her own chambers. There must be respite somewhere from this crowded day, tinged with the horror that had been brought by savage devotion. The ceremony did have meaning; and it was more than the ceremony, the gowns, the crown itself. She, like her father before her, was now the anointed of the Lord, committed to keeping his charge and governing his subjects. But today too there had been bloody spectacle; tragedy marked the triumph of her coronation even as it had marked her life. Once again she had been powerless to interfere, to keep it from happening. Instead she must continue this day as though nothing had touched it. It was the kind of pose to which she had become accustomed. Quietly she obtained the names of the dead; she would send sympathy gifts to their families.

In the great chamber below, Bedford, in his richly furred gown of cloth of gold with a massive chain about his neck, mounted his horse trapped in gold embroidered with red roses and red dragons. Derby, similarly dressed and horsed and displaying his arms of sable lions, joined Bedford in the great hall. The men rode about the hall forcing back the press of spectators.

The queen returned to the banquet. Her ladies sat about her, ready to hold out the napkins, and the trumpets and minstrels performed in the several balconies. The queen chose from the scores of dishes brought before her: roasted boar, venison, trout, pheasant, swan, chicken, eel in gelatin, crane, pike, carp, kid, perch in deep jelly, rabbit, mutton richly garnished, baked raisins, custards, tarts, peacock, egret, partridge, sturgeon, castles of jelly, fruits of all varieties. Sharing in these delights, but again unseen by the curious, the king and his mother sat on a latticed stage built into a window.

As the banquet food was served and devoured, the queen distributed gifts, and her heralds and pursuivants offered their thanks: "Right high and mighty prince, most noble and excellent Princess, most Christian queen, and all our most dread and Sovereign liege Lady, We the Officers of Arms and Servants to all Nobles, beseech Almighty God to thank you for the great and abundant largesse which your grace has given us in honor of your most honorable and rightwise coronation, and to send your grace to live in honor and virtue."

The minstrels of the king and queen struck their instruments and danced about the hall while the queen completed her banquet with fruit and wafers, and then washed her hands. As the trumpets blew, the mayor offered her spices, and received a gold cup in fee. The queen departed the hall "to the rejoicing of many a true Englishman's heart."

On the following day the feasting and celebration continued with the royal family's attendance at mass in St. Stephen's Chapel. The queen, duchesses, and baronesses banqueted again, this time in the Parliament Chamber. After the dinner the ladies, now joined by the gentlemen of estate, danced through the day and into the evening. The festival went on through Tuesday, the 26th, but the queen took her court by barge to Greenwich.[53]

As the royal barge moved down the river, the music of the city drifted across the water:

> *God save King Henry whereso'er he be,*
> *And for Queen Elizabeth now pray we,*
> *And for all her noble progeny;*
> *God save the Church of Christ from any folly;*
> *And for Queen Elizabeth now pray we.*[54]

London sincerely rejoiced at these events. Not only had the marriage of Elizabeth and Henry VII been politically important for the king by securing the allegiance of opposing faction, but also, in a sure but indefinable way, it had somehow sanctified, verified, his crown. Now with the daughter of Edward IV of blessed memory crowned queen, at least the line of descent was clear. The heir already born, and other children she would bear, would unite and contain the royal strains. The throne would pass unquestioned now; God seemed at last to have lifted his scourge of war, penance for the deposition of kings.

For this state of affairs the twenty-year-old queen was largely responsible. Although she was without great power and never sought it, Elizabeth through her reign would be a subtle force behind the policies of her husband. She would attempt to continue the ideals and programs of her father and thus, in a sense, give longevity to his reign. In this way she could give life to her brother, buried God knew where, and keep faith with her father. Hopefully now the souls of the dead might rest, and the living go on with life. For the present, she would focus her attention on her son Prince Arthur and teach him the ideals in which she believed. Not as monarch, not for ambition, not for ego and herself would she reign; but she could stand as an example and as a conscience to those who did. She would teach that a king was first of all a man, subject to all the vicissitudes of fortune; that he must first know himself and the caprice of fortune so that then he might understand other men and govern well. In this way her influence might extend not to just one crown but to many. This would be her stance for the rest of her life.[55]

The king, having brought reasonable calm to domestic matters, was forced to look beyond the sea and entertain matters of international consequence. With Arthur now reaching his first birthday, it was not too early to utilize him by way of a foreign alliance. There were many princesses fit to become queen of England. But the knotty question for the father had been: which princess would insure the most beneficial present and future alliance for the son who would one day be king? France offered several possibilities, but its throne seemed none too secure; in addition the potential French brides were too old for the groom. Italy was in total confusion, and who could tell which hand would become the most valuable in fifteen or thirty years into the next century? On the other hand, Spain as a nation seemed to be growing stronger and more secure all the time; and its royal family had many daughters. Henry therefore decided to seek a Spanish alliance. Negotiations were begun, and by the time Arthur was twelve months old, he was betrothed to a younger daughter of Ferdinand and Isabella named Catherine of Aragon, aged twenty-one months. It was further agreed that the two would not marry, nor would Catherine come to England, until the prince was fifteen years old. When Henry first heard the news that Spain had accepted the marriage offer, he doffed his hat, embraced the ambassador, and whooped loudly a *Te Deum Laudemus.*[56]

For the mother who watched the boy child grow, saw his limbs lengthen, there were mixed emotions. She knew his life could never be complacent, that he would never have the freedom of boyhood, nor even the warmth of home in early days. He was born to be a king and every waking moment of every day must be directed to that end. Only the infant child would be hers. In those brief years she must train him to be loving and kind, to be gentle to the animals he held, to be pleasant to those who served him, to expect only the best from himself—in short, to do his duty. Once his formal schooling began, he had his own household; his training was undertaken by others, and his rare visits to court were treasured events. He was little more than three years old when Henry decided to create him the Prince of Wales. Arthur, as had Elizabeth's brother Edward, would soon be the governor of Wales. The boy was brought from Ashehurst to Sheen, visited his father, and on November 26, 1489, father and son each entered his own barge and traveled the Thames to an elaborate reception in London. Among those witnessing the ceremonies and greeting the prince were the Spanish ambassadors, carefully noting his appearance, his demeanor, and his ready wit. Throughout the public dinners and displays which accompanied such investiture, the boy waited upon his father, holding his towel, offering dishes.

It was late in the evening before they could escape from the ceremony, close the doors behind them, and seek out the mother who was at Westminster Palace awaiting the birth of another brother or sister. How weary the little boy had seemed, how tiny, standing there beside his tall and handsome father. Stiffly formal in his heavy robes, his cap with the ostrich plume, he was the prince. Too well disciplined to shift his feet or hide behind his father in the darkened room, he was a tiny royal guest. Not until he kissed his mother, and she folded him in her arms, did he become the boy he really was. But there he could not linger, for in the evening began the initiation rites to knighthood. In the morning he learned of the birth of a sister, heard mass, mounted his horse, rode in procession about Westminster, and returned to the White Hall. There he received his spurs from the Marquis of Berkeley and the Earl of Arundel. From his father he received his tiny sword; and as the prince knelt before the king he was dubbed Knight of the Bath. In the afternoon Prince Arthur donned his robes of estate and was led to the Parliament Chamber where his father waited. There amidst the nobles of the realm, the boy received his cape, the golden rod, the ring of gold, and was created Prince of Wales.

Once the ceremonies were over, the father left the Parliament Chamber. Today belonged to the prince. The room of ceremony became the banquet hall. The minstrels struck their instruments and the feasting and celebration began. At the center of the high board, in a chair which raised him to table height, presided the three-year-old prince. In another chamber the king visited with the queen, and as they talked of the day's events, they awaited the return of their first daughter from her first public ceremony—her christening. She was named Margaret for her grandmother.[57]

With the ceremonies over, the prince relaxed briefly into the boy, hovered over the cradle of the baby, talked excitedly to his mother of the events he could scarcely comprehend. And for a brief moment, the family was able to knit itself together. The days might be filled with serious affairs of state, but the evenings were kept in the quiet of the queen's chambers. As the family jested with Patch, the queen's fool, or listened to the music of the lute or read aloud the adventures of the great King Arthur, they realized the rarity of the moment and were grateful. There were always forces, events great and small, which converged to push them apart into their separate lives. Even now measles raged about London and struck members of the court circle. It was thought best to leave the city— Arthur must return to his studies and his own estate; the family itself would go to Greenwich for Christmas.

Elizabeth, through fear of contamination, was privately churched; then it was time to turn the boy back to his governors. The farewells and absences they all must learn to endure; tears, it was said, soothed the soul, but what good did they really do? From her chambers in Westminster Palace high above the water's edge, she watched the tiny boy lifted from his father's arms to those of the boatsman. The boy turned and seemed to search the windows. Could he see her, could he possibly sense the longing his mother felt as she stood behind the pane? He was a little boy with the responsibilities of manhood. Never must he be allowed to become dependent, always he must be kept aware of his duty. They both would learn to accept those facts.

Prior to these events England had found herself drawn further into foreign affairs. The central issue was the war between a burgeoning France under the boy-king Charles VIII and the weakening Brittany under the twelve-year-old Duchess Anne. England loathed to see the once mighty duchy absorbed by France, and Henry VII was torn between loyalties cultivated during his years of exile in both countries. Meanwhile Ferdinand and Isabella of Spain, always anxious to attack the French under any pretext, encouraged the English king to wage war on France. In Austria the irresponsible Maximilian I lacked the funds to field even his own armies, but encouraged Henry to fight the French anyway.

Henry, more interested in negotiation than confrontation and convinced that if war came it must pay its own way, convened Parliament. The English still believed that France rightfully belonged to the English crown, or at least provided ground for plunder. Parliament quickly granted funds and imposed levies to begin a war. Collectors went out to secure the tax, but the men of Durham and Yorkshire refused to pay. Led by a commoner John à Chamber, the rebels went so far in their defiance as to kill Henry Percy Earl of Northumberland, who was the collector for the north. The rebellion, however, was quickly put down by Thomas Howard Earl of Surrey, and its leaders captured and tried. At York John à

Chamber was hanged on a high gibbet, with his accomplices symmetrically placed on gallows below him.[58]

In the meantime Edward Woodville, the queen's uncle, mindful of the help from Brittany in the years of exile, requested permission to go secretly to Brittany's aid. Permission was denied, but Woodville went anyway, with an army of four hundred men. To give the illusion of greater English support, some seventeen hundred Bretons were dressed in the white coats with red crosses of the English. Meeting the French in battle on July 27, 1488, the English-Breton army was destroyed almost to a man. Henry VII suddenly found himself in a difficult situation. The French accused him of treaty-breaking, and the English populace screamed for war now that English blood had been spilled. Henry explained himself to the French, who accepted his excuses, but no explanation would satisfy his own people. They would have war, but it would take four years to resolve the issue. Armies were mustered, many of the wealthy bankrupted themselves to field their men, but all were ready to fight and hopeful of rich French plunder.[59]

Charles VIII, however, negotiated his own peace with Brittany, and in 1491 married the Duchess Anne. With the bride went her country, and there was nothing anyone could do to stop the absorption of Brittany into France. Maximilian was furious; he considered the bride to be his. The marriage had been both performed and consummated by proxy. Many had witnessed that bedding of the bride wherein, as she lay naked, Maxmilian's ambassador had entered the bed above the covers, bared his leg to the thigh and touched the protruding foot of the bride. Men might call it the "ceremony of the bootless calf," but the marriage had been called legal in the name of God.[60] Through Anne's marriage to the French King, Maximilian was now bereft of a country, new resources, and a bride; in revenge he would attack from the south if Henry would charge the west coast.

Ferdinand and Isabella continued to offer encouragement but

little real support; they were too deeply involved in fighting the Moors in Granada. Henry was advised to attack anyway. He gathered his army, and with her own hands his wife garnished his helmet and placed it on his head.[61] On October 6, 1492, he landed in Calais. No aid came from Maximilian, only messages of encouragement. After a few minor skirmishes and sieges of Boulogne, Henry began to treat secretly for peace. The French and Bretons were forced to pay his war expenses—725 gold crowns in fifteen yearly installments—and to renew the annuity paid to the late Edward IV. Charles VIII, more anxious to invade Italy than fight the English, readily agreed to Henry's demands. The treaty was signed November 3, and the war was over before it was fought. The armies were frustrated by the lack of plunder, but the king had won a victory and much wealth.[62] On November 9 a letter was read in the Guildhall, proclaiming the peace between England and France; by mid-December, 1492, the king landed at Dover. As he rode homeward toward the Christmas festivities, he was pleased by his venture that had saved lives and made money. But there were many who nursed grudges over their own expenditures and now-empty hands.[63]

There were many abroad, too, who were anxious to build on any discontent in England. In particular three persons in power persisted in threatening the security of Henry VII and his family: King James IV of Scotland was always eager for plunder; Margaret of Burgundy, ever frustrated by Lancastrian victory, suffered new woes and financial losses in England when the Tudor gained the throne; and Maximilian, lately Henry's ally, now felt abused by the English-French treaties.

During the recent wars another Yorkist imposter had emerged. Peter Warbeck, derisively called Perkin by the English, entered the services of a Breton named Pregent Meno. On a trading voyage to Cork in the early 1490's, Perkin arrayed himself in the silks of his master and was immediately noticed by the Irish because of his striking resemblance to the House of York. Could he be the Earl of Warwick, or possibly the bastard of Richard III? Or the young Prince Richard Duke of York, who had disappeared in the Tower? These speculations became so widespread that Perkin finally announced that he was indeed the lost son of Edward IV and heir to his crown. Such a statement, spreading rapidly, was seized upon by dissident Yorkists, and the news was communicated to Charles VIII in France. Charles, thinking he might make use of the imposter, invited him to court. Perkin eagerly journeyed to France and was received royally, even assigned a private guard; but when the English-French truce was concluded, Charles lost interest in the imposter. He left for Flanders and his "aunt," Margaret of Burgundy. There he remained, acquiring a knowledge of literature and manners, and bathing in the adulation heaped upon him. Perkin Warbeck felt glory descending and believed that destiny would one day offer a crown. He watched and waited for his moment of opportunity.

In England Elizabeth of York welcomed home the husband she had come to know and respect, even to love. With his head resting upon her lap, she listened to the adventures of war and its profitable peace. The lines of his forehead, his mouth, his slightly sunken cheeks were more pronounced now than when he had gone away. The strains of kingship were beginning to etch into his flesh. He was being worn away by the duplicity of intrigue abroad and the upstart imposters at home. And these crosscurrents were forcing him to act against his nature. She knew him to be a man of peace forced to war; a man of mercy forced to harsh justice. No doubt, men would remember that he had never lost a battle; but would they remember how he had made war pay its way even when his subjects were too shortsighted to value the policy? Would men remember how he had eliminated wasteful spending by the treasury, had promptly paid his debts, and by so doing, had restored faith in, and respect for, the throne and government? Would men remember how slow he was to act, how anxious he was to hear all sides of a question or an accusation, how he punctuated each decision with "great deliberation and breathing," how he had gained the reputation of a most wise man?[64] Would men remember how he protected the small landholders from more powerful men, how he nurtured the yeomen into sturdy freemen, how he encouraged trade and developed the navy, protected the consumers through price controls and the surveillance of coinage?[65] Would men remember that he wished to be the father of his people? John Morton had long ago understood these things—that the public man was not divorced from the private man who was also a husband and a father. And Morton, now Chancellor of the Realm, tried to explain the point when he defined the king's policy to the nation: "Because it is the king's desire that this peace wherein he hopeth to govern and maintain you, do not bear unto you leaves, for you to sit under in the shade of them in safety, but also should bear you fruit of riches, wealth, and plenty. . . ."[66] But looking down on the weary face, Elizabeth of York wondered if the wars would ever stop, if the imposters would ever leave their nefarious schemes so that the nation might rest and the king might bring it to fruition. It was a dream they both cherished.

5 · THE MOTHER OF KINGS

To the queen looking down from her chambers in West-minster Palace, England, the court, the royal family, life itself in this final decade of the fifteenth century seemed marked by paradox. On the one hand, the country, long scarred by civil war, was a rich and fruitful land. Its rivers teemed with fish and waterfowl. Its forests nourished deer, pheasant, partridge, boar, rabbit—animals of every kind—all free from the ravaging of wolves; for whenever these vicious beasts streaked from the highlands of Scotland, they were im-mediately and savagely hunted down. Sheep, goats, cows, and oxen roamed the hills, and there was so much livestock and farming that England fed and clothed its own. The fields with their rich harvests supplied the tables with food and the goblets with beer and ale. Only wine had to be imported.[1] In the banquet halls of the mighty and the chambers of the clergy, scores of dishes of mutton, boar, venison, each in its own sauce, paraded across the tables. At times sixty-five desserts might be offered; and at the evening's end, the broken foods were dumped into the alms baskets and set outside the door. For there were always some who begged and starved into the night. Though the earth might thrust out its bounty, the plague intermittently

slashed across the land. Indiscriminate in its attacks on rich
and poor alike, it wiped out entire villages, leaving them filled
with stinking carrion and gnawing flies, and no one left to bury
the dead.

To a nation still clothed in Saxon superstition and wrapped
in the robes of the Roman Church, every blessing, every disaster, had its portent, its meaning, its repercussion. Men, women,
and children heard mass every day, sometimes more than once.
In the cities women walked the streets with rosaries in hand
and publicly told their beads.[2] At court and in most wealthy
homes, morning began with private matins and a low mass.
After breakfast there was another service and two more masses.
During mealtimes, especially in the chambers of the queen
and noble ladies, spiritual matters were read and discussed.
At the end of the day there was evensong, and at bedtime
prayers for succor and safety through the night.[3] Always in
some dark chamber of the court or in the thousands of convents and monasteries across the land, priests and nuns
whispered in the darkness for the souls of those long dead
and for the many who still lived and could afford to pay for
heavenly insurance.

Christians might fast and pray, weep and prostrate themselves before the altar and cherish the slaughter of ten thousand
infidels before the victorious Catholic forces of Spain. At
Canterbury a heretic priest might hold adamantly to his erroneous beliefs and be sentenced to the stake. He might be
brought before his sovereign lord, himself on a sacred pilgrimage to the shrine of St. Thomas à Becket. There before
the golden tomb fretted and heavy with gems so rare they dazzled the eye, there before the flickering light playing upon the
crucifix and an agonized, bleeding Christ, that same heretic
might be won again to the faith by the wisdom and argument
of the king. There that heretic priest might admit his error,
even receive the sacrament; but the oils of his body must still

feed the fires of the stake.[4] Throughout the country, bonfires
of Lollard priests with heretical views would burn into the
night, and their fat would smoke and hiss among the scalding
coals.[5]

London, as the capital city, not only mirrored the paradoxes of the nation, it seemed to thrive on them. To the Scottish poet William Dunbar, London was the grandest city of all:

> *Strong be the walls that above thee stand;*
>   *Wise be the people that within thee dwells;*
> *Fresh be thy river with his lusty strands;*
>   *Blythe be thy churches, well sounding be thy bells;*
>   *Rich be thy merchants in substance that excels;*
> *Fair be thy wives, right lovesome, white and small;*
>   *Clear be thy virgins, lusty under kellis:**
> *London, thou art the flower of cities all.*[6]

And so it seemed. The city overflowed its southern banks and
spilled along the "beautiful and convenient" London Bridge
and lined it with houses, markets, and a church. The bridge, of
course, spanned the nation's major highway, the Thames, heavy
with barges and ships, docks and singing workmen, and home
of wheeling gulls and two thousand white swan. But over the
gates of the bridge swarmed the crows and buzzards who
pecked the eyes and ate the flesh from the heads of dead men.

London was a lusty city dominated by that ancient fortress,
the Tower, and protected by mighty walls newly reconstructed.
It was bounded by Aldgate on the north; by Bishopsgate,
Moorgate, and Cripplegate on the northeast; by Ludgate on
the south; by Aldersgate on the southwest; and by Newgate
on the west. Its citizens moved freely to and from the suburbs
and country, secure in the knowledge that in times of war, the
gates would lock and the city walls would hold.[7] The city,

---

* gowns

itself an ancient port and the hub of the nation, exuded prosperity. The handsome houses of timber and brick appeared deceptively small, for their interiors branched into deep halls and open courtyards. Nearly every street had its shop of rich wares of silver, tin, and white lead; in the Strand alone, fifty-two goldsmiths' shops were filled with gold and silver vessels, large and small, more numerous it was believed than all those of "Milan, Rome, Venice, and Florence put together."[8] Each home contained its own silver plate; every church was crammed with crucifixes, candlesticks, censers, patens, and cups of gold and silver; and each innkeeper, however humble, set his tables with silver dishes and drinking cups.[9] But outside, the streets were poorly paved, and because of the constant rain, they disappeared in the mud and sewage which slid into a stinking slime.[10]

Londoners might for pleasure practice with the bow in the fields near Moorgate, or skate upon bone when the ice was on the Thames, ride to the hunt, joust in the streets, or gawk at pageants and royal processions. But the highpoint of any day was eating. The kindest gesture one could make was to invite someone to dinner. Then the main halls would be cleared of the dogs and cats, the floors swept and layered with new rushes often sweetened with lavender and herbs. Oak boards, usually propped against the walls, would be heaved onto trestles geometrically arranged about the room, and the roaring fires lit. Then as the trenchers of fowl, meat, fish, and the bowls of soups and sauces into which each man dipped his bread passed by, as the cups of beer, ale, and wine were shared with friends and the minstrels played, conversation provided respite between servings.[11] There was much to talk of besides the warrings and imposters, the challenges to the throne and to the House of Lancaster, for the horizons of the world were being pushed back against the darkened skies.

Bartholomew Columbus, begging financial backing for the

voyages of his brother, had earlier come to the court of Henry
VII. But storms on the sea, a bout with pirates, and confusions
at court had delayed the meeting, and Christopher Columbus
had sailed under the banner of Ferdinand and Isabella of Spain.
Vasco da Gama had sailed around the Cape of Good Hope to
India and back. These voyages, successful in their missions and
returning with proof of riches beyond the sea, had encouraged
Henry to engage in a similar venture. Outfitting five small ships,
the king commissioned John Cabot to sail west in 1496.

The tiny ships returned in 1497 with descriptions of the
newfound lands and their luscious vegetation. Cabot spoke of
how he had sailed far westward and finding the waters still
open would have sailed farther except that his sailors grew
afraid.[12] Cabot, however, in his most dramatic gesture of all,
presented to the queen three strange men dressed in animal
skins, who tore their raw meat and relished its gore, and who
spoke no language ever heard before.[13] Though fearful at first,
they stayed on at court, came to know its ways and allowed the
court to know theirs. They learned the English language, taught
the court a little of the Indian tongue, and gradually became
so assimilated that in dress and manner they afterwards "could
not be discerned from Englishmen."[14] Somehow, however, the
new countries seemed—were—very remote; men and women
might dream and speculate on what these lands meant to England; more specifically they might envy the Spanish their con-
quests in the New World. But throughout these years, the
main interests of the English were in other exciting events
closer to home and seemingly more relevant.

There were, for instance, the spectacular court events
initiated by the king's creation of his second son as Duke of
York. The boy, born June 28, 1491, and named Henry for
his father, was now a strapping, heavy-set child of three. With
his golden hair and happy demeanor, he reminded everyone of
his grandfather Edward IV. He quickly became the court

favorite. To honor his induction into knighthood, four gentlemen of the court petitioned the king to hold royal jousts, inviting contenders from England and throughout the world. The petition was granted, and preparations went forward at Westminster.

In October, 1494, the king and queen journeyed from Sheen to Westminster Palace to welcome the boy from Eltham. The little prince, in his robes of velvet, straddled his horse and returned the greetings of the mayor and aldermen, the crafts and guilds. The populace that lined the avenues of London led him home to his family.[15]

In the evening Prince Henry waited upon his father at dinner, and like his brother before him, held the towel and dried his father's hands. No women were present, so the child was led to his mother's chambers to babble his news. So great was his excitement, so earnest his attempt to comprehend the meaning of the events about him, that the mother took the son upon her lap and talked of the events to come. Later that night he must take a bath in the linen-lined tub, as part of his initiation as a Knight of the Bath. His father would come to him and mark him with a cross of water and kiss it. Later his men would dry him, dress him in hermit's clothes, and lead him to prayers in the chapel. There he must pray for the souls of his grandfathers and for his grandmother Elizabeth Woodville, dead now two years and buried at Windsor.[16] He must ask God to help him to grow strong in body and wise in mind, to be a faithful servant to his father, to serve his brother Arthur, to do all things well, to be a good prince. As the child was led away to his bath and vigil, the mother watched him with proud but worried eyes.[17]

If Arthur, like his father and her brother Edward, was quiet and restrained, this boy Henry, with his pleasing ways and winning smile, seemed the spirit of her father returned. It was a mixed blessing. Thus the queen decided to spend this night in private vigil and prayer, beseeching God to strengthen the boy, to make him wiser than his grandfather had been, and to make him less lustful, less mindful of the pleasures of the flesh. She believed that Henry, like Edward, would relish life for the sheer joy of living; she only prayed that he would not let it destroy him.

All night in the chapel, with its dim candles and moving shadows, its bleeding Christ and smiling Virgin, those who were to be initiated into the Order of the Knights of the Bath knelt and prayed. In the center of the group and directly before the altar, the tiny prince jammed his fingers into his eyes to keep from going to sleep. At dawn Prince Henry and his fellow knights were shriven and heard mass; only then could they leave the chapel and sleep. At noon each knight was awakened and the earls of Oxford, Northumberland, and Essex helped the prince and the other initiates to dress, and led them to their horses through a secret passage behind St. Stephen's Chapel. There they mounted and rode about the yard in a symbolic pilgrimage. The queen, watching these activities from her chamber, could only admire the ease and agility with which her young son managed his horse. He would now go into the palace, receive his spurs from Buckingham and her half-brother Dorset, and his sword from his father. What she did not know until later was that the king, after dubbing the boy, lifted him, and set him on the table. The child was exhausted, but the services were not yet complete. Then Sir William Sandys, carrying Prince Henry in his arms, led the newly created knights into the chapel. There each man offered his sword to the altar, and Sir William, still holding the prince, helped him to do the same. Afterwards there was banqueting; although it was a fast day, each man was given liberty by the king to eat meat, and the carvers knelt before each knight to carve his food.[18]

The next morning, November 1, 1494, the king donned his robes of estate, and surrounded by Morton, newly created Cardinal of Canterbury, Bedford, Buckingham, Oxford, Essex, and other noblemen, entered the Parliament Chamber to stand under the cloth of estate. From every door came men of rank, the Mayor of London with the aldermen, knights and their squires, judges, and officers of arms. Silently they acknowledged the king's presence. Each man took his place according to rank, and the center of the room cleared. The silence was broken when the Garter King of Arms announced the arrival of the Earl of Suffolk, carrying a rich sword pommel upwards; the Earl of Northumberland bearing a rod of gold; the Earl of Derby, carrying the cape of estate, furred with ermine, and the coronet; and the Earl of Shrewsbury, carrying Prince Henry. At the chamber door the prince was allowed to walk by himself; with Dorset on one side and Arundel on the other, he was led to his father. There, with all ceremony, the cape was wrapped about his shoulders, the coronet settled upon his brow, and Prince Henry became the Duke of York.

The procession reformed. Arundel, bearing the sword of estate, led the way before the king; Derby walked to the right; and Shrewsbury to the left. In Shrewsbury's arms sat Prince Henry, elegant in his new robe and coronet, clutching with both fists his rod of gold. Behind him were the men who witnessed his ceremony. The ladies of the court now joined the proceedings. Elizabeth, crowned and in her robes of estate, led Margaret Beaufort and the ladies of court into the procession, which entered the Abbey to hear the sermon of Cardinal John Morton. It was a day of great rejoicing for all, since it gave the sense of a dynasty's being founded.[19]

Nearly the entire month of November would be given over to the celebrations. Throughout the first days of the month, in preparation for the jousting contests that would be held, hammers nailed scaffolding in place; rich blue hangings, embellished with gold fleur-de-lis, covered the stages; two canopies of estate showed the arms of the king and queen; and cushions of cloth of gold covered the benches. Round about the arena were more modest seats, which grew increasingly plain in accordance with the lower ranks of their intended occupants. On simple wood sat the common folk. From Westminster Hall rode the tournament challengers—the Earl of Suffolk, the Earl of Essex, Sir Robert Curson, and John Peach—accompanied by knights and esquires, helmeted in the blue and murrey of the queen's colors. Their horses were richly trapped in the green and white of the king's colors, fitted with chains of gold and harness furred with ermine. As they rode about the yard with jangling bells, thudding hooves, and cheering crowds, the banners waved and trumpets blew. From King's Street entered the answerers of the challenge—the Earl of Shrewsbury and Sir John Cheney— richly horsed and bravely helmeted.

Throughout the day the challengers and answerers and the knights of their calling raced one against the other. Lances, strongly braced in right hands, met in collision and shattered. With each broken spear, shouts went up and the victor was toasted. Horses careened and screamed with each impact, armor bent and dug into the flesh of man and beast. Sweat and steam oozed from the eye slits of helmets, and dust clogged the air and settled on the clotting blood. The violence, the noise, the smells, the chance of death exhilarated the crowd, caused it to roar in pleasure and anticipation. Too soon the day was over and John Peach, who had won the day, was presented to the five-year-old Princess Margaret. Upon the advice of her father, mother, grandmother, and all the ladies present, she offered the first prize of a ruby set in a gold ring.

In the evening there was dancing and feasting, more music by the minstrels, and antics by Patch, the queen's dwarf. In the corners the courtiers laughed and drank, talked of the jousting and staked their bets on the tourney to come. About the hall strolled the king and queen—the one with Prince Henry, the other with Princess Margaret. Prince Arthur remained at his studies in Ashehurst, but those in the room talked of him and missed his presence. The candles burned low and still the dishes were passed and the dancing continued. On the morrow they would rest for the tourney, which was set for the day after.

On November 11 the galleries were again filled with men, women, and children of all degrees, and the king and queen under their canopies of estate; the trumpets again were blown and the drums struck. From Westminster Hall the challengers again rode, dressed today in the colors of blue and tawny for the Duke of York. The harnesses of their horses were of black velvet bordered with gold and buckled with roses of red and white; above each man waved his banner—Suffolk had his red standard with the words "For to accomplish" above a crest of the golden lion; Essex, his tawny standard with the words "Our promise made" and the crest of the silver falcon with the bruised wing; Curson, his black banner showing the head of a red dragon and the words "There to we be ready." Last rode Peach with a standard of tawny, a crest of a lion's head crowned with ermine, and the words "In everything." From King's Street entered Sir Edward Borough, trapped in green velvet; Sir Edward Darellis, trapped in grey velvet; Thomas Brandon in green velvet; and Rouland de Veilleville in russet sarcenet. This time the opposing sides raced against each other with drawn swords, each man hoping to unhorse the other in less than twelve strokes of the sword. The horses wheeled and crashed, screamed amidst the noise, the dust, and the sweat, while the men in their armor smacked and flailed with the flat of their swords. Suddenly two horses trapped in paper with risqué sayings dashed onto the field. The king and queen and all their court collapsed with laughter as the two clowns thwacked at each other with the pommels of their swords. But neither they nor any of the jousters were sorely hurt.

In the evening there was more banqueting and dancing, and on November 13, the third day's tourney was held. Again

Princess Margaret presented the prizes, although with special pride this time, for the games of the day had been in her honor.[20] These days of festivity would long be remembered as the nation's finest tourneys and an honor to the king and queen and "great gladness to the common people."[21]

The king and queen sitting under the canopies of estate were surrounded by their family, now grown quite large: Margaret, aged five; Henry, aged three; Elizabeth, aged two. They were all handsome children—bright, attentive, excited by the noise and confusions. To the queen, however, sitting upon her golden cushions and watching the delight of the children, the tournament and festival revived the memory of that long-ago day when her handsome uncle Anthony Lord Rivers had jousted so valiantly and overcome every opponent. Then her father had sat upon the stage. He too had been young and strong in the confidence of his youth and the security of his crown. He had had no suspicion then of his death or the murder of his sons; and Rivers, with his love of life and his dazzling ways, had believed he might live forever. Did similar danger and death lurk laughingly behind this pageantry and display of arms? Was death and tragedy even now skulking on padded soles in the guise of Perkin Warbeck? Could there be no joy unshadowed by the past and threatened by the future?

Perkin Warbeck had remained at the court of Margaret of Burgundy. Now it was said that she had given him a personal guard dressed in the murrey and blue of the House of York, and that her court grew with conspirators. Was Perkin, who had dropped the title of Duke of York and assumed that of King Richard IV, even now preparing invasion? Rumors grew, and Henry sent agents into Flanders to search out Perkin's true heritage. To understand the depths of the conspiracy, he sent two spies into Margaret's court. The two, Sir Robert Clifford and William Barley traveled as unhappy Yorkists seeking revenge against the Tudor. To add seeming authenticity to their story, they were cursed at St. Paul's with bell, book, and candle, as traitors to the king.[22]

After infiltrating Margaret's court Sir Robert Clifford and William Barley returned from Flanders, and the news they brought shattered the security of the realm and struck into the heart of the royal circle itself. The conspiracy abroad was growing, King James IV and Maximilian were offering men and materials to Perkin Warbeck to launch an invasion of England. And there were men close to King Henry VII who promised to raise no hand against the invader. Chief among these was the king's own chamberlain, Sir William Stanley. The accusation was difficult, impossible, to understand. Stanley, brother-in-law to Margaret Beaufort and the very man who had saved Henry's life at Bosworth Field, the man who had been so richly rewarded and so highly honored, the man beloved by the royal family, had betrayed them all. He was summoned, tried, and beheaded on Tower Hill at six in the morning, February 16, 1495.[23]

In England, amazement confronted anguish. For those close to the situation, the sacrifice of Stanley was a personal one; but that he and others like him could encourage an imposter, could attempt to bring back from the grave the unfortunate boy prince, was more than could be understood. The queen sought to comfort her mother-in-law; and Margaret Beaufort, in turn, comforted Elizabeth. How unnecessary to gouge open old wounds and feed them with new infection.[24] Margaret, with emotion torn and raw, took her husband Thomas home to Latham Hall. There in privacy they would tend their wounds.

In Europe Perkin, bereft of the support of France and living in the court of Margaret of Burgundy, was inspired to immediate invasion by Maximilian. Ships were outfitted, and Perkin, aware of the earlier Kentish dissatisfaction with Henry VII, set sail. Kent, however, desired no part in new troubles and sought to lure Perkin ashore. He, however, remained on board, but sent a landing party, which was attacked and slaughtered. Perkin then sailed freely on to Ireland. Henry, on a progress to Lancashire visiting his mother and stepfather and trying to soothe the rupture caused by Sir William's death, prepared for a hasty return to London.[25] On the next day, however, having received word of Kentish loyalty, he sent Sir Richard Gilford there with a message "both to praise the fidelity and manhood of the people, and also to render to them his most hearty thanks for their good service to him done, with faithful promise not to forget them hereafter in their suits, requests, and petition."[26] Afterwards the beacons along the coast stood alert to invasion. Henry continued at Latham Hall, home of Margaret Beaufort and Thomas Lord Stanley. Somehow, he explained, they must learn to live with awful events.

Perkin in Ireland received none of the expected support, only open hostility. Forced to flee to Scotland, he threw himself on the mercy of James IV. There the adventurer spun tales of how his brother Edward V had been killed, but he had been allowed to flee to the continent. Wandering from country to country, ignorant of his birth and privilege, he had at last found his way to the court of Margaret. James, if not captivated by the story, was charmed by the prospect of English plunder and of having his puppet on the English throne. To give validity to Perkin's posture, he was allowed to marry into the Scottish royal family and take to wife the beautiful Katherine Gordon. Together the king and pretender plotted and finally exercised a raid into the northern country of England. James burned, pillaged, and noticed that no Englishman rose to Perkin's call. This was the second time his country had ignored him, and James wondered about the placement of his investment.

To Elizabeth these events seemed remote, for her younger daughter, Princess Elizabeth, aged four, a beautiful and happy child, suddenly died. The grief of the loss in turn hurried the birth of another son who also died—too small to survive. The

two were buried in the chapel at Westminster. It was true that
the other children were healthy, would probably grow strong
and live, and for this she was grateful. It was equally true that
deaths must happen where there were many children—but
this knowledge did not ease the pain or stifle the grief. She knew
too that she must grieve alone, for events swirled about them all
and pushed them on to activity. She therefore journeyed as an
act of faith to the shrine of the Virgin at Walsingham.

In London it was necessary to call up Parliament for tax
money for war—this time against Scotland. The tax was granted
but the men of Cornwall refused to pay. John Morton and
Sir Reginald Bray, sent as collectors, were confronted by bands
of Cornishmen under the command of two commoners, Thomas
Flammock a lawyer and Michael Joseph a smith, and the noble-
man Lord Audley in an angry march toward London. Henry
decided to let them come, thus tiring themselves by marching,
and weakening their supply line by distance. James seized this
momentary distraction, and made a hit-and-run attack against
Durham; Perkin in his ship, the *Cuckoo,* made quick sail to
Cornwall. Henry made his plans. He sent Surrey against the
Scots, and the main army under Oxford, Essex, and a Welshman
Rice ap Thomas against the Cornishmen. For additional safety
for his wife and children, he sent them to the security and comfort of the royal apartments at the Tower of London.

To Elizabeth the move was all too familiar; for the third time
in her life she was forced into confinement. Granted, this time
she was not surrounded by hostile guards, but even now men
were marching into the country seeking to destroy her throne
and that of her children. Arthur, she knew, was safe at Ludlow;
Henry and Margaret she would keep with her, try to keep life
for them relatively normal. Their studies would go on, and in
the evenings they would read aloud, practice the lute, play cards.
In these ways, they would fill the hours of waiting while the
spectres and shadows of the past crowded her mind.

The Cornishmen, having received no encouragement in Kent, moved to Black Heath, four miles from London. In the capital there was great fear; the gates were closed and guarded, the walls were manned and armed, and buckets of water were placed on the walls and in the streets. But young Henry insisted on watching from the Tower roof the smoke which marked the Cornish army. He laughed with delight as his father led his army into position. He knew his father would win, but he could not comprehend the danger.[27] The battle itself was brief, and in short order the leaders of the opposition were collected. Lord Audley was sent to Newgate, from which prison he was later dressed in a torn paper coat of his arms reversed, and drawn in a cart through the city to Tower Hill. There he was beheaded. Thomas Flammock and Michael Joseph were hanged, drawn, and quartered, with pieces of their bodies hung on the Tower gates, and their heads on London Bridge. The army of Cornishmen was chastised and pardoned.[28]

In the north Surrey had equally good fortune, for when James heard of his coming, he scurried back to his own country—a journey which, in coming over, had consumed two days, was completed in eight hours of hasty retreat.[29] Although the Scottish king was known for his derring-do, his love of battle for the sake of battle, he could not appreciate that quality in other men. When he challenged Surrey to single combat, he was amazed to hear of Surrey's acceptance. Finding himself at home, the Scottish James decided to stay there, lick his wounds, and listen to the Spanish ambassador urging truce with England. A little peace with his southern neighbors suddenly sounded like a good idea.

In the meantime, Perkin called himself Richard IV, and with an army of three thousand, surrounded and besieged the town of Exeter; but by lowering men over the walls, the town alerted the king. Help came swiftly from noblemen and their armies and Perkin's forces disintegrated. His leaders slipped away

cowardly to sanctuary at Beaulieu Abbey in Hampshire. Quickly
two bands of Henry's lighthorsemen surrounded the sanctuary,
captured Perkin, and brought him to the king. At St. Michael's
Mount, the royal cavalry discovered Perkin's wife, Katherine
Gordon. She too was brought to the king, roped like a bonds-
woman, but Henry was moved to pity and sent her with an
honorable escort to the protection of his queen at the Tower.[30]

Henry came back to London, was greeted in triumph, and
exhibited Perkin to the crowds. Unbound and seemingly unguarded, Perkin rode through the streets of the capital, and
the jeers and mockeries of courtiers and commoners followed
him wherever he went "that one might know afar off where the
owl was by the flight of birds: some wondering, some mocking,
some cursing, some prying and picking matter out of his countenance and gesture to talk of." His confession of imposture and
his common pedigree were published far and wide, while the
upstart was led to imprisonment in the Tower not far from
the Earl of Warwick.[31]

The king and his family, after settling these matters, returned to Sheen and sought to shrug off anxiety through preparations for Christmas. Arthur came home for the holidays, a
tall and handsome youth, looking more like his father now that
childhood plumpness had given way to adolescent leanness. He
was a grave and serious boy, much given to books, and his
mother worried that he would make his life needlessly stern.[32]
There were no such worries, however, about Prince Henry, who
loved his lute as much as his horses, who already danced with
much energy and great abandon. But he brought the family joy
and made them laugh at his antics and smile with pride at his
easy physical ability. Already he rode hard and well, bested his
brother at jousting, and wrestled the servant boys to the floor,
to the delight of his sister. And there was Margaret, already
tall at age eight and giving promise of beauty, who divided her
passion between the lute and cards. When she won, gambling
was her favorite.

The festival of Christmas had scarcely begun, however, when, on December 22 at nine in the evening, the alarm went up—fire in the king's chambers. The family, dropping their games and books, gathered the pet dogs at their feet and raced down the hallways. Already smoke choked the chambers as carpet and tapestries fed the flames. The family stood in the gardens while the fire raged, and men scurried to the roofs with buckets of water. For three hours the fire burned, and much of the building was destroyed. Henry, watching this favorite home die, vowed to rebuild and name it Richmond.[33]

The mixed emotions which closed the year 1497 only signaled paradoxes of the coming year. On the one hand there were happy events: Spanish Ferdinand and Isabella, impressed with King Henry's international strength, were increasingly anxious for the marriage of their daughter Catherine to Prince Arthur; James IV of Scotland, willing now to seal a truce with England, wished to marry Princess Margaret. These alliances were valued ones, not only for the well-being of the nation, but for the eminence of the children. Their parents were pleased, but insisted that both Arthur and Margaret reach their teen years before the weddings went forward. In the meantime they would think of similar matches for Henry and for the new baby, Mary, born in May, 1498.[34]

Other events, however, were taking hold. Perkin Warbeck during these months of imprisonment corrupted the guards and met with Edward Earl of Warwick, long imprisoned in the Tower since the battle of Bosworth Field. Together they planned an escape, and somehow managed it. Once outside the walls, there was nowhere to go. Warwick was captured almost immediately and returned to the Tower. Perkin escaped to the coast to find his passage blocked. He took sanctuary at the priory of Sheen. Again he was captured and returned to London. Once more he was led through the streets and mocked and scorned, only this time he was also pinned to the stocks at Westminster. There, amidst the obscenities and curses of men and the jeers and taunts of women, he was forced to read aloud his confession. Again he outlined his pedigree, named his parents, told how he had traveled from Tournay to Antwerp, and been put in the service of a merchant. He described his coming to England and the encouragement of others which forced him to his disguises. No sooner had he finished speaking than he had to start again, shouting above the vilification of the street mob. The next day he was drawn through the screaming, laughing crowd to Chepe, where he repeated his performance.[35] He was then taken to Tyburn to die upon the gallows. His wife — because of her beauty and royal blood and innocence in these matters—throughout these years and long after continued at court in the service of the queen. Katherine Gordon, assuming again her maiden name, lived for the rest of her life on pensions provided by Henry VII and took in succession three husbands more.[36]

Warwick was arraigned before Oxford, sentenced for treason against the king, and on November 28, 1499, was beheaded at Tower Hill. He was twenty-four years old, a prisoner of his royal blood, a captive of a weakened mind. In all his life he had scarcely known a single day of freedom. His death caused sorrow among those who knew him, for they believed him incapable of plotting anything, let alone the overthrow of the government.[37]

There seemed, however, no end to the line of pretenders. No sooner was one put down than another would rise. Another impersonator of Warwick appeared. This one, named Ralph Wilford, was educated by an Augustinian friar. In the two weeks between the new pretensions and the pretender's hanging in February, 1499, it was noted that the king aged ten years. He was simply being worn out by these frivolous but agonized claims; in spite of the years of white-knuckled hold on the crown, he knew he would never be able to relax his grip.[38]

To rid his spirit of these infections and to escape renewed

ravages of the plague, the king sent his children into the country and took his wife to Calais. Elizabeth, recovering from her seventh confinement in thirteen years and the birth of her third son Edmund Duke of Somerset, felt the trip a welcome change. She and Henry traveled from Greenwich to Dover and took a ship for Calais. It was a good journey, marked not only by the splendor of the court but also by the devotion of the subjects who lined the roads with food and drink to ease the travelers. At Calais arrangements were made to meet Archduke Philip of Burgundy. No, he would not enter Calais, having vowed never to enter the walled city of another. Therefore the two rulers met at St. Peter's Church just outside the city. With much pomp and golden procession, Elizabeth and Henry rode out to meet the archduke. Philip would have gladly held the stirrups of the English king; Henry forbade it, and the two embraced. They talked of old wars and new truces, and agreed to marry their children to strengthen alliances. Prince Henry must marry the archduke's daughter; and the Princess Mary, the archduke's son Charles. To celebrate these events, there were great feastings and jousts, music and pageantry.[39]

Well satisfied with the pleasures of the holiday and the beneficial truces made, Henry and Elizabeth returned to England in June. The plague, which had devoured twenty thousand lives, was over,[40] and the scars of winter were repaired by the brilliance of early summer. Anguish, however, awaited the royal family. Soon after Henry and Elizabeth had settled again at Greenwich and begun to rest and refresh themselves, word came that Prince Edmund, four months old, was dead. Although his parents hardly knew him, their grief was penetrating and severe; they would meet his body at Westminster. The tiny corpse, almost lost in the great procession, was carefully and sorrowfully conveyed from Hatfield through London. Once again the mayor and aldermen, and all the crafts and guilds in their liveries, lined the streets in silent mourning. The child was taken to the Shrine of St. Edward at Westminster Abbey to lie near his infant brother and sister.[41]

Knowing that unabated grief and excessive mourning only provoked the wrath of God, Henry and Elizabeth picked up their lives and renewed their travels from estate to estate. Wherever the king and queen went, ordinary people brought them gifts of puddings and spices, fresh fruit, cherries and strawberries, birds in cages.[42] They held court at Westminster, visited Coventry, and witnessed its splendid mystery plays, stories of the world from Creation to Judgment Day, and rested at Windsor with its fine hunting. It was good to ride again to the singing of the hounds, to race through the forests ducking the limbs and branches. It was good to rest in the evening to the music of the flutes, recorders, and clavichord, to waken in the morning to hear the village children singing in the garden, to watch the folk dancers, the tumblers and jugglers. One could always play tennis, although the king was something of a wild shot and so often sent his tennis balls into oblivion; he much preferred hawking. In the afternoons the entire family, even the baby Mary, might gather around the butts to shoot arrows, but Prince Henry usually won.

Gradually the autumn months and the love of their subjects healed something of the family's earlier sorrow, and thoughts turned toward coming events. Prince Arthur celebrated his fourteenth birthday, and all the court began to talk of Spain and his marriage to Catherine of Aragon the following year. The queen listened with fascination to the reports of the foreign court. She heard of the reception of the English ambassadors by Queen Isabella dressed in a black velvet riding cape slashed to show a dress of cloth of gold bordered with a line of red and white roses of beaten gold, each rose adorned with jewels. She heard that in public processions the Spanish queen often rode a fine mule adorned with pearls and precious stones. She heard how Ferdinand and Isabella would often dance in the evening while their son carried a torch before them in a solo dance of his own.[43]

During the year, correspondence between the four monarchs was heavy; Ferdinand, Isabella, and Henry were most concerned about the timing of the wedding and the terms of the dowry: the marriage was to take place within twelve days of Catherine's arrival in England, and she was to be given a third part of Wales, the duchy of Cornwall, and the county of Chester. In return she would bring part of her dower in ready money and jewels, with the rest to be paid in installments.[44] Elizabeth wrote of her concern for Catherine's safe voyage, the care with which she would be received into the family, and the love and affection the girl would know at the English court.[45]

Previously, Ferdinand and Isabella, fearing more rebellion in England, had been loathe to send their daughter into a land where Warwick still lived.[46] Now, however, with Warwick dead, Arthur past his fifteenth birthday, and the terms of the dowry settled, Catherine left her family and set sail in May, 1501. Violent storms and raging seas forced the ship's return, and the wise men interpreted this as a sign that boded ill. All nature, it was said, intervened to keep the girl from England. Nevertheless, politics being the force of nations, she again left her family, her home, and her country, and reached Plymouth October 2.[47] The carefully planned journey to Exeter, Sherbourne, Shaftsbury, Amesbury, Chester, and around London to Croyden was taken in slow stages. Before each new town, companies of knights rode out to meet the princess and her party to escort her to the night's lodging. Thus with great pomp and increasing procession she moved sometimes in her litter, other times on muleback. Outside of London, in St. George's field, she was met and welcomed by a great host of noblemen; foremost among them, and chief receiver, was the handsome nine-year-old Prince Henry. They moved forward to the great London celebration. The city, always rising to the occasion, had swept and sanded its streets for the better footing of the horses, hung out its banners and tapestries, and practiced and positioned its minstrels and trumpets. Its people, gaily dressed in their own fine costumes, craned and peered at the curious foreigners.

Catherine, wearing a broad round felt hat, with heavy long black plumes, draped in a mantilla of orange-red satin, rode a handsome black mule. Her sidesaddle, like those of her ladies, was fashioned not unlike a small armchair. Each of the Spanish ladies upon a mule was escorted by an English lady upon a horse; but since the Spanish mounted to the right and the English to the left, the ladies rode back to back—the impression being that they had quarreled.[48] Thus with Prince Henry at her right and the papal legate at her left, Catherine of Aragon rode through Southwark and across London Bridge toward St. Paul's Church to offer thanks for her safe journey.[49] Along the way were pageants of welcome; one elaborate scene represented St. Katherine and St. Ursula, who concluded her speech with:

> *As Arthur your Spouse, than the second now*
> *Succeedeth the first Arthur in dignity,*
> *So in likewise, Madame Catherine, you*
> *As second Ursula shall succeed me.*

Other pageants welcomed her as "the Bright Star of Spain," told of the auspicious signs of the zodiac which sanctioned the wedding, and described her husband as "a prince of all princes the very flower." Henry and Elizabeth, with their court, watched these proceedings from a private home in Chepe; they saw the mayor and his men ride forward to meet the princess, and heard the voice of "Honor" speak from the pageant:

> *Wherefore, noble princess, of that you persevere*
> *With your excellent spouse, there shall ye*
> *Reign here with us in prosperity forever.*

With these words sounding in her ears, Catherine of Aragon the Princess of Wales entered St. Paul's Church to offer thanks for her safe journey and, no doubt, to ask for strength to adjust to this new and foreign land. She would not meet her husband until they met at the altar.[50]

Catherine and her attendants rested the night at Bishop's Palace; in the morning she entered her litter for the short trip to Baynard's Castle, where Elizabeth held court. Once the formalities were over, the queen embraced the sixteen-year-old girl, and speaking Latin—for neither understood the language of the other—Elizabeth sought to comfort the girl, assure her of welcome and warmth, and tried to ease the strangeness and confusion of a foreign place. How difficult must be the girl's life. Unable to communicate except with other Spaniards, how alone and lonely she must feel. She too must learn to accept her fate as they all must do, for it was the role which God had assigned them. For royalty, especially women, there were few choices; that one must understand and accept. The two spoke together of Spain, of the parents Ferdinand and Isabella, and of Prince Arthur, newly arrived from Wales and anxious for his wedding day.

Sunday, November 14, 1501, the family, Catherine, and the Spanish attendants gathered at the Tower. Leading the procession was Prince Henry, resplendent in cloth-of-silver tissue trimmed in gold Tudor roses. Among the handsomely furnished nobles rode King Henry in robes of red velvet, a breastplate set with diamonds, rubies, and pearls, and his belt of rubies. The trappings of his white horse with its gilded hooves were of splendid damask and gold. Behind Henry, in a chariot drawn by white horses, sat Elizabeth of York handsomely garbed in white satin with a train of purple velvet. Beside her sat the bride, elegant in white and gold, a coronet of rich stones upon her head, her auburn hair hanging loose halfway down her back. Throughout the procession the musicians played, trumpets sounded, and crowds pressed into each other, pointing, waving, amazed at the display of magnificence.[51]

Prince Arthur waited within St. Paul's Cathedral. The church itself had been nearly transformed. Gigantic hangings stretched from the ceiling to within six feet of the floor; two long bridges, complete with elevated stages, spanned the church—one for the wedding party, the other for the king and queen. As the procession neared the church, the trumpeters standing high in the eaves took up the welcome and played the princess, escorted by Prince Henry, to the high stage and the waiting bridegroom. Here the marriage was challenged as planned, since the bride and groom—like nearly all royalty—were within the bonds of kinship; and in defense of the marriage, a papal dispensation was read. Then with the trumpets sounding, the prince and princess moved to the high altar for the ceremony itself.

For Elizabeth of York, surrounded by her children, watching the proud figure of the young Henry and the kneeling figure of Arthur and Catherine, there were mixed emotions. The wedding pleased her, for Catherine and Arthur were both young and would grow up together; perhaps life would thus be easier for them. But what of the young Henry, so handsome there in his dignity? When would he too kneel at the altar? Who would be then the bride? And what of Margaret, too young to assume the cares of adulthood but soon to be a wife? Perhaps time and life were taking new hope from these young ones, would treat them more gently. But were there not shadows lurking even now to take away their joy? The ghosts and horrors of the past had been ever close, and there was no reason to believe they were not still so. The innocent must be happy while they could.

At the altar the bride and groom separated. Arthur left, while Prince Henry took Catherine of Aragon by the hand and led her home. There in Bishop's Palace, the wedding banquet took place, and amidst the gaiety Catherine and her ladies danced alone and played the castanets. Arthur danced the volte with his sister Margaret, and Henry so excited himself in dancing that he ripped away his jacket in order to move more freely.[52] In the streets conduits ran with wine, so that all London might celebrate the day.[53]

In the evening, the Duchess of Norfolk and Princess Margaret led the bride to her chamber, and Henry led his brother. In the morning Arthur rang early for a drink, commenting: "I have this night been in the midst of Spain which is a hot region, and that journey maketh me so dry."[54]

On Tuesday the king and queen came from Baynard's Castle to St. Paul's for mass, and then to Bishop's Palace to see the bride and groom.[55] From there each took a richly decorated barge for the trip by water to Westminster Palace and the jousts and tourneys of celebration. The chief challenger was the Duke of Buckingham in his colors of green and white and his plumed helmet. The defenders arrived in richly decorated pageants of allegorical settings: Dorset appeared in a black tower trimmed with cloth of gold, surrounded by thirty gentlemen in black satin with beads of silver worn about their necks; Guilliam de Rivers was in a ship, cross-sailed; Essex, on a mountain drawn by a red dragon. Every day for a week men jousted and tourneyed, displaying their arms for the court and the Spanish visitors. And every evening there were banquets and dancing.[56]

On Sunday the court again took their barges and headed upriver to the newly completed manor of Richmond. There it was drizzling, and Elizabeth and Henry played chess, other lords and ladies played at backgammon and cards and dice at little tables, while Catherine and the princes danced and sang. By afternoon the weather cleared, and the entire company visited the gardens to watch Spanish acrobats walk a tightrope. In the evening after the banquet, the pageant was of a great rock drawn into the hall by representations of sea horses. Once the rock was in place, it opened to reveal the Children of the Royal

Chapel playing their musical instruments and singing. The rock closed, only to open again, and this time it released into the hall white pigeons, doves, and rabbits, after which there was great chase and much merriment.[57]

The pleasures of the days lightened the winter days, and Arthur and his bride were sent away with the good wishes of their parents and London to Ludlow Castle in Wales, there to assume the duties of governing the country. In December the Scottish ambassadors came to court to negotiate the betrothal of Princess Margaret to King James IV of Scotland. The marriage service was celebrated on January 25, 1502, between the princess and the Earl of Bothwell, proxy for James, in the queen's chapel at Richmond. There in the presence of her parents, her brother Henry, and her sister Mary, she received their blessings and exchanged vows with Bothwell:

> I Margaret, the first begotten daughter of the right excellent, right high and mighty Prince and Princess Henry by the grace of God King of England, and Elizabeth Queen of the same, wittingly and of deliberate mind, having twelve years complete in age in the month of November last be passed, contract matrimony with the right excellent, right high and mighty, Prince James King of Scotland, the person of whom Patrick, Earl of Bothwell, is Procurator; and take the said James King of Scotland unto and for my husband and spouse and all other for him foresake, during his and mine lives natural; and thereto I plight and give to him, in your person as procurator, aforesaid, my faith and truth.[58]

With these words the Princess Margaret became Queen of Scotland. She would not reign, however, for two more years. Her mother insisted upon the point. Her daughter, the mother maintained, might be tall and comely, but she was still very much a girl—not ready to assume the duties of a woman. Let her remain at home for a while, have more of the responsibilities of court before she left forever. It was painful to have the children leave even though they must.

The betrothal was followed by banqueting and jousts, the pleasures of masquing and dancing, dominated by an enormous lantern filled with singing folk. At the tourneys and games, spears twelve inches in diameter were matched one against the other, but to the amazement and delight of the company, these spears too were broken.[59]

With the two marriages completed, the court settled into peace and comfort for the remainder of the winter. The land at last was quiet: there had been no new word of foolish impostors; Arthur and Catherine were settled at Ludlow; Margaret and Mary were gay young girls uninvolved in worldly affairs in spite of Margaret's marriage; and Prince Henry kept them all entertained, playing upon their moods, cavorting madly, or delicately sounding his lute. It was a pleasant and happy time for them all.

Gradually the greenery of spring pushed through the deadened limbs of winter and London shrugged off a shade of grey. Spring was in the air, and the family moved outside to their horses and hunts, their games at Greenwich—that home by the sea which seemed in its greenery and openness a symbol of spring. Suddenly out of the west came the anguished news that Prince Arthur was dead. Never of the strongest physique, his constitution had suddenly broken down, and he died April 2, 1502, at fifteen years of age.

The news was brought first to the confessor of the king so early in the morning that Henry had not yet risen. The priest entered the chamber with the words: "If we receive good things at the hand of God, why may we not endure evil things"; and he told of the prince's death. Henry, believing that the queen should not hear these "most sorrowful and heavy tidings alone," sent for her to come to his chamber. The king was distracted with grief and Elizabeth took him in her arms and rocked him with gentle words, reminding him that he could not give way to despair, for he was her comfort and the comfort of the realm. She spoke of his mother, who had had only one son; and yet God had preserved him and brought him to the crown. Softly she continued speaking of the fair prince and two fair princesses which God had granted them. God, she said, was still where he was, and she and her husband were young enough to have more children. Slowly Henry's sobs subsided, and the two continued together quietly, praying for Arthur, praying for themselves.

When words had been exhausted, Elizabeth left the king and returned to her chamber. There, unable to control her private grief, she fell prostrate upon the floor and sobbed. No comfort offered by her ladies, no words of the priest, could erase the pain or ease the sorrow. The king was sent for, and he came. Ordering the room emptied, he lifted his wife "with true, gentle, and faithful love" into his arms. With warm words and soft, he repeated her words of hope and promise, and together they thanked God for their remaining son. Together they had endured much, and somehow they survived this day.[60]

Throughout the land dirges were sung for the lost prince, the boy who had promised so much hope, the boy who had combined the roses red and white, the boy who offered promise of King Arthur come again.

At Ludlow, Arthur's body was prepared for burial, placed in its black velvet-covered coffin, and carried for the last time. amidst tapers and mournful dirges, to his chapel. There it lay under a canopy of black cloth of gold stitched with a white cross, until the grieving procession formed for the journey to Worcester, the final resting place. Then with banners of the Trinity, the *Patible,* the Virgin, and St. George held at each corner of the coffin, the banner with the prince's arms following, and Thomas Howard the Earl of Surrey as chief mourner, the procession moved by slow stages from Ludlow to Bewdley to Worcester. Each night the procession stopped, and the body was placed under good watch in chapels along the way. In the morning the six horses trapped in black would be harnessed again to the hearse, the banners lifted, and through rain and mud, the mourners ushered their sad burden. At times the weather was so foul that extra cloths were placed over the hearse to protect it from the chilling rain; the mud so deep that oxen replaced the horses.

At Worcester all the torches of the town were lighted in mournful greeting, and the streets filled with tearful folk, quiet and sad in this day of grief. Seventeen torches preceded the bier, and banners of the kings and queens of England and Spain joined those of the prince in wordless tribute. After the lessons and prayers, the offerings of the mourners, the reading of the gospel, Prince Arthur's own horse was ridden into the chapel and became, with his arms and poleax, the most moving gift of all. At the sight of the horse which Arthur had dearly loved, there was no man in the church who did not weep.

The body of Arthur was then carried to the south end of the altar where it was buried. The men who lowered the coffin wept; the Bishop of Lincoln, offering prayers, mingled his tears with the holy water and earth dropped upon the coffin. Each Officer of Arms weepingly cast his coat of arms into the grave; Sir William Ovedall, Comptroller of Arthur's household, with sobs of anguish and woe broke over his head his staff of office. Each man in Arthur's service repeated the gesture; and to those who watched, it was a poignant sight.[61] Throughout England "all the honest inhabitants of every parish" said prayers for the peace of the dead prince's soul and wept in the April rain. His bride came again to court, but the gladness of earlier days shrouded itself in the robes of mourning.[62]

For months the court waited with anxious concern to see if Catherine of Aragon were pregnant, but she was not. With all

doubt removed, Henry Duke of York was created on February
18, 1503, the Prince of Wales. He was an able prince and those
who knew him believed him capable of effective rule. Joy,
however, went out of the occasion, and was replaced by quiet
dignity, for there were many who remembered the earlier ceremony and thought of the transitory quality of human life.[63]

Earlier in the year, on January 13, the first stone of Our Lady
Chapel had been laid at Westminster Abbey.[64] Henry VII
wished to build a monument to himself, his family, and his
dynasty that would circumvent days and years and would last
for all time. For its construction he would spare no expense, no
labor, and its mighty work with its lofty spires would speak
across the ages of a man who loved God. He would have it so.

Somber as these thoughts were, life continued to push
through, sought to renew itself. Elizabeth of York was again
pregnant. For the eighth time Margaret Beaufort busied herself
with all the preparations that preceded a royal birth. The queen's
chamber must be readied at Richmond. The room became heavy
with rich tapestries of a floral pattern only, for it was believed
that representations of human figures might affect the newborn
child. All the windows were covered over save one, and that was
arranged so that the queen might have light when she desired it.
Her chapel was newly dressed, and furnished with crucifixes and
ornaments of gold and relics of saints. The floors were carpeted
with heavy oriental rugs, and the room outfitted with chairs and
deep cushions. On the bed there were down pillows; a coverlet
of scarlet, furred with ermine and embroidered with crimson
velvet upon velvet; a head sheet of cloth of gold furred with
ermine; a mattress stuffed with wool; and a featherbed with a
bolster of down. All were tasseled with gold and embroidered
with crowns and devices of the king and queen.

It was, however, while resting at the Tower of London that
Elizabeth suddenly knew she must take to her chamber. So the
room was hastily and honorably prepared, and the tapestries

quickly changed. With the men and women of the court about her, she climbed the one hundred fifty-two steps to her rooms, where together they heard mass. Then she turned to thank them all and to beseech their prayers that God would send her a good hour. With her ladies, she entered her room, now hung with blue tapestries covered with golden fleur-de-lis.[65] Again she knelt before her altar and prayed, but a great weariness of spirit descended upon her. Amidst the gorgeous hangings of the room, she lay down.

Outside the winds howled and whipped about the Tower. The Thames churned and tossed its boats, and the sounds of the sea birds screamed and pitched against the chilling rain. During the night, within the warmth and security of the Tower, a baby cried. A princess had been born.

FEBRUARY 10–11, 1503

WITH *the onset of darkness, the Tower slowly settled into quiet and the night watch took up its solitary march in muffled silence. Amidst the deepening shadows, servants broke off their labors, shivered by the fires, ate their suppers and smiled as they spoke of the christening, the child, the queen much beloved. She would be well soon—Dr. Hallywurth had said so, as he left for home. It would be good to have her back among them; she always brought joy, a pleasant word, a smile, sometimes a gift. Life was different, somehow darker, without her. It was no wonder the king liked to sit away the evening in her chamber. Of these things, the servants talked against the night, the dark, and the shadows.*

In the chambers of the queen, the heat huddled in corners and beneath the covers. The voices of Henry Tudor and Margaret Beaufort lifted and settled almost with the shadows. Softly they spoke of the christening, always a splendid affair with canopies and candles, processions and song. Yes, it was well to have it done; the child Catherine seemed frail. With tiny ones, one never knew. But God be praised, the other children were well. Prince Henry was a fine boy, growing handsomely; he would live long unless he broke his neck in the hunt.

Voices came and went, riding upon the shadows. It was all familiar to the queen as she lay under the heavy covers of down. It was warm and comforting to hear the others talk so, for long ago the resentment and frustration had given way to pleasures of family and home. Drifting now on the sounds of voices, Elizabeth of York heard the king and his mother speak of Henry and Catherine. Of marriages and dowries, while far away midnight tolled and tomorrow came as yesterday fled. Time and marriages. Catherine and Arthur. Marriages and time. Of Margaret and James and time. Time. Margaret must have time. And Mary. Mary and Charles, marriage and time. And Henry and Elizabeth and time and Margaret and Henry. Time.

Darkness streaked with dawn. The seabirds began again their screech against the morning cold. The air hung heavy with moisture while the winds chased and fretted about the Tower. The king roused himself and approached the bed of his wife. He wanted to be the first to wish her well on this, her thirty-eighth birthday. But when he took her hand, he knew that she was dead.

EPILOGUE

D EVASTATED by the death of his wife "Elizabeth the Good," as her subjects would continue to call her, Henry VII, with his most trusted servant, privately withdrew to a solitary place "to pass his sorrow and would that no man should resort to him."[1] To Elizabeth's servants he sent Sir Charles Somerset and Sir Richard Gilford to offer gentle, comforting words. He sent for the children and told them the sorrowful news. Together they reentered the queen's chamber where she now lay dressed in her robes of estate, and together they prayed for her soul. Throughout the day high masses were sung; the bells of St. Paul's were rung in mournful song, and each bell in the city took up the dirge while the people came to the Tower and stood in the morning mist.

On Sunday, February 12, the body was embalmed; and its place on the bed of state was taken by a wax effigy in the likeness of the queen dressed in her robes of velvet and cloth of gold. The body was placed in a lead coffin bearing her name and boarded over with black velvet and a white damask cross. It was carried under a canopy into the Norman Chapel of St. John within the Tower. There, against windows lined with black crepe and walls heavy with black silk damask, five hundred candles lighted the chapel. The ladies of the queen's household, dressed in their most somber and simplest gowns and wearing kerchiefs over their heads, entered two by two. The queen's sister, Lady Catherine, as chief mourner, took her place at the head of the coffin. After the mass the ladies stood watch by the body for the next twelve days. At every Kyrie Eleison an officer of arms said a Pater Noster for the soul of the queen.

At noon Wednesday, February 22, the coffin was placed on "a carriage covered with black velvet with a cross of white cloth of gold, very well draped." Seven horses trapped in black velvet drew the hearse. Behind and above it, and seated in a chair was an image exactly representing the queen "in her rich robes of state, her very rich crown on her head, her hair about her shoulders, her sceptre in her right hand, her fingers well garnished with rings and precious stones." On the hearse, beside the coffin and the chair, were six gentlewomen kneeling in prayer. Horses trapped in black velvet, bearing the arms of the queen, carried knights in black mourning hoods. By every horse walked a knight, bearing banners of the Virgin, the Assumption, the Salutation, and the Nativity, to symbolize that the queen died in childbed. Eight ladies of honor upon black horses rode behind the hearse, and beside them walked gentlemen in mourning gowns. The Mayor of London and important citizens followed the sorrowful procession. At Fenchurch Street the cortège was met by thirty-seven young ladies, one for every year of the queen's life.[2] They were dressed in white and wreathed in white flowers. Every hundred yards a guild or religious group stood with lighted torches and with children, some dressed as angels with golden wings, singing prayers and dirges.

Throughout the streets from the Tower to the Abbey, the procession moved its sorrowful way. Every church was shrouded in black but illuminated with thousands of candles. Every citizen stood in a doorway or at a window holding his lighted candle. And as the procession moved and the priests chanted their litanies, the people of the streets offered their responses. At Temple Bar, the abbots of Westminster and Bermondsey met and censed the body, and the entire procession, led by Thomas Stanley Earl of Derby entered Westminster Abbey. The body, removed from the hearse and carried under a canopy, was placed on a catafalque covered with a "cloth of majesty"; its fringed valance bore the queen's motto, Humble and Reverent.

There the body rested under watch while the lords and ladies removed to Westminster Palace for supper. Throughout the night, ladies, squires, and heralds took their places in sorrowful attendance. In the morning, the ladies of the queen, including her four sisters, placed upon the coffin thirty-seven palls; a high mass for the dead was sung; and the Bishop of Rochester preached the funeral sermon: "Have pity, have pity on me, my friends, for the hand of God hath touched me."[3] The palls were removed, the effigy representing the queen was placed on the Shrine of St. Edward, and the mourners left the Abbey. Elizabeth of York was alone with the priests and her grave. They hallowed the place, and the body was given to the vault.[4]

Upon her death, Sir Thomas More, who knew her, wrote the following elegy as though the queen were speaking:

> *Yet was I lately promised otherwise*[5]
> *This year to live in weal and in delight,*
> *Lo, to what cometh all they blandishing promise,*
> *O false astrology and divinitrice,*
> *Of God's secrets vaunting thyself so wise?*
> *How true for this year is thy prophecy?*
> *The year yet lasteth, and lo, here I lie!*
>
> *Adieu, mine own dear spouse, my worthy lord,*
> *The faithful love that did us both combine*
> *In marriage and peaceable concord*

Into your hands here do I clean resign,
To be bestowed on your children and mine;
Erst were ye father, now must ye supply
The mother's part also, for here I lie.

Where are our castles now? where are our towers?
Goodly Richmond, soon are thou gone from me,
At Westminster, that costly work of yours,
Mine own dear lord, now shall I never see;
Almighty God, vouchsafe to grant that ye,
For you and children well may edify;
My palace builded is, for lo, here I lie!

Farewell, my daughter, Lady Margaret,
God wot full oft it grieved hath my mind,
That ye should go where we might seldom meet,
Now I am gone, and have left you behind,
O mortal folk, but we be very blind,
What we least fear full oft is most nigh,
From you depart I first, for lo, now here I lie!

Farewell, madame, my lord's worthy mother,
Comfort your son, and be of good cheer,
Take all at worth, for it will be no other;
Farewell, my daughter Catherine, late the phere*
Unto Prince Arthur, late my child so dear.
It booteth not for me to wail and cry,
Pray for my soul, for lo, now here I lie!

Adieu, lord Henry, loving son, adieu,
Our Lord increase your honor and estate;
Adieu, my daughter Mary, bright of hue,
God make you virtuous, wise and fortunate;

---

* companion

Adieu, sweetheart, my little daughter Kate,
Thou shalt, sweet babe, such is thy destiny,
Thy mother never know, for lo, now here I lie!

Lady Cecily, Lady Anne, and Lady Catherine!
Farewell, my well-beloved sisters three,
Oh lady Bridget, other sister mine,
Lo here the end of worldly vanity,
Now are you well who earthly folly flee,
And heavenly things do praise and magnify,
Farewell, and pray for me, for lo! here I lie!

Adieu, my lords, adieu; my ladies all;
Adieu, my faithful servants every one;
Adieu, my commons, whom I never shall
See in this world—wherefore to Thee alone,
Immortal God, verily three in one,
I me commend; thy infinite mercy,
Show to thy servant, for now here I lie![6]

The king's poet and biographer, Bernard André, wrote of the
queen: "She manifested from her infancy an admirable fear
and devotion toward God; toward her parents, a singular
reverence; toward her brothers and sisters, an unbounded at-
tachment; and toward the poor and the ministers of religion, a
wonderful respect and affection."[7] Polydore Vergil in his *Anglia
Historia* wrote that Elizabeth of York "was a woman of such a
character that it be hard to judge whether she displayed more
of majesty and dignity in her life than wisdom and modera-
tion."[8]

There can be no doubt that the life of Elizabeth of York was
a full one, set against tapestry rich in the purple of royalty, the
gold of wealth, the red of death and destruction, and the black
of mourning. Though she spent her life in the shadows of more

flamboyant figures, they in no way diminished the significance of the life she led and of her impact on history. Most profound was her influence on those who knew her and those she came to love. Her husband, Henry VII, is perhaps the clearest example. For once the queen was dead, the character of the king disintegrated. Struggling with the insecurities which traced his life as the child in prison and as the adult in exile, he found temporary strength in his crown, his wife, and his family. But when Elizabeth was gone, the old insecurities seemed to return, and he sought security in wealth. His tax levies became increasingly severe, and the pleasures of court were curtailed. Toward his daughter-in-law Catherine of Aragon, Henry became stingy and penurious, denying her rightful sums till it reached the point where the girl could no longer clothe her servants or pay their wages. In spite of the demands of Ferdinand and Isabella to return Catherine to Spain, Henry held tenaciously to her and her dowry. To secure both, he considered with immodest haste to marry her himself, but Spain, England, and the world were repulsed at the idea. The king then arranged a betrothal between the girl and Prince Henry. This move was more than a political one; it was a financial one. It was a gesture which dominated the remaining years of his life. Where earlier his hand had been eased open by his wife to generosity and pleasure, that same hand literally counted the coins in the growing treasury.

First among his immediate concerns was the marriage of his daughter Margaret to James IV. She was thirteen years old when she and her father, with many of his court, left Richmond on June 27, 1503. They journeyed first to Collyweston, home of Margaret Beaufort, and visited the grandmother as final preparations were made for the journey. On July 8, the king handed his daughter to the Earl of Surrey and his wife, who escorted her to her husband and throne in Edinburgh. Wherever the procession moved, each town set out its welcome of foods and drink and costly pageants, as the little Queen of Scotland, riding sometimes on her horse, other times in her litter, moved steadily onward. It was not until early August that she reached Edinburgh and met the king. No sooner had she settled into her new court when fire struck in the night to destroy her favorite palfrey. James came to her court to comfort her, and when he left, he leapt into the saddle without touching the stirrups.[9]

There were days of jousts and tourneys, pageants and processions, all marked by James' great courtesy and devotion. The couple was married August 8 amidst celebrations in both England and Scotland; but the young Margaret, thrust into a strange land, encountering a dialect difficult to comprehend and ways and customs she did not understand, grew lonely for the familiar life of home. She wrote her father: "For God's sake, sir, hold me excused that I write not myself to your Grace, for I have no leisure this time, but with a wish I would I were with your Grace now, and many times more. . . . And for this that I have written to your Grace, it is very true, but I pray God I may find it well for my welfare hereafter."[10]

Time proved the marriage politically propitious. Margaret's granddaughter was the unhappy and ill-fated Mary Queen of Scots. And when in England the Tudor reign of Elizabeth I seemed doomed to extinction by the death of the Virgin Queen in 1603, Margaret's great-grandson, James VI of Scotland, assumed the English crown as James I. In this way the crowns of Scotland and England were united by a single monarch.

The fortunes of Henry and Elizabeth's other daughter were also mixed. Although the young Mary was several times married by proxy to Charles of Castile, the marriage was never consummated. After the death of her father, and during the reign of her brother Henry VIII, the English came to resent the chicanery of Charles' politics. Prompted therefore by her brother and his chief adviser Wolsey, Mary renounced Charles on July 30, 1514. A month later the exquisitely beautiful princess

was married by proxy to the fast-aging and decrepit Louis XII.
The marriage made her Queen of France. In September of the
same year Mary was escorted by her brother and his court to
Dover. Although rough seas and multiple storms delayed her
departure, she finally sailed into the turbulence. Her own ship
grounded on the French coast, and the young bride was carried through the waves by her gentleman Sir Christopher
Garnish.

On October 9 she married King Louis at Abbeville, and to
her horror, the next day he dismissed all of her English attendants. She despaired and fretted. Marriage to the old man
was bad enough, but to be also bereft of friends and familiar
faces was intolerable. Her coronation at St. Denis' in November did little to lift her gloom; she sustained herself with the
promise of her brother that if she survived the French king,
she might marry whom she liked. Louis died January 1, 1515,
and Mary was free. Fearing, however, that Henry VIII would
force her into another political alliance, she secretly married her
early love Charles Brandon Duke of Suffolk. At first the marriage brought down Henry's wrath and forced Mary and her
husband's absence from court. Gradually the girl won again her
brother's heart, and she and Brandon were accepted if not welcomed. Their only daughter Frances later became the mother
of Lady Jane Grey, tool of ambitious men and usurpers. She was
Queen of England for nine days upon the death of Edward VI;
she was then beheaded for treason.

The founder of the dynasty, Henry VII, pieced out the last
dark days of his reign with one debased act after another. Ever
anxious now to fatten his growing treasury, he contemplated
numerous marriages—the most macabre of all being that to
Catherine of Aragon's older sister, Joanna of Castile. Lured by
the vast wealth of her country, Henry discounted reports of
Joanna's increasing madness and the fact that she carried every-
where the embalmed body of her husband Philip. Madness,

Henry maintained, interfered little with the queen's ability to have children. The marriage never took place, but Henry's desire amazed even King Ferdinand. Isabella, no doubt, would have been mortified at the suggestion had she not already died November 26, 1504.

Among Henry VII's most positive actions was the building of his chapel at Westminster. In his will, he outlined the purposes of its creation: first, to honor the Virgin and contain on the high altar "the greatest image of Our Lady that we now have in our Jewel House"; secondly, to be the tomb of his queen, himself, and all his descendants; and thirdly, to be the final resting place of Henry VI, a man Henry much revered as his sainted uncle. This final hope was never realized, and Henry VI remained at Windsor, buried not too distant from the man who took his throne—Edward IV. The chapel, "painted, garnished, and adorned in as goodly and rich a manner as such work requireth and as to a king's work appertaineth," would contain a black and white marble tomb for himself and his wife. Before it, effigies of the royal couple must kneel in perpetual prayer. This design was never completed, for when Henry VII died of bronchitis at Richmond on April 21, 1509, his son ordered the Florentine sculptor Peter Torrigiano to design the tomb with recumbent statues of Henry VII and Elizabeth of York. Among the ornaments about the tomb is the repetitive design of a crown in a hawthorn bush—symbol of the victory and reward of Bosworth Field.[11]

Shortly before his death, Henry VII—mindful perhaps of his recent avarice—sought to rectify his life to the better comfort of his soul. He therefore granted pardon to those in prison, with the exception of thieves and murderers. For the debtors imprisoned in London jails, the king himself paid their fees.[12] He was only fifty-two when he died and in the twenty-fourth year of his reign, but his life had worn away with insecurity and the complexities of government; with grief for the loss of his son Arthur, who had crystallized much joy and hope; and with despair at the death of his wife, who had offered solace and comfort and balanced his life. Unfortunately, that portrait drawn by Sir Francis Bacon of the miserly king, who was unkind to his wife, distanced from his children, and harsh and vindictive to his subjects, is an erroneous one, but it has stuck tenaciously to his every portrait. He was, after all, a man who had usurped a crown tainted with suspicion and blood, and polished it with respect and dignity, thus renewing faith in government. He was a man superstitious enough to execute a falcon for attacking an eagle and to kill mastiffs for attacking a lion.[13] But he was also pious and devout, true to his faith, and founder of that magnificent monument to God, the Henry VII Chapel at Westminster. He was a man attentive and generous to his wife, giving her gifts of jewels and ornaments in joy, and offering comfort and solace in grief. Above all, however, he was a man who stabilized a nation, giving it the security and prosperity he sought in his own life. The poet spoke of "The Twelve Triumphs of Henry VII" and noted:

> *Of his virtue and illustrious dignity*
> *According to my poor ability,*
> *I will speak, that it may be known*
> *How victoriously he reigns.*
> *Treacherous Envy is always raging*
> *To destroy him by her venomous fate,*
>   *But in the end he resists in such wise*
>   *That he will confound the envious traitors.*[14]

This he managed to do.

When he died, his funeral was marked by a great procession and sorrow, and he was laid in the vault with great reverence next to his wife. After the archbishop cast earth upon the coffin and the men of the household broke their staves of office, the vault was closed. The heralds took off their coat armor, hung them about the rails of the hearse, and cried "lamentably": "The noble King Henry the Seventh is dead." Every herald dressed himself in a new coat and cried joyfully: "God send the noble King Henry the Eighth long life."[15]

In the Tower, in mourning, waited the youthful Henry VIII. Encouraged by policy, and perhaps by the fantasies of the nine-year-old boy who escorted the bride of his brother, Henry on June 11 married his brother's widow—Catherine of Aragon. Together they rode, with splendid retinue and magnificent display, to their coronation at the Abbey on June 25. Already Henry was tall and athletic, first at tennis and tourneys, delicate at the lute, buoyant at the dance, ebullient in personality, quick and sensitive of mind. With his handsome virile physique, his golden hair, his warm smile, and easy fellowship, he reminded many of that great carnal man, his charismatic and able grandfather Edward IV.

The brilliance of his youth moving through the early summer offered promise and joy to the cheering throng and dispelled the gloom of mourning and the clouds of the last years of his father's reign. A new era had begun, the century was yet young, and Henry VIII on his coronation day personified the dream of a new age. He was more Yorkist than Tudor in his joy of life and all that it offered—the lusts, the loves, the pleasures of sport. He would have them all. In turn he would beget the grandest monarch England would ever know, and name her for his mother—Elizabeth.

In Westminster Abbey the dust settled on the tomb and memory of Elizabeth of York. Her story, like her life, forced into the shadows by more startling events, became a footnote to history. She became her epitaph:

Here rests Queen Elizabeth
Daughter of Edward IV some time monarch of this realm;
Sister of Edward V who bore the title of king,

Wedded to King Henry VII
The illustrious mother of Henry VIII
Who closed her life
In the Tower of London,
On February 2, 1502[16]
Having completed her 37th year

These words, however, say little of the woman who brought hope to those in despair, comfort to those in pain, and restraint to those in power. Though she built no monuments and led no armies, she combined piety with ability and marked the lives of all who knew her. She was foremost a daughter, a sister, a wife, a mother, who lived as her motto stated—"Humble and Reverent"; but she carried in her veins the blood of virile, effective kings, and her legacy brought England to its Golden Age.

NOTES

CHAPTER ONE

1. Robert Fabyan, *New Chronicles of England and France*. ed. Henry Ellis (London, 1811), p. 655.
2. *Calendar of the Patent Rolls Preserved in the Public Records Office, 1467–1477* (London, 1914), p. 44. The text reads: "October 9, 1467. Westminster. Grant for life to the King's daughter the Princess Elizabeth of the manor of Great Lynford, county of Buckingham, lately belonging to James, late Earl of Wiltshire, and in the King's hands by reason of an act in Parliament at Westminster. 4 November, 1, Edward IV."
3. John Stow, *The Chronicles of England* (London, 1580), p. 752.
4. Henry T. Riley, trans. and ed., *Ingulph's Chronicles of the Abbey of Croyland with the Continuation by Peter of Blois* (London, 1893), pp. 425–426 (hereinafter cited as *Croyland*).
5. The Croyland chronicler speaks of Henry VI's confinement: "Being captured in the northern parts, he was led by a strong body of men to the Tower of London, where King Edward ordered all possible humanity to be shown towards him, consistently with his safe custody; and, at the same time, gave directions that he should be supplied with all suitable necessaries, and treated with becoming respect." Riley, *Croyland*, p. 439.

6. William Gregory, *Chronicle 1189–1469,* ed. by James Gaird-ner as *The Historical Collections of a London Citizen in the Fifteenth Century* (Westminster, 1876), p. 215.

7. Raphael Holinshed, *Chronicles of England, Scotland, and Ire-land* (London, 1807), 3, 360. *See also* "The Travels of Leo Von Rozmital," in A. R. Myers, ed., *English Historical Docu-ments 1327–1485* (New York, 1969), 4, 1168–1169.

8. Riley, *Croyland,* p. 426.

9. Edward Hall, *Chronicle Containing the History of England* (London, 1809), p. 365.

10. Holinshed, *England, Scotland, and Ireland,* pp. 201-202.

11. Riley, *Croyland,* p. 440; Holinshed, *England, Scotland, and Ireland,* p. 203.

12. Holinshed, *England, Scotland, and Ireland,* p. 202.

13. James Gairdner, ed., *Letters and Papers Illustrative of the Reigns of Richard III and Henry VII* (London, 1861), 1, 223–239.

14. Cora L. Scofield, *Life and Reign of Edward the Fourth* (Lon-don, 1923), 1, 506 (hereinafter cited as *Life and Reign of Edward IV*).

15. Riley, *Croyland,* p. 444.

16. *Ibid.,* p. 458.

17. Holinshed, *England, Scotland, and Ireland,* p. 289.

18. Stow, *Chronicles of England,* p. 724; John Warkworth, *A Chronicle of the First Thirteen Years of the Reign of King Edward the Fourth,* ed. J. O. Halliwell (London, 1839), p. 13 (hereinafter cited as *First 13 Years of Edward IV*).

19. Warkworth, *First 13 Years of Edward IV,* p. 11.

20. From a note in which Edward IV thanks William Gould, butcher, for weekly provisions of "half a beef and two mut-tons," in Henry Ellis, ed., *Letters Illustrative of English His-tory,* series 2, 1 (London, 1827), p. 141.

21. Fabyan, *New Chronicles of England and France,* p. 659; Riley, *Croyland,* p. 463.

22. Stow, *Chronicles of England,* p. 725.

23. Edward's pretense of devotion to the crown and his claiming that he "came but for his own" is reminiscent, of course, of

Bolingbroke (later Henry IV), who ostensibly returned to England in 1399 for his rights as Duke of Lancaster and ended by seizing the crown of Richard II.

24. Warkworth, *First 13 Years of Edward IV*, p. 14.
25. John Bruce, ed., *Historie of the Arrivall of Edward IV in England and the Finall Recoverie of His Kingdomes from Henry VI. A.D. MCCCCLXXI.* (London, 1838), pp. 4–5 (hereinafter cited as *Arrival of Edward IV*).
26. Bruce, *Arrival of Edward IV*, p. 7.
27. *Ibid.*, pp. 9–11.
28. As they are today, all images in churches were covered throughout the period of Passiontide.
29. Bruce, *Arrival of Edward IV*, pp. 13–14.
30. *Ibid.*, p. 15.
31. Cited by Scofield, *Life and Reign of Edward IV*, p. 576.
32. Bruce, *Arrival of Edward IV*, p. 17.
33. *Ibid.*, pp. 18–21; Fabyan, *New Chronicle of England and France*, pp. 660–661.
34. Warkworth, *First 13 Years of Edward IV*, p. 5.
35. Eric N. Simons, *The Reign of Edward IV* (London, 1966), p. 232.
36. There is much conjecture as to how Prince Edward died, but the following account seems to have been widely accepted: "In the which battle [at Tewkesbury] she [Margaret] was taken, and Sir Edward her son, and so brought unto the king. But after the king had questioned with the said Sir Edward, and he had answered unto him contrary his pleasure, he then struck him with his gauntlet upon the face; after which stroke so by him received, he was by the king's servants incontinently slain upon the fourth day of the month of May." Fabyan, *New Chronicles of England and France*, p. 662.
37. Charles L. Kingsford, ed., *Chronicles of London* (Oxford, 1905), p. 184.
38. Riley, *Croyland*, p. 446.
39. Bruce, *Arrival of Edward IV*, p. 38. Fabyan also adds a widely believed, but unprovable, notion: "Of the death of this prince [Henry VI] diverse tales were told; but the most common

fame went that he was sticked with a dagger, by the hands of the Duke of Gloucester, which, after Edward IV usurped the crown. . . ." *New Chronicles of England and France,* p. 662.

40. Henry VI was later reinterred at Windsor, not far from the tomb of Edward IV.

41. Fabyan, *New Chronicles of England and France,* p. 656; Holinshed, *England, Scotland, and Ireland,* p. 486.

42. Richard Davey, *The Pageant of London* (New York, 1906), p. 315.

43. A. R. Myers, ed., *The Household of Edward IV: The Black-book and the Ordinance of 1478.* (Manchester, 1959), n. 4.

44. Myers, *English Historical Documents,* p. 1158.

45. Riley, *Croyland,* pp. 481–482.

46. *Ibid.,* p. 475.

47. Commenes, cited by P. J. Helm, *England under the Yorkists and Tudors* (London, 1968), p. 7.

48. Riley, *Croyland,* p. 472; Hall, *History of England,* p. 313; Holinshed, *England, Scotland, and Ireland,* p. 342.

49. Hall, *History of England,* p. 338.

50. Holinshed, *England, Scotland, and Ireland,* p. 330.

51. *Ibid.,* pp. 342–343.

52. Riley, *Croyland,* p. 479.

53. Kingsford, *Chronicles of London,* p. 188; Holinshed, *England, Scotland, and Ireland,* p. 346; Hall summarizes well the circumstances of Clarence's death: "The fame was that the King or the Queen, or both, were sore troubled with a foolish Prophecy, and by reason thereof began to stomach and grievously to grudge against the Duke [of Clarence]. The effect of which was, after King Edward should reign, one whose first letter to his name should be a G . . . [men] said afterward that that Prophecy lost not its effect, when after King Edward, Gloucester usurped his kingdom. Others alledge this to be the cause of his [Clarence's] death. That of late, the old rancour between them being newly revived the Duke being destitute of a wife [Isabella had died], by the means of Lady Margaret Duchess of Burgundy, his sister, procured to have the Lady Mary, daughter and heir to Duke Charles her husband, to be

given him in matrimony; which marriage King Edward (envying the felicity of his brother) both again-said and disturbed. This privy displeasure was openly appeased, but not inwardly forgotten, nor outwardly forgiven, for that, not withstanding a servant of the Duke's was suddenly accused of poisoning, sorcery, or enchantment, and thereof condemned, and put to taste the pains of death. The Duke, which might not suffer the wrongful condemnation of his man . . . nor yet forbear, nor patiently suffer the unjust handling of his trusty servant, daily did oppugne, and with ill words murmur at the doing thereof. The King much grieved and troubled with his brother's daily querimonye [complaining], and continued exclamation, caused him to be apprehended, and cast into the Tower, where he being taken and adjudged for a Traitor, was prively drowned in a Butt of Malvesey." *History of England,* p. 326.
54. Holinshed, *England, Scotland, and Ireland,* pp. 360–361.
55. Dominic Mancini, *The Usurpation of Richard the Third,* trans. C. A. J. Armstrong (Oxford, 1969), p. 59 (hereinafter cited as *Usurpation of Richard III*).
56. Hall, *History of England,* pp. 343–344.
57. Holinshed, *England, Scotland, and Ireland,* pp. 357–358.

CHAPTER TWO

1. Gairdner, *Reigns of Richard III–Henry VII,* I, I–10.
2. Edward IV's armor continued to hang above his tomb until it was seized in the mid-seventeenth century by one of Oliver Cromwell's followers. The armor was then destroyed.
3. "The Death of Edward IV," in Rossell Hope Robbins, ed., *Historical Poems of the XIVth and XVth Centuries* (New York, 1959), p. 11.
4. Holinshed says of Edward's children: ". . . much fair issue, that is to wit, Edward the Prince, thirteen years of age, Richard, Duke of York, two years younger; Elizabeth, whose fortune and grace was after to be queen, . . . Cecily, not so fortunate as fair; Bridget, whose representing the virtue of her, whose

name she bare, professed and observed a religious life in Dertford, an house of close nuns; Anne, that was after honorably married unto Thomas, then Lord Howard, and after the Earl of Surrey; and Katherine, which long time tossed in either fortune, sometime in wealth, oft in adversity. . . ." *England, Scotland, and Ireland,* p. 360.

5. Mancini, *Usurpation of Richard III,* p. 7.

6. *Calendar of Patent Rolls: 1467–1477,* pp. 414, 417; Holinshed, *England, Scotland, and Ireland,* p. 365; Paul Murray Kendall, *The Yorkist Age* (New York, 1965), p. 162.

7. Mancini, *Usurpation of Richard III,* p. 93.

8. Riley, *Croyland,* pp. 484–485.

9. Mancini, *Usurpation of Richard III,* pp. 63–65.

10. Holinshed, *England, Scotland, and Ireland,* p. 366.

11. Riley, *Croyland,* p. 486; Holinshed, *England, Scotland, and Ireland,* pp. 366–367.

12. Riley, *Croyland,* p. 487.

13. Holinshed, *England, Scotland, and Ireland,* p. 368.

14. *Ibid.*

15. *Ibid.,* pp. 368–369.

16. Mancini, *Usurpation of Richard III,* p. 85.

17. Holinshed, *England, Scotland, and Ireland,* pp. 369–370.

18. E. F. Jacob, *The Fifteenth Century: 1399–1485* (Oxford, 1961), pp. 612–613.

19. Riley, *Croyland,* p. 487; Hall, *History of England,* p. 351.

20. Riley, *Croyland,* p. 487.

21. Mancini, *Usurpation of Richard III,* p. 83.

22. Holinshed, *England, Scotland, and Ireland,* pp. 379–380.

23. "Great Chronicle of London," in Myers, *English Historical Documents,* p. 334.

24. Hall, *History of England,* pp. 360–361; Holinshed, *England, Scotland, and Ireland,* p. 381.

25. "Great Chronicle of London," p. 334.

26. Hall, *History of England,* p. 362.

27. Holinshed, *England, Scotland, and Ireland,* pp. 374–377.

28. Mancini, *Usurpation of Richard III,* p. 89; Kingsford, *Chronicles of London,* p. 190.

29. Mancini, *Usurpation of Richard III,* p. 89.

30. Riley, *Croyland,* p. 488.

31. Upon the death of Henry V in 1422, the throne passed to his son Henry VI, who was then nine months old.

32. The confusions of the frantic year of 1483 have never really been settled, and there are many students of the period who see Richard III as a victim of Tudor plots and lies. An interesting if obtuse letter found in *The Cely Papers,* however, points clearly to the confusions and anxieties of the period. The style of the letter is so veiled that it makes exact transcription impossible. *See* Henry Elliot Malden ed., *The Cely Papers 1475–1488* (London, 1900), pp. 132–133.

33. Dominic Mancini, who was in England during 1483, offers an interesting comment on Gloucester's activities after the removal of Hastings and the other "conspirators": "When Richard felt secure from all these dangers that at first he feared, he took off the mourning clothes that he had always worn since his brother's death, and putting on purple raiment, he often rode through the capital surrounded by a thousand attendants. He publicly showed himself so as to receive the attention and applause of the people as yet under the name of protector; but each day he entertained to dinner at his private dwellings an increasingly large number of men. When he exhibited himself through the streets of the city he was scarcely watched by anybody, rather did they curse him with a fate worthy of his crimes, since no one now doubted at what he was aiming." *Usurpation of Richard III,* p. 95.

34. Holinshed, *England, Scotland, and Ireland,* pp. 386–390.

35. *Ibid.,* p. 390.

36. Fabyan, *New Chronicles of England and France,* p. 669.

37. Holinshed, *England, Scotland, and Ireland,* pp. 390–393.

38. Rivers was not only a poet but also a patron of William Caxton, and contributed money and writings to Caxton's press. Among these are four translations from French to English: *Dictes and Sayings of Philosophers,* which also contains an explanatory prologue by Rivers; *The Four Last Things; The Cordyale;* and *Moral Proverbs,* for which Rivers possibly wrote

the first stanza of the epilogue. William Caxton, *The Prologues and Epilogues,* ed. W. J. B. Crotch. *EETS,* orig. ser. 176 (London, 1928).

39. Mancini, *Usurpation of Richard III,* p. 113. *See also* Rivers' will as reprinted in Gairdner, *Reigns of Richard III–Henry VII.*

40. Joseph Ritson, *Ancient Songs* (London, 1877), pp. 87–88.

41. Riley, *Croyland,* p. 489; Fabyan, *New Chronicles of England and France,* p. 668; Hall, *History of England,* p. 364.

42. Fabyan, *New Chronicles of England and France,* p. 668.

43. *Ibid.,* p. 669.

44. *Rotuli Parliamentorum,* 6, 240–242.

45. Holinshed, *England, Scotland, and Ireland,* p. 396.

46. *Ibid.;* Riley, *Croyland,* p. 489.

CHAPTER THREE

1. Claude de la Roche Frances, *London Historical and Social,* vol. 1 (Philadelphia, 1901), p. 97.

2. Riley, *Croyland,* pp. 469–470.

3. *Ibid.,* p. 469.

4. Holinshed, *England, Scotland, and Ireland,* pp. 397–398.

5. Riley, *Croyland,* p. 490; Hall, *History of England,* pp. 375–376; Holinshed, *England, Scotland, and Ireland,* pp. 398–400. For the complete description of Richard's coronation, *see* Gairdner, *Reigns of Richard III–Henry VII,* pp. 379–384.

6. Stow, *Chronicles of England,* p. 846.

7. Edward Carpenter, *A House of Kings: The History of Westminster Abbey* (London, 1966), p. 91.

8. Hall, *History of England,* p. 363; Holinshed, *England, Scotland and Ireland,* pp. 384 ff.

9. *Calendar of Patent Rolls: 1476–1485,* p. 496.

10. Riley, *Croyland,* p. 490.

11. *Ibid.*

12. Fabyan, *New Chronicles of England and France,* p. 670.

13. Riley, *Croyland,* p. 490.

14. After the deaths of Edward V and his brother, Wakefield Tower

was commonly called "the Bloody Tower." Frances, *London Historical and Social,* p. 98.

15. From MS. 433 of the Harleian collection in the British Museum library, which includes an authorization for the payment of wages to thirteen men for services to Edward IV and Edward "bastard."

16. Mancini, *Usurpation of Richard III,* p. 93.

17. "Great Chronicle of London," in Myers, *English Historical Documents,* p. 337. Though the fate of the princes was never discovered, it is generally assumed that they were slain, and there is much conjecture as to who was responsible for the murders. The most comprehensive review of possibilities is that of Paul Murray Kendall, whose case against Buckingham becomes a formidable one: "There are, roughly, three possibilities regarding the situation of Edward's two sons at the time that Buckingham, at Brecon, was beginning to take the Bishop of Ely into his confidence. They may have been alive, in which case they probably either were dwelling in the Tower or had been conveyed northward to take up a secret residence at Sheriff-Hutton in the custody of the Earl of Lincoln. Should this conjecture be true, then Buckingham and Morton devised the report of the Princes' deaths, knowing that it would find ready credence and that if they accomplished their end, no one would be in a position to produce the Princes in any case. There is the second possibility, that Buckingham, for reasons unsuspected by the King, persuaded Richard to snuff out the lives of the two boys by convincing him that the deed was necessary to the safety of his throne. It is also possible that Richard had begun his progress, and Buckingham remained briefly in London in order to murder the Princes himself. Being Constable, he could open all doors and command what he would. . . ." *Richard the Third* (New York, 1956), p. 317.

18. Mancini, *Usurpation of Richard III,* p. 93.

19. J. Masselin, "Journal des Etats Généraux de France tenus à Tours en 1484," in Myers, *English Historical Documents,* pp. 37–39.

20. Hall, *History of England,* pp. 377–378; Holinshed, *England, Scotland, and Ireland,* pp. 401 ff. Although many students of the period have dismissed Hall and Holinshed as little more than Tudor propagandists, the fact remains that the bones of two boys were found in July 1674 at the foot of stone steps leading to St. John's Chapel in the White Tower. The bones were removed in 1678 and reburied in Henry VII's chapel at Westminster Abbey by order of Charles II. Twice the bones have been examined and they seem to be of boys the ages of Edward V and the Duke of York. *See* Frances, *London Historical and Social,* pp. 95–96.

21. Jacob, *Fifteenth Century,* p. 625.

22. Hall, *History of England,* pp. 379–380.

23. Riley, *Croyland,* p. 490; Fabyan, *New Chronicle of England and France,* p. 670.

24. The grants to Buckingham seem excessive: "May 16, 1483. Grant for life to the king's kinsman, duke of Buckingham, of the offices of chief justice and chamberlain in south and north Wales, constable of the castles and counties of Kermondyn and Cardigan, the castles of Abrustwith, county Cardigan, and Deneover in south Wales, the castle and town of Tonebigh, county Pembroke, the castle and lordship of Kylgarvan in south Wales, the castle and Town of Llan Stephan in south Wales, the lordship of Wallewynscastell, county Pembroke, and the castle and lordship of Westhavorford in south Wales, constable, steward, and receiver of the castle, lordship, and manor of Uske, the castle and lordship of Carlion, the castle, lordship, and manor of Dynas, the castle and a moiety of the lordship and manor of Ewyas Lacy, the castles, lordships, and manors of Belth, Clifford, Radnore, Melenyth, Mongomery, Dynbigh, Elvell and Nerberth, the castles, lordships, and manors of Wygmore, and Holte in the marches of Wales, the lordship and manor of Bromfield in the same marches, steward and receiver of the lordship and manors of Norton, Knighton, Raydor, Guerthreuyon, Comotoyder, Glasbury, Weryfreton, Cherbury, Terthic, Halcetur, Kadewyn, Newton, Kyry in the marches of Wales, Stanton Lacy by Ludlow, Bewdely, North-

cleobury, Cleobury, Barnes, Mortymers Cleobury, Hugely, Ernewode, Cherylsmersshe, Cleoton, Pembrugge, Greslane, Hynton, Orleton, Nethwode, Wolfreylowe, and Malmeshill Lacy in Wales and the marches and all other lordships, manors, lands and hereditaments of the King in north and south Wales and the marches, constable, steward, treasurer and receiver of the castle, county, lordship and manor of Pembroke in south Wales, constable and captain of the castles and towns of Abrustwith, county Cardigan, Kernervan and Conwey, county Carnarvon, Beaumarys, county Anglesey, and Harlech, county Merioneth, and all other castles of the king in the north and south Wales and the marches, with authority to place soldiers in the castles for their safe-custody, master or keeper of the forest of Snowden, county Carnarvon, and all other forests and chaces of the king in south and north Wales and the marches and master of the game of deer in the same, receiving the accustomed fees. . . ." *Calendar of Patent Rolls: 1476–1485,* pp. 349–350.

25. Hall, *History of England,* p. 383; Holinshed, *England, Scotland, and Ireland,* p. 403.
26. Holinshed, *England, Scotland, and Ireland,* pp. 410 ff.
27. Hall, *History of England,* p. 389; Holinshed, *England, Scotland, and Ireland,* p. 411.
28. Riley, *Croyland,* p. 491.
29. Hall, *History of England,* p. 390.
30. Holinshed, *England, Scotland, and Ireland,* pp. 412–413.
31. *Ibid.,* pp. 413–414.
32. Edward IV's will makes it clear that Elizabeth of York existed mainly as a marriageable commodity and her prime duty was to form a valuable political alliance. The will states: *"Item: We will that our daughter Elizabeth have* X^m *marks toward her marriage, and that our daughter Mary have also to her marriage* X^m *marks, so that they be governed and ruled in their marriages by our dearest wife the Queen and by our said son the Prince if God fortune him to come to the age of discretion; And if he decease afore such age, as God defend, then by such as God disposeth to be our heir and by such Lords and other as then*

shall be of their counsel; and if either of our said daughters do marry themselves without such advice and assent so as they be thereby disparaged, as God forbid, that then she so marrying herself have no payment of her said X^m marks but that it be employed by our Executors toward the hasty payment of our debts and restitutions as is expressed in this our last Will." Samuel Bentley, ed., *Excerpta Historica* (London, 1833), p. 369.

33. Holinshed, *England, Scotland, and Ireland,* p. 414.
34. Riley, *Croyland,* p. 490; A. L. Rowse, *Bosworth Field: From Medieval to Tudor England* (New York, 1966), pp. 200–201.
35. Hall, *History of England,* p. 394; Holinshed, *England, Scotland, and Ireland,* pp. 417 ff.
36. In Hall, *History of England,* the name is given as Humphrey Bannister. Ellis notes that Hall is in error, that Bannister's Christian name was Ralph. *Letters Illustrative of English History,* ser. 3, 1 (London, 1846), p. 100.
37. Hall, *History of England,* pp. 393–394; Fabyan, *New Chronicles of England and France,* p. 670.
38. Hall, *History of England,* p. 395; Fabyan, *New Chronicles of England and France,* pp. 670–671.
39. Ellis, *Letters,* ser. 3, p. 101. To the historian Edward Hall, Bannister was used as an object lesson and considered a recipient of heavenly justice. After Buckingham's death, Hall speaks of Bannister's family: ". . . his son and heir waxed mad and so died in a boar's sty, his eldest daughter of excellent beauty was suddenly struck with a foul leprosy, his second son very miraculously deformed of his limbs and made decrepit, his younger son in a small puddle was strangled and drowned, and he [Bannister] being of extreme age arraigned and found guilty of a murder and by his clergy saved. And as for his one thousand pounds King Richard gave him not one farthing. . . ." Hall, *History of England,* p. 395. As the following shows, there seems no basis for Hall's conclusion: "August 15, 1484. Grant to the King's servant Ralph Bannister and the heirs male of his body, for his good service against the rebels, of the manor of Ealding, county Kent, of the yearly value of £50, to hold with knight's fees, wards, marriages, stanks [pools], mills, parks,

woods, underwoods, liberties, and commodities by knight-service and a rent of £4 yearly." *Calendar of Patent Rolls: 1476–1485,* p. 482.

40. Caroline Halstead, *Life of Margaret Beaufort, Countess of Richmond and Derby* (London, 1839), p. 125.

41. *Rotuli Parliamentorum,* p. 250.

42. Hall, *History of England,* p. 397; Holinshed, *England, Scotland, and Ireland,* p. 422.

43. Hall, *History of England,* pp. 395–396.

44. Riley, *Croyland,* p. 497.

45. Hall, *History of England,* p. 409.

46. Riley, *Croyland,* p. 497.

47. Holinshed, *England, Scotland, and Ireland,* p. 429.

48. Ellis, *Letters,* ser. 2, pp. 149–150.

49. John Heneage Jesse, *Memoirs of King Richard the Third* (Boston, 1911), p. 253.

50. Holinshed, *England, Scotland, and Ireland,* p. 430.

51. Riley, *Croyland,* p. 497.

52. Hall, *History of England,* p. 401.

53. Richard III is unduly maligned by the Tudor chroniclers. Hall, for instance, says of the king: "As he was small and little of stature so was he of body greatly deformed, the one shoulder higher than the other, his face small but his countenance was cruel, and such, that a man at first aspect would judge it to savor and smell of malice, fraud, and deceit; when he stood musing he would bite and chew his nether lip, as one who said, that his fierce nature in his cruel body always chafed, stirred and was ever unquiet; beside that, the dagger that he wore he would, when he studied, with his hand pluck up and down in the shief to the midst, never drawing it fully out, his wit was pregnant, quick and ready . . . and apt to dissemble, he had a proud mind and an arrogant stomach. . . ." *History of England,* p. 421. Holinshed adds: "Richard . . . was in wit and courage equal with either of them [Edward IV and Clarence], in body and prowess far under them both, little of stature, ill featured of limbs, crook backed, his left shoulder much higher than his right, hard favored of visage . . . he

was malicious, wrathful, envious, and from afore his birth ever forward. It is for truth reported, that the duchess his mother had so much ado in her travail, that she could not be delivered of him uncut; and that he came into the world with the feet forward . . . and . . . not untoothed." *England, Scotland, and Ireland,* p. 362. *See also* Stow, *Chronicles of England,* p. 755.

54. Stow, *Chronicles of England,* p. 847.
55. Holinshed, *England, Scotland, and Ireland,* p. 422.
56. Sir George Buck in his book describes a letter supposedly written by Elizabeth of York to Thomas Howard Duke of Norfolk in which ". . . she desire him to be a mediator for her to the king, in the behalf of the marriage propounded between them, who, as she wrote, was her only joy and maker in this world; and that she was his in heart and thought; with all insinuating, that the better part of February was past, and that she feared the Queen would never die. All these be her own words, written with her own hand; and this is the sum of her letter, which remains in the autograph, or original draft, under her own hand, in the magnificent cabinet of Thomas Earl of Arundel and Surrey, . . ." *Life of Richard III* (London, 1646), pp. 128–129. No one else has seen the letter; and the possibility of such expression seems incongruous with the life and ambitions of Elizabeth of York. Buck must have confused the hand of the letter.
57. Riley, *Croyland,* pp. 498–499.
58. *Ibid.,* p. 499.
59. Polydore Vergil, *Anglia Historia,* trans. Denys Hay (London, 1950), p. 3.
60. Holinshed, *England, Scotland, and Ireland,* p. 431.
61. "Acts of the Mercers' Company," in Myers, *English Historical Documents,* p. 173.
62. Riley, *Croyland,* p. 499.
63. Hall, *History of England,* p. 406.
64. Holinshed, *England, Scotland, and Ireland,* pp. 433–434.
65. I. Heywood, ed., *Most Pleasant Song of the Lady Bessy* (London, n. d.).

66. Fabyan, *New Chronicles of England and France,* p. 672.
67. E. M. G. Routh, *Lady Margaret: A Memoir of Lady Margaret Beaufort, Countess of Richmond and Derby, Mother of Henry VII* (London, 1924), pp. 54–55.
68. Holinshed, *England, Scotland, and Ireland,* p. 436.
69. After Richard's defeat at Bosworth Field the name of the inn was changed to the Blue Boar.
70. Holinshed, *England, Scotland, and Ireland,* pp. 437–438.
71. *Ibid.,* p. 438.
72. Riley, *Croyland,* pp. 502–503.
73. Hall, *History of England,* p. 414.
74. *Ibid.;* Holinshed, *England, Scotland, and Ireland,* pp. 438–439.
75. Mancini, *Usurpation of Richard III,* p. 99.
76. Riley, *Croyland,* p. 503.
77. Hall, *History of England,* pp. 416–418.
78. *Ibid.,* p. 418.
79. Riley, *Croyland,* p. 504; Hall, *History of England,* p. 418.
80. *See also* Vergil, *Anglia Historia,* p. 77.
81. Hall, *History of England,* p. 420; Holinshed, *England, Scotland, and Ireland,* pp. 443–445.
82. Hall, *History of England,* p. 422.
83. Richard's body remained with the Grey Friars until the dissolution of the monasteries in 1536. When the monastery was destroyed, Richard's tomb was robbed and his body was thrown into the river. See Hall, *History of England,* p. 421; Fabyan, *New Chronicles of England and France,* p. 673; Holinshed, *England, Scotland, and Ireland,* pp. 446–447.

CHAPTER FOUR

1. The parents of Henry VI were Henry V and Catherine of Valois. Upon Henry's death (1422), Catherine married the Welshman, Owen Tudor; they had two sons, Edmund and Jasper Tudor, who were half-brothers to King Henry VI and much honored by him.
2. James Gairdner, *Henry the Seventh* (London, 1889), p. 6.

3. The legitimacy of Gaunt's second family had been reaffirmed by Richard II's successor, Henry IV, who confirmed the rights of the Beaufort line but added the words *excepta dignitate regali.* How valid the note of exclusion was remains a questionable point. *See* Gairdner, *Reigns of Richard III–Henry VII,* 2, xxx.

4. Vergil, *Anglia Historia,* p. 3.

5. The often repeated statement that Henry VII entered London covertly in a closed chariot is an erroneous one based on Bacon's mistaken reading of Andreas' use of *laetenter* (joyfully) as *latenter* (covertly).

6. Hall, *History of England,* p. 423.

7. John Leland, *Itinerary,* Lucy Toulmin Smith, ed. (Carbondale, Pa., 1964), 1, 65.

8. Hall, *History of England,* p. 422.

9. *Ibid.,* p. 423.

10. Robbins, *Historical Poems,* no. 34, pp. 93–94.

11. Riley, *Croyland,* p. 495; Vergil, *Anglia Historia,* pp. 7–9; Holinshed, *England, Scotland, and Ireland,* p. 483.

12. Sir Francis Bacon, *History of the Reign of King Henry VII,* eds. James Spedding et al. (New York, 1869), p. 92.

13. Gairdner, *Henry the Seventh,* p. 35.

14. C. R. N. Routh. *They Saw It Happen* (Oxford, 1956), pp. 60–61.

15. Hall, *History of England,* p. 425; Holinshed, *England, Scotland, and Ireland,* p. 483.

16. The "Device for the Coronation of King Henry VII" had offered detailed planning for a double coronation of Henry and Elizabeth. The following is typical of the suggested ordering of events: "Soon after the King is passed out of the Tower, the Queen shall follow upon cushion of white damask cloth of gold, bare-headed, wearing a round circle of gold set with pearls and precious stones, arrayed in a kirtel of white damask day cloth of gold furred with miniver, garnished with anletts [small rings] of gold. . . ." p. 6; ". . . the Cardinal shall bless the Queen's crown saying *Oremus Deus tuorum;* then he shall set the same crown upon the Queen's head, having then

a coif put thereon by the said great lady, for conservation of the said unction, which is afterward to be dried . . . the Queen thus crowned shall be led of the abovesaid Bishops of Exeter and Ely unto her seat of estate near to the King's seat royal. . . ." William Jerdan, ed., *Rutland Papers* (London, 1842), p. 20.

17. John Duncan Mackie. *The Earlier Tudors 1485–1558* (Oxford, 1952), p. 55.

18. Bacon, *Reign of King Henry VII*, p. 48.

19. Holinshed, *England, Scotland, and Ireland*, p. 424.

20. Riley, *Croyland*, pp. 511–512.

21. Mackie, *Earlier Tudors*, p. 65; Gairdner, *Henry the Seventh*, pp. 40–41.

22. Bacon, *Reign of King Henry VII*, p. 67.

23. Hall, *History of England*, p. 425.

24. John Leland. *De Rebus Britannicus Collectanae* (London, 1770), pp. 185–190.

25. Bacon, *Reign of King Henry VII*, p. 52.

26. *Ibid.*, p. 68.

27. Holinshed, *England, Scotland, and Ireland*, pp. 483–484; Gairdner, *Henry the Seventh*, p. 46.

28. *Camden Miscellany* (London, 1848), 1, 5.

29. Leland, *Collectanae*, pp. 190–193.

30. *Ibid.*, "Ordinances of Margaret Countess of Richmond," pp. 173–183.

31. Fisher's account cited by Routh, *Lady Margaret*, p. 19.

32. Riley, *Croyland*, p. 446; Hall, *History of England*, p. 423; Charlotte Augusta Sneyd, trans., *A Relation, or Rather True Account, of This Island of England, c. 1500* (London, 1847), p. 19: "The Welsh people are generally supposed to have been the original inhabitants of the island, and they themselves say, and it is also believed by the English, that they are descended from the Trojans. . . ."

33. Henry VII and his family encouraged the development of the so-called Tudor myth, part of which stressed the Tudor descent from King Arthur; the descent was intentionally underscored by the choice of name for Henry's firstborn son. King Arthur,

of course, is a legendary rather than an historical figure; but one is moved to agree with Sir Winston Churchill that had Arthur not lived one would have been forced to invent him.

34. Routh, *Lady Margaret,* p. 62.
35. Halstead, *Margaret Beaufort,* p. 204.
36. Robbins, *Historical Poems,* p. 95.
37. Sir Francis Bacon's account of Arthur's birth and his forebear is of interest: "In September following, the Queen was delivered of her first son, whom the King (in honor of the British race, of which himself was) named Arthur, according to the name of that ancient worthy King of Britons; in whose acts there is truth enough to make him famous, besides that which is fabulous. The child was strong and able, though he was born in the eighth month, which the physicians do prejudge." *Reign of King Henry VII,* p. 69.
38. Leland, *Collectanae,* pp. 204–207; John Stow, "Memoranda," in James Gairdner, ed., *Three Fifteenth Century Chronicles* (London, 1880), pp. 104–105.
39. Leland, *Collectanae,* p. 183.
40. Robbins, "The Roses Entwining," *Historical Poems,* pp. 94–95.
41. Kingsford, *Chronicles of London,* p. 200.
42. Leland, *Collectanae,* pp. 234–237.
43. *Ibid.,* pp. 207–208.
44. Holinshed, *England, Scotland, and Ireland,* p. 486.
45. Leland, *Collectanae,* pp. 209–211.
46. Hall, *History of England,* p. 433. Dorset had remained under watch in France until invited home by Henry VII.
47. Leland, *Collectanae,* pp. 212–214; Hall, *History of England,* pp. 433–435; Holinshed, *England, Scotland, and Ireland,* pp. 486–489.
48. Gairdner, *Henry the Seventh,* p. 56.
49. James III, in one of his frequent battles with his own aristocracy, lost a pitched battle, fled into a mill where he was caught, murdered, "and left naked like stinking carrion." Hall, *History of England,* p. 448.
50. Holinshed, *England, Scotland, and Ireland,* p. 485.
51. *Ibid.* The belief that Henry VII was needlessly cruel to

his mother-in-law is counterbalanced by certain facts: (1) she, rather than his own mother, stood as godmother for the firstborn, Arthur. (2) There are numerous accounts of payments to her, for instance: *"Item 21.* April 3, 1486 . . . for payments to Elizabeth queen of England late wife of King Edward IV, in full satisfaction of her dower, with arrears since Michaelmas last for term of her life. . . . *Item 429.* February 26, 1490. Order to pay Elizabeth, widow of King Edward IV, the arrears since 19 February last of an annuity of £400 which the King by letters patent of that date granted her for her life out of the exchequer." *Calendar of the Close Rolls Preserved in the Public Records Office 1476–1485* (London, 1963), pp. 5–6; 122. (3) Henry VII had pursued marriage negotiations on her behalf with the King of Scotland.

52. Leland, *Collectanae,* p. 218.
53. *Ibid.,* pp. 216–231.
54. Davey, *Pageant of London,* p. 302.
55. A similar conclusion regarding Elizabeth of York's influence over her husband is offered by Henry VII's biographer, Gairdner, who states that Elizabeth was "a woman much beloved by the people, who undoubtedly had exercised much influence over him for good, although it is true, in the words of Bacon, that towards her 'he was nothing uxorious.' Henry, indeed, was too much a king to be greatly under the control of women, and with matters political she had certainly nothing to do. But we notice a deterioration of Henry's character after he became a widower." *Henry the Seventh,* p. 182.
56. Mackie, *Earlier Tudors,* p. 93.
57. Leland, *Collectanae,* pp. 250–254.
58. Hall, *History of England,* p. 443; Holinshed, *England, Scotland, and Ireland,* p. 493.
59. Holinshed, *England, Scotland, and Ireland,* pp. 490–491.
60. Hall, *History of England,* p. 449.
61. Bentley, *Excerpta Historica,* p. 86.
62. Hall, *History of England,* pp. 456–458; Holinshed, *England, Scotland, and Ireland,* pp. 496–502.
63. Fabyan, *New Chronicles of England and France,* p. 684.

64. Hall, *History of England,* p. 504.

65. Bacon, *Reign of King Henry VII,* pp. 143–147.

66. *Ibid.,* p. 123.

CHAPTER FIVE

1. Sneyd, *This Island of England,* pp. 10–11.

2. *Ibid.,* p. 23.

3. Myers, *English Historical Documents,* p. 837.

4. Kingsford, *Chronicles of London,* p. 222.

5. Fabyan, *New Chronicles of England and France,* p. 686.

6. Mackie, *Earlier Tudors,* pp. 41–42.

7. *Ibid.,* p. 42.

8. Sneyd, *This Island of England,* pp. 42–43.

9. *Ibid.,* pp. 28–29.

10. Routh, *They Saw It Happen,* pp. 1–3.

11. Sneyd, *This Island of England,* p. 21; Routh, *They Saw It Happen,* pp. 1–3.

12. Holinshed, *England, Scotland, and Ireland,* p. 520.

13. Davey, *Pageant of London,* pp. 315–316.

14. Holinshed, *England, Scotland, and Ireland,* p. 528.

15. Kingsford, *Chronicles of London,* p. 201; Fabyan, *New Chronicles of England and France,* p. 485.

16. Elizabeth Woodville died at Bermondsey Abbey in 1492 in the presence of her daughters Cecily, Catherine, Bridget, and Anne. The queen was not present because she was awaiting the birth of her daughter Elizabeth. Elizabeth Woodville was then buried at St. George's Chapel, Windsor, near her husband Edward IV.

17. Gairdner, *Reigns of Richard III–Henry VII,* pp. 388–390.

18. *Ibid.,* pp. 390–391.

19. James Gairdner, ed., *Paston Letters* (London, 1872), 3, 385; Gairdner, *Reigns of Richard III–Henry VII,* pp. 392–393.

20. Gairdner, *Reigns of Richard III–Henry VII,* pp. 394–403.

21. Kingsford, *Chronicles of London,* pp. 202–203.

22. *Ibid.,* p. 203; Hall, *History of England,* p. 464; Holinshed, *England, Scotland, and Ireland,* p. 504.

23. The remaining evidence of Sir William Stanley's betrayal is in a reputed remark made to Clifford which, in substance, was that if Perkin were the Duke of York then Stanley would raise no hand against him. Kingsford, *Chronicles of London,* pp. 203–204; Hall, *History of England,* pp. 464–465; Holinshed, *England, Scotland, and Ireland,* pp. 504–506.

24. Hall, *History of England,* p. 465.

25. *Ibid.,* p. 471.

26. *Ibid.,* pp. 472–473.

27. Mackie, *Earlier Tudors,* p. 142.

28. Holinshed, *England, Scotland, and Ireland,* pp. 511–519.

29. Henry Colet's letter cited by Charles Williams, *Henry VII* (London, 1937), pp. 129–130.

30. Vergil, *Anglia Historia,* p. 109; Hall, *History of England,* p. 485.

31. Holinshed, *England, Scotland, and Ireland,* p. 519; Bacon, *Reign of King Henry VII,* p. 291.

32. Comments regarding Arthur are rare, as Sir Francis Bacon notes: "Only thus much remaineth, that he was very studious and learned beyond his years, and beyond the custom of great Princes." *Reign of King Henry VII,* p. 320.

33. The manor Richmond was completed in 1500; and although Henry's choice of name seems clear enough, the following offers an interesting interpretation: "In this year the King, after he had finished a great part of the building of his manor of Sheen, which as before is said was consumed by fire, for consideration that in the time of the said burning great substance of riches, as well in jewels and other things of riches, was perished and lost; and also that the reedifying of the said manor had cost, and after should cost before it were pursued, great and notable sums of money, where before that season it was once called or named Sheen, from this time it was commanded by the King that it should be called or named Rich mount." Kingsford, *Chronicles of London,* p. 233. *See also* Fabyan, *New Chronicles of England and France,* p. 686.

34. Holinshed, *England, Scotland, and Ireland*, p. 521.
35. Hall, *History of England*, pp. 488–489.
36. Mackie, *Earlier Tudors*, pp. 145–146.
37. Vergil, *Anglia Historia*, p. 119; Hall, *History of England*, pp. 490–491. Hall also briefly outlines the history of Clarence's children, and their sad story is worthy of repetition: Clarence ". . . left behind him two young infants, engendered of the body of the daughter to Richard, late Earl of Warwick, which children by destiny, or by their own merits, following the steps of their ancestors, succeeded them in like misfortune, and similar ill chance. For Edward his heir, whom King Edward [IV] had created Earl of Warwick was three and twenty years after, in the time of King Henry VII, attainted of treason, and on Tower Hill beheaded. Margaret his sole daughter was married to Sir Richard Pole, knight, being much bound to King Henry VII for her advancement in marriage, besides manifold benefits, by her of him received. But most of all obliged to that excellent prince King Henry VIII, for restoring her as well to the name and title of Countess of Salisbury, as to the possessions of the same; she forgetting the miserable chance [fortune] of her father, and less remembering the kindness and kindred of her said sovereign lord, committed against his Majesty, and his realm, abominable and detestable treason, for the which she was in open Parliament adjudged and attainted, and two and sixty years after her father was put to death in the Tower, she on the green within the same place, with an axe suffered execution." *History of England*, pp. 326–327.
38. Hall, *History of England*, p. 490.
39. Fabyan, *New Chronicles of England and France*, p. 687; Hall, *History of England*, p. 492.
40. Fabyan, *New Chronicles of England and France*, p. 687.
41. Kingsford, *Chronicles of London*, pp. 231–232.
42. "Privy Purse Expenses, Henry VII," in Bentley, *Excerpta Historia;* N. H. Nichols, ed., *Privy Purse Expenses of Elizabeth of York* (London, 1830).
43. "Journals of Roger Machado," in James Gairdner, ed., *Memorials of Henry VII* (London, 1858), pp. 340–363.

44. *Ibid.,* pp. 405–407.
45. Gairdner, *Reigns of Richard III–Henry VII,* pp. 111–112.
46. Holinshed, *England, Scotland, and Ireland,* p. 524.
47. Gairdner, *Henry the Seventh,* p. 178.
48. Davey, *Pageant of London,* pp. 321–322.
49. Gairdner, *Reigns of Richard III–Henry VII,* pp. 404–410.
50. Kingsford, *Chronicles of London,* pp. 234–248.
51. Davey, *Pageant of London,* pp. 322–323.
52. *Ibid.,* p. 324.
53. Gairdner, *Reigns of Richard III–Henry VII,* p. 415.
54. Holinshed, *England, Scotland, and Ireland,* p. 527.
55. Gairdner, *Reigns of Richard III–Henry VII,* p. 416.
56. Kingsford, *Chronicles of London,* pp. 249–252.
57. Davey, *Pageant of London,* pp. 324–325.
58. Leland, *Collectanae,* p. 262.
59. *Ibid.,* pp. 252–264.
60. *Ibid.,* pp. 373–374.
61. *Ibid.,* pp. 373–381.
62. Kingsford, *Chronicles of London,* p. 255.
63. Hall, *History of England,* p. 497.
64. Holinshed, *England, Scotland, and Ireland,* p. 529.
65. Leland, *Collectanae,* p. 249.

EPILOGUE

1. Cited by Agnes Strickland, *Lives of the Queens of England,* vol. 4 (Boston, 1863), p. 56.
2. The old style of counting one's age numbered the years as begun rather than as presently done with the year as it is completed.
3. Job 19:21, from the eighth lesson read at the service of the dead.
4. Kingsford, *Chronicles of London,* pp. 258–259; Davey, *Pageant of London,* pp. 325–326; Strickland, *Queens of England,* pp. 57–59.
5. The predictions for Elizabeth of York, as drawn by the astrologers, had been for a profitable year.

6. Cited by Strickland, *Queens of England,* pp. 59–60.

7. Cited by Jesse, *Memoirs of Richard III,* p. 423.

8. Vergil, *Anglia Historia,* p. 133.

9. Leland, *Collectanae,* pp. 258–299.

10. Ellis, *Letters,* ser. 1, 1, 41–43. *See also* Jerden, *Rutland Papers,* pp. 25–27.

11. Carpenter, *House of Kings,* pp. 95–96.

12. Holinshed, *England, Scotland, and Ireland,* p. 541.

13. Christopher Morris, *The Tudors* (New York, 1957), p. 58.

14. Gairdner, *Memorials of Henry VII,* p. 307.

15. Leland, *Collectanae,* pp. 303–309.

16. The date in the inscription on Elizabeth of York's tomb is, of course, in error. The actual date of her death was February 11, 1503.

BIBLIOGRAPHY

Ames, Joseph. *Typographical Antiquities of Great Britain.* London, 1749.

Andréas, Bernard. "Life of King Henry VII," *Memorials of King Henry the Seventh.* London, 1858.

Bacon, Sir Francis. *History of the Reign of King Henry VII.* Edited by James Spedding et al. New York, 1869.

Bagley, J. J., and Rowley, P. B., eds. *A Documentary History of England,* vol. 1. New York, 1966.

Bayley, John. *The Histories and Antiquities of the Tower of London.* London, 1821.

Bentley, Samuel, ed. *Excerpta Historica.* London, 1833.

Bergenroth, G. A., ed. *Calendar of Letters, Dispatches, and State Papers Relating to the Negotiations between England and Spain: 1485–1509,* vol. 1. London, 1862.

Biddle, Richard. *Life of Sebastian Cabot.* Philadelphia, 1830.

Bowle, John. *Henry VIII.* London, 1964.

Bruce, John, ed. *Historie of the Arrivall of Edward IV in England and the Finall Recouerie of His Kingdomes from Henry VI. A.D. MCCCCLXXI.* London, 1838.

Buck, Sir George. *The History of the Life and Reign of Richard the Third.* London, 1646.

Busch, Wilhelm. *England under the Tudors.* Translated by Alice M. Todd. New York, 1965 (first published 1895).

Calendar of Documents Relating to Scotland. London, 1888.

Calendar of the Close Rolls Preserved in the Public Records Office, 1461–1468; 1468–1476, 2 vols. London, 1954. *1476–1485; 1500–1509.* London, 1963.

Calendar of the Patent Rolls Preserved in the Public Records Office, 1461–1467; 1467–1477; 1476–1485. London, 1914.

Camden Miscellany, vol. 1. London, 1848.

Campbell, William, ed. *Materials for a History of the Reign of Henry VII.* London, 1877.

Carpenter, Edward. *A House of Kings: The History of Westminster Abbey.* London, 1966.

Caxton, William. *The Prologues and Epilogues of William Caxton.* Edited by W. J. B. Crotch. *EETS,* orig. ser. 176. London, 1928.

Chambers, R. W., ed. *A Fifteenth-Century Courtesy Book. EETS,* orig. ser. 148. London, 1914.

Chastellain, G. *Chronique.* Paris, 1868.

Chronicles of the White Rose of York. London, 1845.

Comines, Phillipe de. *Mémoirs.* Paris, 1860.

Cook, E. Thornton. *Royal Elizabeths: The Romances of Five Princesses.* London, 1928.

Cooper, Charles Henry. *Memoir of Margaret, Countess of Richmond and Derby.* Cambridge, 1874.

Davey, Richard. *The Pageant of London.* New York, 1906.

Davies, R. *English Chronicle.* London, 1856.

Denton, William. *England in the Fifteenth Century.* London, 1888.

Douglas, David C., ed. *English Historical Documents,* vols. 4, 5. New York, 1969.

Ellis, Henry, ed. *Letters Illustrative of English History,* series 1, vol. 1. London, 1824; series 2, vol. 1. London, 1827; series 3, vol. 1. London, 1846.

Fabyan, Robert. *New Chronicles of England and France.* Edited by Henry Ellis. London, 1811.

Fenn, John, ed. *Original Letters Written during the Reigns of Henry VI, Edward IV, Richard III,* 2 vols. London, 1787.

Fisher, John. *The English Works of John Fisher.* Edited by J. E. B. Mayer. London, 1876.

Fortescue, Sir John. *The Governance of England.* Edited by C. Plummer. Oxford, 1885.

Frances, Claude de la Roche. *London Historical and Social,* vol. 1. Philadelphia, 1901.

Gairdner, James. *Henry the Seventh.* London, 1889.

————, ed. *Letters and Papers Illustrative of the Reigns of Richard III and Henry VII,* 2 vols. London, 1861.

————, ed. *Memorials of King Henry the Seventh.* London, 1858.

————, ed. *Paston Letters,* 3 vols. London, 1872.

————, ed. *Three Fifteenth-Century Chronicles.* London, 1880.

Grafton, Richard. *Chronicles.* London, 1809.

Great Britain Stationery Office. *Indexes and bibliographical publications of H. M. Stationery Office.* London, 1939.

Gregory, William. *Chronicle 1189–1469.* Edited by James Gairdner as *The Historical Collections of a London Citizen in the Fifteenth Century.* Westminster, 1876.

Grose, Francis. *The Antiquities of England and Wales,* 8 vols. London, 1783.

Habington, Thomas. *Historie of Edward IV.* London, 1640.

Hall, Edward. *Chronicle Containing the History of England.* London, 1809 (reprinted New York, 1965).

Halliwell, J. C., ed. *Letters of the Kings of England,* vol. 1. London, 1846.

Halstead, Caroline. *Life of Margaret Beaufort, Countess of Richmond and Derby.* London, 1839.

Harding, J., ed. *Chronicle.* London, 1809.

Harleian MS. London, British Museum Library.

Hays, Denys, ed. *Europe in the Fourteenth and Fifteenth Centuries.* New York, 1966.

Helm, P. J. *England under the Yorkists and Tudors.* London, 1968.

Heywood, I., ed. *Most Pleasant Song of the Lady Bessy.* London, n. d.

Holinshed, Raphael. *Chronicles of England, Scotland, and Ireland,* vol. 3. London, 1807.

Jacob, E. F. *The Fifteenth Century 1399–1485.* Oxford, 1961.

Jerdan, William, ed. *Rutland Papers*. London, 1842.

Jesse, John Heneage. *Memoirs of King Richard the Third*. Boston, 1911.

Kendall, Paul Murray. *Richard the Third*. New York, 1955.

————, *The Yorkist Age*. New York, 1965 (first printed 1962).

Kesteven, G. R. *1485: From Plantagenet to Tudor*. London, 1967.

Kingsford, Charles L., ed. *Chronicles of London*, Oxford, 1905.

————, *English Historical Literature in the Fifteenth Century*. Oxford, 1913.

————, ed. *The Stonor Letters and Papers 1290–1483*, 2 vols. London, 1919.

Lander, J. R. "The Treason and Death of the Duke of Clarence: A Reinterpretation," *Canadian Journal of History*, 2 (1967), pp. 1–28.

————, *The Wars of the Roses*. London, 1965.

Leland, John. *De Rebus Britannicus Collectanae*. London, 1770.

————, *Itinerary*, vol. 1. Edited by Lucy Toulmin Smith. Carbondale, Pa., 1964.

Letts, Malcolm. *As the Foreigner Saw Us*. London, 1935.

Lindsay, Philip. *The Tragic King Richard III*. New York, 1934.

McElroy, Mary M. Davenport. "Literary Patronage of Margaret Beaufort and Henry VII: A Study of Renaissance Propaganda (1483–1509)" *DA*, 25, 4127. Austin, University of Texas, 1965.

Mackie, John Duncan. *The Earlier Tudors, 1485–1558*. Oxford, 1952.

Malden, Henry Elliot, ed. *The Cely Papers 1475–1488*. London, 1900.

Mancini, Dominic. *The Usurpation of Richard the Third*, 2d ed. Translated by C. A. J. Armstrong. Oxford, 1969.

Marche, Olivier de la. *Mémoirs*. Paris, 1883.

Meagher, John C. "The First Progress of Henry VII," *Ren D*, n.s. 1 (1968), 45–73.

More, Sir Thomas. *Life of Richard III*. Edited by Richard S. Sylvester. New Haven, Conn., 1963.

Morris, Christopher. *The Tudors*. New York, 1957.

Mumby, Frank Arthur. *The Youth of Henry VII*. London, 1913.

Myers, A. R., ed. *English Historical Documents 1327–1485,* vol. 4; *1485–1558,* vol. 5. New York, 1969.

———, ed. *The Household of Edward IV: The Blackbook and the Ordinance of 1478.* Manchester, 1959.

———, "The Household of Queen Elizabeth Woodville, 1466–1467," *BJRL,* 50 (1967), 207–235; 443–481.

Nichols, John Gough, ed. *Chronicle of the Grey Friars of London.* London, 1857.

Nichols, N. H., ed. *Boke of Noblesse.* London, 1860.

———, *Privy Purse Expenses of Elizabeth of York.* London, 1830.

Ogilvy, James S. *Relics and Memorials of London City.* London, 1910.

Pickthorn, Kenneth. *Early Tudor Government.* Cambridge, 1934.

Pollard, A. F. *The Reign of Henry VII from Contemporary Sources,* 3 vols. London, 1913.

Ramsay, Sir J. H. *Lancaster and York.* London, 1898.

Rickert, Edith, ed. *The Babees Book.* London, 1923.

Riley, Henry T., trans. and ed. *Ingulph's Chronicles of the Abbey of Croyland with the Continuation by Peter of Blois.* London, 1893.

———, ed. *Memorials of London and London Life in the XIIIth, XIVth, and XVth Centuries.* London, 1868.

Ritson, Joseph. *Ancient Songs and Ballads.* London, 1877.

Robbins, Rossell Hope, ed. *Historical Poems of the XIVth and XVth Centuries.* New York, 1959.

———, ed. *Secular Lyrics of the XIVth and XVth Centuries.* London, 1952.

Robson-Scott, W. D. *German Travellers in England 1400–1800.* Oxford, 1953.

Rotuli Parliamentorum, 6.

Routh, C. R. N. *They Saw It Happen.* Oxford, 1956.

Routh, E. M. G. *Lady Margaret: A Memoir of Lady Margaret Beaufort, Countess of Richmond and Derby, Mother of Henry VII.* London, 1924.

Rowse, A. L. *Bosworth Field: From Medieval to Tudor England.* New York, 1966.

Scofield, Cora L. *Life and Reign of Edward the Fourth,* 2 vols. London, 1923.

Simons, Eric N. *The Reign of Edward IV.* London, 1966.

Smith, George, ed. *The Coronation of Elizabeth Woodville.* London, 1935.

Sneyd, Charlotte Augusta, trans. *A Relation, or Rather True Account, of This Island of England, c. 1500.* London, 1847.

Stapleton, Thomas, ed. *Plumpton Correspondence.* London, 1838.

Storey, R. L. *The End of the House of Lancaster.* London, 1966.

Stow, John. *Annals of London.* London, 1615.

————, *The Chronicles of England from the Brute Unto This Present Year 1580.* London, 1580.

————, *Survey of London.* London, 1598.

Strickland, Agnes. *Lives of the Queens of England,* vol. 4. Boston, 1863.

Tanner, L. E., and Wright, W. "Recent Investigations regarding the Fate of the Princes of the Tower," *Archaeologia,* 84 (1934), pp. 1–26.

Third Report of the Deputy of Public Records. London, 1842.

Thomas, A. H., and Thornley, I. D., eds. *The Great Chronicles of London.* London, 1938.

Traherne, J. M., ed. *Historical Notices of Sir Matthew Craddock.* London, 1840.

Vergil, Polydore. *Anglia Historia.* Translated by Denys Hay. London, 1950.

Warkworth, John. *A Chronicle of the First Thirteen Years of the Reign of King Edward the Fourth.* Edited by J. O. Halliwell. London, 1839.

Watson, Vera. *A Queen at Home.* London, 1952.

Wedgwood, J. C., ed. *History of Parliament 1439–1509.* London, 1936.

Williams, Charles. *English Historical Documents 1485–1558,* vol. 5. London, 1967.

————, *Henry VII.* London, 1937.

Woods, Mary Everett, *Royal and Illustrative Ladies,* vol. 1. London, 1846.

Worcester, William of. *Annales Rerum Anglicarum.* Oxford, 1774.

Wright, Thomas, ed. *Political Poems and Songs Composed between the Ascension of Edward IV and that of Richard III,* vol. 2. London, 1861.

Wriothesley, Charles. *A Chronicle of England 1485–1559.* Edited by William Douglas Hamilton. London, 1875.

INDEX

Sussex, Robert Radcliff Earl of, 8, 158, 169, 170
Swart, Martin, 142, 144
Sweating sickness, 123–124
Swynford, Catherine, 119

Talbott, Sir Gilbert, 108
Tewkesbury, battle of, 25, 50, 73
Thomas, Rap ap, 105–106
Thomas, Rice ap, 177
Tiptoft, John Earl of Worcester, 17
Tirrell, Sir James, 81–82
Torrigiano, Peter, 205
Tower of London, 4, 5, 7, 11, 12, 13, 14, 17, 21, 22, 25, 26, 32, 37, 45, 46, 47, 48, 51, 54, 60, 64, 68, 72, 74, 81–82, 83, 94, 100, 130, 142, 144, 148, 160, 165, 174, 177–178, 180, 186, 209, 231; White Tower, 72, 193–194, 197, 218; Wakefield, or Bloody Tower, 74, 80, 217; Chapel of St. Peter ad Vincula, 78
Tudor, Catherine, 194, 201
Tudor, Edmund, 117, 136, 168, 224
Tudor, Elizabeth, 173, 176
Tudor, Henry. *See* Henry VII
Tudor, Jasper, as Earl of Pembroke, 16–17, 24–25, 26, 89, 98, 117–118; as Duke of Bedford, 124, 133, 142, 149, 150, 152, 170, 224
Tudor, Margaret, 156, 172–173, 177, 179, 180, 187, 189, 190, 200, 202–203
Tudor, Mary, 180, 182, 183, 190, 201, 203–204

Urswick, Christopher, 98, 124

Vaughan, Sir Thomas, 38, 48, 60, 65, 67
Veilleville, Rouland de, 172
Vergil, Polydore, 201

Warbeck, Perkin, 160, 173–178, 180, 229
Warwick, Edward Earl of, 29, 60, 61, 104, 121–122, 141–142,
143, 178, 180–181; impersonations of, 160, 181, 184, 230–231
Warwick, Richard Neville Earl of, 4, 5, 6, 7, 8, 9–20, 21, 22, 23, 24, 31–32, 51, 72–73, 85, 118
Westminster Abbey, 3, 13, 15, 27, 36, 44, 56, 70, 74, 76, 94, 128, 148, 150–151, 176, 182, 198–199, 200, 207; St. Stephen's Chapel, 36, 153, 169; Our Lady Chapel (later Henry VII's Chapel), 193, 205, 206
Westminster Palace, 3, 4, 21, 22, 27, 30, 32, 42, 43, 45, 50, 51, 56, 57, 60, 67, 69, 76, 96, 118, 122, 125, 130, 150, 151, 156–157, 168, 182, 199
Whitehall, 74
Willoughby, Sir Robert, 113, 121–122
Wiltshire, Thomas Boleyn Earl of, 75
Winchester, 136–137
Winchester Cathedral, 137–138
Windsor, 4, 24, 27, 28, 36, 45, 78, 79, 168, 182, 212; St. George's Chapel, 27, 36, 45, 78, 229
Wolsey, Thomas Archbishop of York, 204
Woodstock, Thomas Duke of Gloucester, 47
Woodville, Anne, 8
Woodville, Anthony. *See* Rivers
Woodville, Catherine, 8, 48
Woodville, Sir Edward, 37, 44, 49, 55, 90, 137, 158
Woodville, Eleanor, 8
Woodville, Jacquette, 8
Woodville, John, 7
Woodville, Mary, 8
Woodville, Sir Richard, 6, 7

York, 11, 12, 19, 39, 79, 102, 104, 109, 131–133, 145
York, archbishops of. *See* Neville, George; Rotherham, Thomas; Wolsey, Thomas
York, Edward of Langley Duke of, 118
York Minster, 79